Post-Conviction Relief: The Advocate

Kelly Patrick Riggs

FREEBIRD
PUBLISHERS

Freebird Publishers
www.FreebirdPublishers.com

Freebird Publishers

221 Pearl St. Ste. 541, North Dighton, MA 02764

Info@FreebirdPublishers.com

www.FreebirdPublishers.com

Copyright © 2022
Post-Conviction Relief: The Advocate
By Kelly Patrick Riggs

All Freebird Publishers titles, imprints, and distributed lines are available at special quantity discounts for bulk purchases for sales promotions, premiums, fundraising educational or institutional use.

ISBN: 978-1-952159-39-8

Printed in the United States of America

SCOPE AND PURPOSE

This book completes the *Post-Conviction Relief* series. Therefore, it is my humble opinion that this publication should be the final step in preparing you, the reader, for the real world of post-conviction litigation. In that effort, I have written this book as the toolbox of *pro se* filing.

This book contains the many filings that I have used over the years. Although there is no way that anyone could list every type of filing that a prisoner or a court may encounter, I have listed many of the filings that have been used in the many aspects of advocating for others. With this book, advocates can hone their skills to a fine point, which I hope to see expressed in courts around the country.

With the end of my work in sight, I hope that you see an opportunity for yours to begin. I hope that you pick up where I left off; I hope that you can see the need to fight for those who cannot fight for themselves.

TABLE OF CONTENTS

CHAPTER ONE

THINGS YOU SHOULD KNOW

After reading this book's summary, I'm sure you realize that it contains more of the writings I used as a "jailhouse lawyer." I'm also sure you're ready to get down to business, but let me share a few things with you before we start state.

I can imagine many different reasons that would explain why you picked up this book. One of the most obvious and probable is because you're locked away in federal prison. That's the reason I started writing. Then, others unknowingly picked up my first book and have now been through the whole collection. Of course, it would stand to reason they would follow their study to the end.

It doesn't matter why you started reading, what matters is what you do now. For some of you, all that will ever matter is your case and the life you want to get back. But for others, post-conviction practice becomes a passion. If it has become a passion for you, you are now one of today's most important individuals among incarcerated people: you are an Advocate.

The word "Advocate" is defined as "a person who publicly supports or recommends a particular cause or policy; a person who pleads on someone else's behalf; a pleader in a court of law, a lawyer." It is highly unlikely that you will ever appear in court or actively litigate a case. Nonetheless, if you're writing for other people, you're no less an Advocate than any lawyer.

The difference between a lawyer and an Advocate is the passion to learn a case and give your all for the good of your client. As you likely know from either personal experience or the study of federal criminal cases, lawyers are quick to sell their clients up the river for an easy buck. This is where you can be much different.

THE WRIT WRITER

One of the most important characteristics of a good prison Advocate is humility – knowing your limitations. Always remember that it is very little you can do in most cases. That is not because you are wrong or that the client is undeserving, it is because all prisoners are predetermined to be guilty. This prejudice is why politicians accuse each other of criminal conduct. The accuser will win by default if politicians can get Americans to believe their opposition is a criminal. You do realize that because of this prejudice, your limitations will often begin and end with writing the writ.

Another important characteristic is the ability to recognize opportunities. As Advocates, we all want that big win to hang our hats. Unfortunately, those big wins are rare. I'm not saying that they are impossible to find, they do happen from time to time. But, if you concentrate on the little things, you will have a large number of little wins. With many little wins, you develop a reputation for winning consistently. That is much more important than being known for never achieving anything.

In my time as a jailhouse lawyer, I stumbled upon a few good opportunities in the very beginning. The first was the "Drugs Minus Two," or Amendment 782 to the United States Sentencing Guidelines (U.S.S.G.). The next was the invalidation of the residual clause in 18 U.S.C.: 924(e). This sent me on a trend of looking for law and court precedent changes. I suggest that anyone interested in making a name for themselves in post-conviction relief practice do the same.

FINDING OPPORTUNITY

I know this sounds like a no-brainer, but it's not. If you think back to before your first interaction with the legal system, you'll realize that you had little exposure to federal criminal law, if any. But now you are most likely surrounded by people complaining about one aspect of it or another. Likewise, before sentencing, you had little reason to think about sentence correction. Just like before you thought about advocacy, you had little reason to consider the many opportunities that exist to help other people with sentence reduction.

This means that you will be required to start thinking about things much broader than your own needs. You will have to have answers to questions that you ordinarily would never consider. And you will have to study subjects that you never imagined you would ever need. Along with this, you will also have to know where to find new opportunities if you plan to be an effective advocate. I came to this realization early in my confinement.

When I found myself locked away in federal prison, I was a first-time offender. So, as you can imagine, I did not need to worry about the career offender enhancement found in the United States Sentencing Guidelines. But to my surprise, people who noticed I studied law started to ask me questions, even about the Career Criminal Act. See U.S.S.G.: 4b1.

Needless to say, I was helpful, so I would research the subject and find the answers. I soon became the go-to guy for all legal questions. I discovered that the many questions I faced were because of some news of change or acts of Congress. I also learned that I could stay ahead of the game by doing a little pre-study on subjects that were made public. The bottom line is that if it was about criminal law or prison issues, prisoners would hear about it sooner or later.

So, to save myself time, I learned to find it first. Now for the golden question: where does a beginner find the answers to what is going to happen next? The answer was simple for me. I would spend the first hour of every day reading the updates in the law library. I would also read any law journal I could find after hours. If you're wondering about my TV time, forget it. I quit watching TV years ago. Remember what I said about post-conviction litigation becoming a passion? Sometimes, it is more like an all-consuming obsession.

CHAPTER TWO

PRO SE FILINGS RELATED TO NEW CHARGES

My career as a jailhouse lawyer started at the Federal Transfer Center in Oklahoma City, Oklahoma. On my first day there, I started to look up the statute I was charged with. Of course, the computers at OKC are in the center of the common area, and everyone can see exactly what you're doing. I was spotted looking up law in the first fifteen minutes.

The man who noticed what I was doing was on his way to prison for being a felon in possession of a firearm. Of course, I thought that they already had him, and his legal process was over. I was wrong. He had yet another pending charge, and his appointed lawyer told him he didn't have to worry about it. This was completely untrue.

The facts of his case were a problem. He had a second indictment for possessing the same firearm he was already convicted of possessing. Double jeopardy? No, not really. He was charged with possessing the same weapon on two different days. Was his counsel ineffective? Sure, he was, but proving that in 2255 would have taken more time than the young man could spare. In that case, the young man had already spent enough time in prison to be ready to apply for a halfway house. Unfortunately, he was not eligible for a halfway house because of the other charge. Luckily for him, he was eligible for relief under The Interstate Agreement on Detainers Act.

Ultimately, this young man's case was my wake-up call. His case is the one that made me realize that even when incarcerated, we need to learn how to conduct a criminal case. This chapter is dedicated to *pro se* filings needed to address new charges.

It is important to pay special attention to this section because criminal cases are not usually considered post-conviction processes. To start with, in most criminal cases, counsel will be appointed as soon as the Interstate Agreement on Detainers is invoked. What does that mean exactly? Well for starters, the court expects your case through your appointed counsel. Unfortunately, your appointed counsel will have no intention to do anything except collect fees for work he's not doing. This also means that you ordinarily won't have access to the court, nor will they allow you to file motions on your behalf.

Therefore, it is very important to present your motions as *pro se* motions. When you use the term "*pro se*" you invoke the Supreme Court controlling *pro se* doctrine of *Haines v. Kerner* 404 U.S. 519 (1972). Why do I bring this up? It's because I expect you to alter these filings to fit your own needs but do not under any circumstances exclude the term "*pro se.*"

Legal experts around the country are familiar with the problem of overbroad or just plain vague federal criminal laws that are used to pad the cells and the pockets of the profiteers who operate today's criminal justice system. These laws are used to ensnare unsuspecting defendants and shock the few honorable lawyers who defend them. It is a recurring scheme in today's federal criminal courts and was prominently featured in Justice Kagan's dissent in *Yates v. United States*, where she described "the real issue" in the case as being "overcriminalization and excessive punishment in the U.S. Code."

Justice Kagan is not the only expert to raise this issue. Legal scholars have been writing about this very problem for years on end. Many have gone straight to the Constitution as the solution to this problem, specifically the Due Process Clause. They even raise issues about fair notice to draw attention to vaguely worded statutes that even Federal Judges don't understand.

This is all a good idea, but it overlooks the common and simple legal mechanism that was specifically drafted for combating overcriminalization. The federal criminal procedure rules readily available methods for defendants to secure a legal ruling before trial on whether their alleged conduct constitutes a federal crime. In the motion that follows, you will be introduced to Federal Rules of Criminal Procedure, rules 7, 12, and 47. I do suggest that you read them in full for your understanding.

IN THE UNITED STATES DISTRICT COURT
FOR THE NORTHERN DISTRICT OF ALABAMA
SOUTHERN DIVISION

UNITED STATES OF AMERICA plaintiff	§ § §	Case no.:
v.	§ §	2:12-cr-297-KOB-JEO
	§	
JOHN DOE defendant	§ §	

MOTION FOR DISMISSAL OF INDICTMENT

The defendant John Doe, filing this motion in pro se and without the assistance of appointed counsel, and pursuant to Fed. R. Crim. P. 12(b)(2) and (3), and 7(c)(2), requests that the Court dismiss the indictment because, on its face, it: (i) fails to charge an essential element of all 42 counts against Mr. Doe – the "materiality" of his alleged "inside information;" (ii) is so vague as to lack the constitutional sufficiency needed to allow Mr. Doe to mount a defense and to protect his due process rights; and (iii) contains facially deficient forfeiture allegations.

I. STATEMENT OF THE CASE

On December 20, 2005, Mr. Doe was indicted in a six-page indictment on 42 counts of insider trading. The indictment alleges that Mr. Doe, while employed as the CEO and a board member at Qwest Communications International, Inc. ("Qwest"), sold stock with a gross sales price totaling $100,812,582.02. The indictment further alleges that such sales occurred between January 2-May 29, 2001, during which period Mr. Doe:

[W]as aware of material, non-public information about Qwest's business, including, but not limited to: (a) that Qwest's publicly stated financial targets, including its targets for 2001, were extremely aggressive and a "huge stretch"; (b) that in order to achieve its publicly stated financial targets for 2001, Qwest would be required to significantly increase its recurring revenue business during the first few months of 2001; (c) that Qwest's past experience or "track record" in growing recurring revenue at a sufficient rate to meet its publicly stated financial targets was poor; (d) that Qwest's recurring revenue business was underperforming from early 2001 and was not growing at a sufficient rate to meet Qwest's publicly stated financial targets; (e) that there were material undisclosed risks relating specifically to Qwest's recurring and non-recurring revenue streams that put achievement of Qwest's 2001 publicly stated financial targets in jeopardy; (f) that the gap between Qwest's publicly stated financial targets and Qwest's recurring revenue was increasing, thus increasing Qwest's reliance on risky and unsustainable one-time transactions; and (g) that there would be insufficient non-recurring revenue sources to close the gap between Qwest's publicly stated financial targets and its actual performance.

The heart of the Government's case is that Mr. Doe was told of a concern that Qwest might not be able to meet its publicly stated financial targets or, in the common parlance, "make its numbers." As a

7

matter of law, this is insufficient to charge the crime of insider trading, especially given the government's explicit concession that Qwest's financial reporting during the relevant period was fully accurate and complete.

It is not alleged that Mr. Doe knew Qwest could not make its numbers, or even that he believed Qwest could not make its numbers, but merely that he had been told that Qwest might not be able to make its numbers. This Court has previously held that a failure to disclose financial "risks" is not the concealment of material information. See *McDonald v. Kinder-Morgan, Inc.*, 287 F.3d 992,998 (10th Cir. 2002) (aff'g Nottingham, j.). As Mr. Doe is not charged with possessing any material information that would restrain him from exercising and then selling his stock options, the indictment does not charge an offense and should be dismissed.

Alleging that Mr. Doe was told that Qwest's publicly stated financial targets were "extremely aggressive" and "a 'huge stretch'" also fails to allege the requisite materiality. What does a "huge stretch" or "extremely aggressive" mean – especially when Qwest undisputedly did make its numbers from January 2 - May 29, 2001, the period during which Mr. Doe made the stock sales alleged in the indictment? What was he told before May 29, 2001? Of what was Mr. Doe allegedly aware of the date specified in each of the remaining 41 counts?

Additionally, the Government has asserted in a filing with this Court, that Mr. Doe is "criminally responsible for insider trading if he was aware of material inside information at the time of his trades and acted with the requisite scienter? And, most importantly, that this is true "even if Qwest accurately reported its financial results, and disclosed every fact required to be disclosed by law ..." The Prosecution has put forth an impossible proposition. As will be shown, under the circumstances here, the federal common law under section 10(b)(5) is clear that there is but a single definition of "material information," applicable equally to the company and its officers. Indeed, the law tells us that knowledge by an officer is necessarily imputed to the company. It cannot, therefore, simultaneously be alleged that (1) Mr. Doe is guilty of insider trading because of things had been told before he sold his stock – that the stated financial targets were "a huge stretch" and "extremely aggressive" – were material information, and (2) that Qwest was not required to disclose this identical, supposedly "material," information. On the contrary, no insider can be guilty of a crime for trading in his company's stock if the company has accurately disclosed all that the law requires it and him to disclose. Any other standard would bring the marketplace into chaos.

In short, since the Government has charged Mr. Doe with nothing more than a failure to disclose financial risks and has explicitly admitted that Qwest's disclosures as to its financial targets for 2001 were accurate and complete throughout the relevant period, it necessarily follows that the indictment fails to allege the "materiality" of Mr. Doe's "inside information" – an essential element of all 42 counts against Mr. Doe. This failure renders the indictment facially deficient.

Further, the indictment is so vague as to lack constitutionally requisite sufficiency. The law is clear that the sufficiency of an indictment must be measured by the document's four corners and that a deficient indictment may not be saved by extraneous facts. Indeed, a court should refrain from considering evidence outside the indictment when testing its legal sufficiency. In other words, an indictment so vague as to lack constitutionally requisite sufficiency cannot be cured by a bill of particulars. That is to say, the answers to the bill of particulars that we have demanded will not save the indictment if it is constitutionally deficient. See *Russell v. United States*, 369 U.S. 749, 770 (1962) ("But it is a settled rule that a bill of particulars cannot save an invalid indictment."). The answers to the bill cannot substitute for words the grand jury did not charge and did not have in mind when it made the charges that it did. Since the words that this grand jury chose to adopt are insufficient as a matter of law, the indictment should be dismissed.

The indictment should also be dismissed for failure to allege materiality as a matter of law under the "efficient market test." The judicially noticeable facts are dispositive that the alleged insider information could not have been material.

Finally, the indictment makes a demonstrably deficient forfeiture allegation. Even though the Government recognized the statutory restriction on the face of the indictment by stating that it was seeking proceeds obtained "as a result of the offense," it then ignored this restriction by demanding forfeiture of the entire gross sales price. The law is clear that arriving at the proceeds requires some type of calculation of profit deriving from the charged offense. Here, the Government has failed to deduct from the gross sale price the amount of the monies paid by Mr. Doe for the shares. Furthermore, the proper amount of forfeiture is the difference between the value of the shares before disclosure of the material, non-public information, and the market value of the shares after the marketplace assimilated the alleged material information.

For each one of these reasons, it is respectfully submitted, the indictment should be dismissed.

II. ARGUMENT

A. The Elements of the Charged Offense

The indictment alleges insider trading in violation of 15 U.S.C.: 78(j), 17 C.F.R.: 240.10(b)(5), and 17 C.F.R.: 240.10(b)(5)(1). Section 10(b) of the Securities Exchange Act of 1934, 15 U.S.C.: 78(j)(b), and SEC Rule 10(b)(5) which is promulgated thereunder, 17 C.F.R.: 240.10(b)(5), prohibit fraudulent acts done in connection with securities transactions. See *Dura Pharmaceuticals, Inc. v. Broudo*, ___ U.S.___, 125 S.Ct. 1627, 1630-31 (2005); see also *Basic Inc. v. Levinson*, 485 U.S. 224, 230 (1988). Although: 10(b) does not use the term "insider trading," ":10(b) and Rule 10(b)(5) are violated when a corporate insider trades in the securities of his corporation based on material, nonpublic information." *United States v. O'Hagan*, 521 U.S. 642, 651-52 (1997).

In this District:

The following are the elements … to establish a misrepresentation violating rule 10(b)(5): "(1) a material misrepresentation, (2) in connection with the purchase or sale of a security, (3) scienter, and (4) use of a jurisdictional means." Depending on the circumstances, the first element may be satisfied in alternative ways, such as by showing an omission where there is a duty to speak.

German v. S.E.C., 334 F.3d 1183, 1192 (10th Cir. 2003) (citations omitted); accord, *City of Philadelphia v. Fleming Companies, Inc.*, 264 F.3d 1245, 1257-58 (10th Cir. 2001), citing *Grossman v. Novell, Inc.*, 120 F.3d 1112, 1118 (10th Cir.1997); see also *Anixter v. Home-Stake Products*, 77 F.3d 1215, 1225 (10th Cir. 1996) (similar definition); and see *Shriners Hospitals For Children v. QWEST Communication Intl Inc.*, 2005 WL 2350569, at *6 (D. Colo. 2005) (Blackburn, J.) (citing Anixter), and *S.E.C. v. C. Jones & Co.*, 312 F.Supp.2d 1375, 1379 (D. Colo. 2004) (Miller, J.) (citing German).

Thus, to prove insider trading, the Government must allege the existence of a material representation or omission and Mr. Doe's knowing use of that information while trading. Having failed to make the requisite allegations on the face of the indictment, the indictment should be dismissed.

B. As a Matter of Law, the Allegations of the Indictment Fail to Allege the Requisite Materiality

As a matter of law, "[a] statement is material only if a reasonable investor would consider it important in determining whether to buy or sell stock.'" *McDonald*, 287 F.3d at 998, quoting *Grossman*, 120 F.3d at 1119. In *McDonald*, the plaintiff alleged that the company had made materially misleading statements because "they do not disclose the existence of the significant risks associated with the Bushton-related 'keep whole' contracts while reporting the incremental operating revenue and operating income attributable to the operation of the Bushton Plant." 287 F.3d at 996. This Court dismissed the McDonald complaint on its face under Rule 12(b)(6), for failure even to state a claim. The Tenth Circuit then upheld this Court's conclusion that "the accurate reporting of historic successes does not give rise to a duty to further disclose contingencies that might alter the revenue picture in the future," *id.* at 998.

This indictment suffers from an identical lethal disability.

There is no allegation in the indictment that Qwest's historical reporting was anything but accurate and complete. McDonald outlawed 10(b)(5) claims based upon non-disclosure of vague contingencies, that is, "failure to disclose risks" in connection with earnings, yet it is precisely these vague contingencies – "extremely aggressive," "a huge stretch," "risky," and "jeopardy"– which the prosecution had the grand jury specify as the "material" information known to Mr. Doe. Claiming that Mr. Doe had been told that Qwest's "publicly stated financial targets, including its targets for 2001, were extremely aggressive and a 'huge stretch' " is just a different way of saying that Mr. Doe was aware that there were "contingencies that might alter the revenue picture in the future," which is exactly what this Court, and the Tenth Circuit sitting in review of this Court, have held to be immaterial, as a matter of law.

Consequently, McDonald instructs that these types of contingencies do not give rise to a duty to disclose. The indictment is not saved by the other vague and conclusory allegations of Paragraph 6. Whether taken individually or as a whole, they merely establish the reality faced by every public company when future earnings are projected based on history: not all expectations may be met, and the actual sources of revenue often do not precisely line up, either with those of the past or with those expected in the future. See, *e.g.*, *Stevelman v. Alias Research Inc.*, 174 F. 3D 79, 85 (2nd Cir. 1999)("Management's optimism that is shown only after the fact to have been unwarranted does not, by itself, give rise to an inference of fraud."); see also *In re* Ikon Office Solutions, Inc. Securities Lit., 131 F.Supp.2d 680, 702 (E.D. Pa. 2001) ("The fact that a future prediction turns out to be wrong does not mean it was fraudulent when made."), aff'd, 277 F.3d 658 (3d Cir. 2002).

For example, ¶ 6(b) alleges that Mr. Doe was told, "[n]o later than December 4, 2000," "that to achieve its publicly stated financial targets for 2001, Qwest would be required to significantly increase its recurring revenue business during the first few months of 2001." Putting aside the factual issue that there is no difference between making the target via non-recurring rather than recurring income, such an allegation is insufficient to establish that the earnings guidance had to be changed to render it not misleading. See *Kushner v. Beverly Enterprises, Inc.*, 317 F.3d 820, 831 (8th Cir. 2003) ("[T]here is no duty to disclose 'soft information,' such as a matter of opinion [or] predictions ... 'Soft information must be disclosed only if virtually as certain as hard facts.'") (Quoting *In re Sofamor Danek Group, Inc.*, 123 F.3d 394, 402 (6th Cir. 1997), cert. denied, 523 U.S. 1106 (1998)). In any event, as we show in Point C, *infra*, the Government admits that the guidance was materially sufficient.

The same circumstance holds true of Paragraph 6(d), which alleges that "[n]o later than December 4, 2000," "Qwest's recurring revalue business [Which was not its only source of income] was underperforming from early 2001: and was not growing at a sufficient rate to meet Qwest's publicly stated financial targets" (emphasis added). In plain English, the indictment alleges that between December 4, 2000, and September 10, 2001, the rate of growth of the recurring revenue business imperiled the achievement of the target. It alleges no more than a contingency, a mere possibility that was always subject to change and which might well have evolved at any point during or after the period from December 4, 2000, through May 29, 2001. And May 29, 2001, is the last date that should matter for this indictment since that is the last date of any crime charged. This bare allegation of a contingency is so far different from the accusation of knowledge that more recurring revenue could not or would not be realized, let alone that any shortfall in expected recurring revenue could not be made up from other revenue sources, that it is directly forbidden by McDonald.

Paragraph 6(c) alleges that "[n]o later than December 4, 2000," "Qwest's past experience or 'Track record' in growing recurring revenue at a sufficient rate to meet its publicly stated financial targets was poor." Whatever "poor" means and that is anyone's guess, the prosecution does not allege that Qwest's historical disclosures were in any manner deficient or false, or misleading, or that Mr. Doe knew or even believed that Qwest could not make its numbers. And this allegation is made notwithstanding that this Court has specifically held, as affirmed by the Tenth Circuit, that accurate reporting of historic financial results does not give rise to a duty "to further disclose contingencies that might alter the revenue picture" 287 F.3d at 998 (emphasis added). It simply cannot be denied that these allegations impermissibly attempt to convert such historical information into "material" statements.

Paragraph 6(e) alleges "that there were material undisclosed risks relating specifically to Qwest's recurring and non-recurring revenue streams that put the achievement of Qwest's 2001 publicly stated financial targets in jeopardy" (emphases added). The prosecution's deliberate use of these inherent uncertainties, alleging that achieving the revenue target was "risky" or "in jeopardy," is directly prohibited by McDonald.

Paragraph 6(f) alleges that "later than December 4, 2000, through and including September 10, 2001," "the gap between Qwest's publicly stated financial targets and Qwest's recurring revenue was increasing, thus increasing Qwest's reliance on risky and unsustainable one-time transactions" (emphasis added). Again, we are presented with an indictment that fails to charge a crime and instead contains language that this Court has ruled requires dismissal on its face. What is this, if not a contingency, something that may or may not come to pass and that may or may not prove relevant in hindsight after all other sources of revenue are considered?

As no other allegations of materiality have been made, the indictment fails to allege this requisite element of the offense and the indictment should, therefore, be dismissed. See United States v. Coia, 719 F.2d 1120, 1123 (11th Cir. 1983), cert, denied, 466 U.S.973 (1984) ("It is perfectly proper, and mandated, that the district court dismiss an indictment if the indictment fails to allege facts which constitute a prosecutable offense").

C. The Government's Judicial Admission Renders the Allegations Against Mr. Doe Immaterial

Putting aside the strictures of McDonald, this indictment should be dismissed because the Government has taken the position in a filing with the Court that Qwest's financial guidance and disclosures were accurate and complete, even as it alleges in the indictment that Mr. Doe had a duty to disclose that same information. The information cannot logically or legally be both material and immaterial at the same time. Because the Government concedes that Qwest's filings were accurate and complete it follows, *a fortiori*, that Mr. Doe cannot have acted inappropriately in trading on the same information and that the indictment, therefore, fails to allege materiality, a necessary requisite of the offense.

The prosecution has stated to this Court that Mr. Doe "is still criminally responsible for insider trading if he was aware of material inside information at the time of his trades and acted with the requisite scienter," "[e]ven if Qwest accurately reported its financial results, [and] disclosed every fact required to be disclosed by law...." (Doc. 26 at 2). To the extent the Government is conceding that, during the operative time in question, Qwest accurately reported its financial results and disclosed every fact required to be disclosed by law, this Court may deem this a judicial admission, having "the effect of withdrawing a fact from issue and, dispensing wholly with the need for proof of the fact" *Guidry v. Sheet Metal Workers Inc. Ass 'n, Local No. 9*, 10 F.3d 700, 716 (10th Cir. 1993), cert. denied, 514 U.S. 1063 (1995); accord, *United States v. Alvarez-Becerra*, 33 Fed. Appx. 403, 406-07 (10th Cir.), cert. denied, 536 U.S. 931 (2002) (citing *Towerridge, Inc. v. T.A.O., Inc.*, 111 F.3d 758, 769 (10th Cir. 1997) and Guidry); see also *Plastic Container Corp. v. Continental Plastics of Oklahoma, Inc.*, 607 F.2d 885, 906 (10th Cir. 1979), cert. denied, 444 U.S. 1018 (1980) (same doctrine, drawn from Second and Fifth Circuit authority).

As a matter of law, Mr. Nacchio's knowledge is imputed to the company. See, *S.E.C. v. Texas Gulf Sulphur Co.*, 401 F.2d 833, 860-62(2d Cir. 1968), cert. denied, 394 U.S. 976 (1969). Qwest's knowledge cannot, therefore, be less than Mr. Doe's. Accordingly, the Government's concession that, throughout the period that Mr. Doe was trading his stock, Qwest had "accurately reported its financial results, [and] disclosed every fact required to be disclosed by law" compels the conclusion that Mr. Doe had no undisclosed material information about Qwest when he made the trades that are the subject of the 42-count indictment. Accordingly, by the government's own admission, whatever possible contingencies Mr. Doe was told about were not material and he was free to sell his stock. See, *e.g.*, *Grossman*, 120

F.3d at 1119 ("unless the statement 'significantly altered the "total mix" of information available, it will not be considered material"), quoting *TSC Indus.*, 426 U.S. at 449; and see *Garcia*, 930 F'.2d at 829 ("The [Supreme] Court has explained that it deliberately did not set the materiality standard too low because of cancer that a minimal standard would result in avalanches of information that would bury stockholders in trivia ..."), citing basic, 485 U.S. at 231.

The Government seems to be suggesting in the alternative that the knowledge Mr. Doe (and Qwest) had was material but nevertheless did not have to be disclosed. (See Doc. 26 at 2-3 ("Qwest...had a good faith belief or a recognized legal right to withhold material information under one of the exceptions to disclosure under the securities laws ... In fact, it is the essence of at least one type of insider trading that the defendant has material inside information that is not legally required to be disclosed.")) An example of this exception would be undisclosed news about a pending merger. See, *e.g.*, *Garcia v. Cordova*, 930 F.2d 826, 828-29 (10th Cir. 1991), citing *Chiarella*, 445 U.S. at 226-29. This, however, is not the allegation in Paragraph 6 of the indictment. This is not a charge concerning withheld news as to a subject that is not released because of a legal right to be silent, this is a charge that Mr. Doe heard that there was something wrong with Qwest's publicly stated financial targets to the effect that they were "extremely aggressive and a 'huge stretch.'" If this were material as to Mr. Doe, it would have had to be disclosed by Qwest as well, since it would not fall under any "exceptions to disclosure under the securities law."

D. The Indictment Fails to Allege an Offense

The Paragraph 6 laundry list of things Mr. Doe was allegedly told is not only anything more than a list of contingencies, but the words also themselves are too vague to state a crime. Words like "stretch," "aggressive," "risky" and "jeopardy" are the accordion-type language that in reality says nothing definite enough to be understood and, certainly, nothing definite enough to be defended against. The language connotes nothing meaningful. This, in the final analysis, is why such language cannot be "material."

Accordingly, the indictment fails to apprise Mr. Doe with reasonable certainty of the nature of the accusation against him. That is, the prosecution has failed to allege the operative facts of the crime of insider trading with the constitutional sufficiency that would allow Mr. Doe to mount a defense and comport with his due process rights. This omission is a facial deficiency that, respectfully, requires the dismissal of the indictment.

The Tenth Circuit has consistently held that a vague indictment does not pass constitutional muster. In *United States v. Hall*, 20 F.3d 1084, 1087 (1041 Cir. 1994) (some citations omitted), the Court affirmed the district court's dismissal of an indictment, stating:

An indictment is deemed constitutionally sufficient if it (1) contains the essential elements of the offense intended to be charged, (2) sufficiently apprises the accused of what he must be prepared to defend against, and (3) enables the accused to plead an acquittal or conviction under the indictment as a bar to any subsequent prosecution for the same offense. *Russell v. United States*, 369 U.S. 749, 763-64... (1962); *United States v. Walker*, 947 F.2d 1439, 1441 (10th Cir. 1991) ... An indictment should be tested solely based on the allegations made on its face, and such allegations are to be taken as true. *United States v. Sampson*, 371 U.S. 75, 78-79 (1962). Courts should refrain from considering evidence outside the indictment when testing its legal sufficiency.

Accord, *United States v. Welch*, 327 F.3d 1081, 1090 (10th Cir. 2003) (citing *Hall*).

Constitutional sufficiency does not merely require that the allegations of an indictment be detailed enough to provide for mounting a defense, it also safeguards the due process protection that a grand jury affords as a check on an overzealous prosecutor. A grand jury may not give a prosecutor a blank check. See *United States v. Kilpatrick*, 821 F.2d 1456, 1464-65 (10th Cir. 1987).

In *United States v. Curtis*, 506 F.2d 985, 990 (10th Cir. 1974) (emphases added), the Court explained that an indictment requires:

Some substantial indication of the nature or character of any scheme or artifice to defraud or to obtain money or property by using false pretenses, representations, or promises is requisite. And it is not sufficient in this regard to merely plead the statutory language. *Cf. Russell v. United States*, 369 U.S. 749 ... (1962); *Lowenburg v. United States*, 156 F.2d 22 (10th Cir. 1946). A reference to the cases cited first above will disclose that in each instance, the nature of the schemes or artifices is identified or described, including the particular pretenses, representations, or promises claimed to have been false.

The Curtis Court was confronted with a mail fraud indictment in which "then salient facts vital to the government's claim of an unlawful scheme or artifice is masked, if not concealed, by the conclusionary language of the indictment as framed," *id.* at 987. Similarly, here, the wholly vague contingencies of Paragraph 6 mask the salient facts vital to the prosecution's claim. When the contingencies are stripped away – that is, when words like "extremely aggressive," "huge stretch," "risky" and "jeopardy" are removed from the indictment, as they must be under *McDonald* as well as for vagueness – all that is left is the bare language of the statute. Such charging language, using only the words of the statute (*e.g.*, willfully sold based on inside information), is what *Curtis* prohibits. As the Curtis Court observed:

What the 'scheme and artifice to defraud or the 'false and fraudulent pretenses, representations and promises' referred to in the indictment were is left to speculation. And by the curious commingling of references to the scheme, with allegations of various means utilized to carry it out, the indictment is confusing as well as vague.

Id. at 989. The Curtis Court reversed and remanded because:

In sum, the indictment here, after all that has been said and done, pleads little more than the statutory language without any fair indication of the nature or character of the scheme or artifice relied upon or the false pretenses, misrepresentations, or promises to form a part of it …

Id. at 992.

In addition to violating the legal requirements for pleading securities fraud as announced, McDonald's indictment is confusing and internally inconsistent. It uses terminology that no one can define and time segments that are impossible to assess. It was brought in a hurry, notwithstanding a three-year investigation, on the very eve of the discharge of the grand jury which had been investigating a case of fraud, but which was left only with this product instead. It was not brought in this form to simplify the case, as the Government has repeatedly represented to this Court, but because the Government had no case at all. The prosecution is attempting, by its incorrect and inconsistent declarations of what it must prove, to avoid the accounting issues which cannot be sidestepped in determining the accuracy of the public guidance as to Qwest's future income and earnings. Thus, if the Court permits the case to go forward – which we respectfully submit it should not do – all of Qwest's accounting during the relevant period will be material to the accuracy of its public guidance, as will be the reasonableness of the views of that guidance's internal critics, and the reasonableness of Mr. Doe's rejection of those views.

Because the Government failed to satisfy the requisites of the Constitution in seeking the instant indictment, the indictment should, we respectfully submit, be dismissed.

E. The Allegations of the Indictment Are Also Immaterial, As a Matter of Law, Under the "Efficient Market Test" of Materiality

A court may find non-public information to be immaterial as a matter of law by employing the "efficient market" test. See *Texas Gulf Sulphur Co.*, 401 F.2d at 858-59 ("The disclosure of information materially important to investors may not instantaneously be reflected in market value, but despite the intricacies of security values truth does find relatively quick acceptance on the market") (emphasis added). Similarly, the SEC has itself argued that "market reaction" reflects materiality. See, *e.g.*, *S.E.C. v. Hoover*, 903 F. Supp. 1135, 1146-47 (S.D. Tex. 1995).

In a series of cases beginning with *Burlington Coat Factory Securities Litigation*, 114 F.3d 1410 (3d Cir. 1997), then Circuit Judge Alita championed the "efficient market" test as a method of determining those times when, as a matter of law, an alleged failure to disclose was not material and, consequently, could not support an insider trading or 10b-5 claim. This is just such a situation. As will be discussed, the reality is that the market failed to react negatively to Mr. Doe's disclosures of the allegedly material non-public information asserted in the indictment, rendering that information immaterial as a matter of law.

In *Burlington Coat Factory*, the Third Circuit explained:

Because the market for BCF stock was "efficient," and because the July 29 disclosure did not affect BCF's price, it follows that the information disclosed on September 20 was immaterial as a matter of law. Ordinarily, the law defines "material" information as information that would be important to a reasonable investor in making his or her investment decision. ...In the context of an "efficient" market, the concept of materiality translates into information that alters the price of the firm's stock. ...This is so because efficient markets are those in which information important to reasonable investors (in effect, the market) ...is immediately incorporated into stock prices. ...Therefore, to the extent that information is not important to reasonable investors, it follows that its release will have a negligible effect on the stock price. In this case, plaintiffs have represented to us that the July 29 release of information did not affect BCF's stock price. This is, in effect, a representation that the information was not material.

114 F.3d at 1425 (multiple citations omitted).

This is precisely the fact pattern presented in the present matter. The Court may take judicial notice that the material information Mr. Doe is alleged to have traded on was conveyed to the marketplace in two disclosures, one on August 7, 2001, and the second on September 10, 2001. The Court may also take judicial notice as to the market's "immediate" reaction to each disclosure, as the daily trading price of Qwest shares is certainly not in dispute. Fed. R. Evict. 201(f) ("Judicial notice may be taken at any stage of the proceeding."); see also *United States v. Gordon*, 634 F.2d 639, 642 (1st Cir. 1980) ("The district judge was free to dispose of the motion [to dismiss the indictment]...by taking judicial notice...."); and see *United States v. Briddle*, 212 F. Supp. 584, 589 (S.D. Cal. 1962) ("This Court has the power to receive evidence – including evidence adduced using judicial notice – upon the hearing of the defendant's motions to dismiss the indictment at the bar."). Indeed, in *Hall*, the Tenth Circuit observed that:

[I]t is permissible and may be desirable where the facts are essentially undisputed for the district court to examine the factual predicate for an indictment to determine whether the elements of the criminal charge can be shown sufficiently for a submissible case.

Hall, 20 F.3d at 1087 (quoting *United States v. Brown*, 925 F.2d 1301, 1304 (10th Cir. 1991)).

The *Hall* Court found additional support in another Tenth Circuit decision for "the proposition that under certain circumstances a trial court is within its jurisdiction in ordering a pretrial dismissal based on the insufficiency of the evidence," concluding that "our affirmance of the district court's dismissals in *Wood* is an implicit recognition of a district court's authority, under certain limited circumstances, to go beyond the allegations of the indictment and make predicate findings of fact" 20 F.3d at 1087-88 (discussing *United States v. Wood*, 6 F.3d 692 (10th Cir. 1993)).

What will be seen is that after the first disclosure, not only did the price of Qwest stock not drop, but it also actually rose. Similarly, Qwest shares rose over three dollars per share on the day of the second disclosure and, despite the events of September 11, 2001 (which came only a day later), despite that the financial markets were then shut down for a week, and even though the general market suffered a significant downturn when trading resumed, the price of Qwest stock retained its gain, then remained virtually unchanged for the next week of trading. In other words, there was no immediate negative reaction to the news, which is dispositive, as a matter of law, that the disclosures were not material.

Judge Alito's subsequent opinion in *Oran v. Stafford*, 226 F.3d 275 (3d Cir. 2000), is an even more dramatic demonstration that the indictment against Mr. Doe should be dismissed due to the non-materiality of the disclosures at issue because the market's reaction to disclosures there was virtually identical to those in the matter sub judice, and that court held that the disclosure was therefore not material as a matter of law. In *Oran*, after the disclosure took place, not only did the stock not drop, but it also actually "rose by $3.00 during the four days after the…disclosure" 226 F.3d at 283. Here, Qwest was trading at $24.29 when the market opened on August 7, 2001, the date of the first alleged disclosure. Over the next week, the price of Qwest stock rose, closing at $24.66 on August 13 (the fifth day of trading). See Exhibit D. The second alleged disclosure was on September 10, 2001. On that day, Qwest stock opened at $16.34 and immediately rose, closing at $19.90, a gain of more than three dollars a share, or more than 21%. Once the markets reopened on September 17, the Qwest stock bucked the huge general downward trend, preserved the September 10 gain, then held steady for the next 5 days, *id.* "Under Burlington's market test, this price stability is dispositive of the question of materiality" *Oran*, 226 F.3d at 283. Subsequently, in *In re* NAHC, Inc. Securities Litigation, 306 F.3d 1314, 1330 (3d Cir. 2002), the court concluded that "no negative effect" on a company's stock price immediately following the date of disclosure rendered the disclosed information immaterial as a matter of law. This, notwithstanding that the company's stock price plunged 75% just three weeks after the disclosure was made, *id.* at 1321.

In re Merck & Co., Inc. Securities Litigation, 432 F.3d 261 (3d Cir. 2005) is the most recent Third Circuit "efficient market" opinion. There, "the disclosure occurred on April 17, and there was no negative effect on Merck's stock" until a Wall Street Journal article was published two months later, *Id.* at 269. Finding the facts similar to those found in *In re NAHC Inc.*, the court again deemed the initial disclosure immaterial as a matter of law, *id.*

Although the Tent Circuit has never addressed the "efficient market" test of materiality, courts throughout the country have employed the test. In Basic Inc., the Supreme Court observed that "recent empirical studies have tended to confirm Congress' premise that the market price of shares traded on well-developed markets reflects all publicly available information, and, hence, any material misrepresentations," 485 U.S. at 246. See also, *e.g.*, *Grimes v. Navigant Consulting, Inc.*, 185 F.Supp.2d 906, 914 (N.D. Ill. 2002) (the court deemed a disclosure immaterial when the stock rose that same day, instead of falling as expected).

Here, where it is undisputed that the price of Qwest stock rose following each of the two disclosures, and there was no negative reaction by the end of a week of trading, this Court should, respectfully, find as a matter of law that these disclosures were immaterial. Because these disclosures are alleged to be the material non-public information Mr. Doe traded on, and they are immaterial as a matter of law, the indictment should be dismissed for failure to allege a requisite element of the offense.

F. The Forfeiture Allegations of the Indictment Are Demonstrably Deficient

The indictment makes a forfeiture allegation that the $100,812,582 gross sales price of Mr. Doe's sales "represent[s] the number of proceeds obtained as a result of the offenses" (Doc. 1, Forfeiture Allegations at 6). This is demonstrably, and fatally, deficient. The Federal Rules of Criminal Procedure, the forfeiture statute itself, and the applicable federal common law are unequivocal that the words "proceeds obtained as a result of the offense" necessitate a "profits" calculation and can never consist solely of the gross sales price. Because the indictment fails to employ a profit calculation and instead demands forfeiture of the gross sale price, the forfeiture allegations of the indictment are facially defective and should be dismissed.

Fed. R. Crim. Pro. 7(c)(2) states:

Criminal Forfeiture. No judgment of forfeiture may be entered in a criminal proceeding unless the indictment … provides notice that the defendant has an interest in property that is subject to forfeiture by applicable statute.

The forfeiture statute asserted in the indictment (Doc. 1, Forfeiture Allegations at 6), 18 U.S.C. § 981(a)(1)(C), defines property subject to forfeiture as any property…which…is derived from proceeds traceable to a violation." Thus, the starting point – as mandated by the statute and conceded on the very face of the indictment – is that there must be a causal relationship between the property sought by forfeiture and the charged offense.

One of the deficiencies in the indictment's forfeiture demand is the failure to credit Mr. Doe with the price he paid for the shares. How can any conceivable definition of "proceeds gained" from the sale of stock ignore the costs of purchasing the stock in the first place? As fatal as this deficiency is alone, equally serious deficiencies exist from claiming the entire gross sale price as the "proceeds obtained as a result of the offenses." Unlike most situations where insider trading is alleged, Mr. Doe did not purchase the shares in question on the open market. Rather, he executed options that were granted to him as part of his compensation. The only accusation in the indictment is that he sold these shares while in possession of certain information (Doc. 1 ¶ 9 at 4). Consequently, it would be demonstrably false to suggest that proceeds could be derived solely by subtracting the purchase price from the gross sales price. This is because Mr. Doe's profit from buying at an option price and selling at the market price was at least partly attributable to his compensation, not the alleged offense of insider trading. A different formula must be employed, a formula that has found wide acceptance.

The First, Second, and D.C. Circuits have concluded that:

In an insider trading case, the proper amount of disgorgement is generally the difference between the value of the shares when the insider sold them while in possession of the material nonpublic information and their market value a reasonable time after public dissemination of the inside information," *SEC v. MacDonald* 699 F.2d 47, 54-55 (1st Cir. 1983). See also *SEC v. Patel*, 61 F.3d 137, 139 (2d Cir. 1995); *SEC v. Shapiro*, 494 F.2d 1301, 1309 (2d Cir.1974).

SEC. v. Happ, 392 F.3d 12, 31 (first Cir. 2004); accord, *SEC v. First City Fin. Corp.*, 890 F.2d 1215, 1231 (D.C. Cir. 1989).

When this analysis is applied to the instant facts, the amount subject to a forfeiture would not be the gross sales price, or even the net sales price (the gross sales price minus the amount paid) but, rather, the difference between (i) the value of the shares just before Mr. Doe disclosed the allegedly material non-public information, and (ii) the value of the shares "a reasonable time after that disclosure." As shown in the discussion of the "efficient market" test for materiality, *supra*, the market failed to react negatively to either of the two disclosures. Thus, even if the charged offense is proven beyond a reasonable doubt, for purposes of forfeiture there were no "proceeds obtained as a result of the offenses." Critically, while the Government might quibble over just what starting value should be applied to the formula, it is clear that under any permissible methodology some amount must be deducted from the net – not gross – sales price. This double factual infirmity is fatal to the indictment.

It is, therefore, necessary to employ the method of valuing the profits, or proceeds, from alleged insider trading as adopted by most Circuits, which defines "profits" as the difference between the value of the shares to the disclosure of the insider information, and the value of the shares after the market assimilated that information. Only in this manner can the "proceeds obtained as a result of the offenses" be separated from the proceeds to which Mr. Doe was legitimate– and uncontestably – entitled as part of his compensation as the CEO of Qwest.

Because the Government lists the full gross sales price as the proceeds obtained as a result of the offense, not even crediting the cost of purchasing the shares let alone tying the amount sought in forfeiture to the offense charged, the forfeiture allegations of the indictment are facially deficient.

CONCLUSION

For the foregoing reasons Defendant, John Doe respectfully asks for entry of an Order dismissing the indictment,

Respectfully submitted this 16th day of February 2020, by.

X_____

John Doe, *pro se*
Reg. No.: _____-___
Federal Correctional Institution
P.O. BOX 9000
Seagoville, TX 75159

CERTIFICATE OF SERVICE

I hereby certify, that on this 16th day of February 2020, a true and correct copy of the foregoing MOTION FOR DISMISSAL OF INDICTMENT was served on all parties as required by rule and law.

Respectfully submitted this 16th day of February 2020, by:

X_____

John Doe, *pro se*
Reg. No.: _____-___
Federal Correctional Institution
P.O. Box 9000
Seagoville, TX 75159

UNITED STATES DISTRICT COURT
FOR THE NORTHERN DISTRICT OF ALABAMA
SOUTHERN DIVISION

UNITED STATES OF AMERICA plaintiff	§ § §	Case no.:
v.	§ §	2:12-cr-297-KOB-JEO
KELLY PATRICK RIGGS, defendant	§ § §	

MOTION TO WITHDRAW GUILTY PLEA

Now comes the above-named defendant, prose, and pursuant to Rule 11(d) F. R. Crim. P., hereby moves to withdraw the guilty plea entered in this matter. As grounds, the undersigned alleges and shows to the court as follows:

1. In entering his guilty plea Kelly Patrick Riggs (Riggs) believed that the temporal scope of the conspiracy to which he was admitting began in 2011 and continued through May 16, 2012.

2. Riggs' belief was reasonable because ¶ 4 of the plea agreement alleges that the conspiracy began sometime in 2011 and continued through May 16, 2012. Additionally, the "factual basis" attachment to the plea agreement only recites conduct that occurred in the year 2012. Finally, when the court orally examined Riggs on a factual basis Riggs told the court that he distributed cocaine in 2012.

3. Riggs' reasonable belief concerning the temporal scope of the conspiracy is material to his decision to plead guilty because the government seeks to present evidence of offense-specific guideline conduct that occurred well before 2005. Specifically, the government seeks to present evidence of a murder that occurred in 2002; and, further, the government's testimony concerning the weight of the drugs involved in the conspiracy focuses on Riggs' alleged drug activities in the summer of 2003.

4. Had Riggs understood that the temporal scope of the alleged conspiracy began in 2002 he would not have entered a guilty plea. Riggs is, in fact, not guilty of the Benion homicide nor did he distribute drugs during 2003.

Wherefore, it is respectfully requested that the court grant Riggs leave to withdraw his guilty plea. This motion is further based upon the attached Brief in Support.

UNITED STATES DISTRICT COURT
FOR THE NORTHERN DISTRICT OF ALABAMA
SOUTHERN DIVISION

UNITED STATES OF AMERICA plaintiff	§ § §	Case no.:
v.	§ §	2:12-cr-297-KOB-JEO
KELLY PATRICK RIGGS, defendant	§ § § §	

BRIEF IN SUPPORT OF MOTION TO WITHDRAW GUILTY PLEA

Factual Background

The history of this case, in terms of its duration and its Byzantine complexity, rivals any Grisham novel. In June 2012, the defendant, Kelly Patrick Riggs (Riggs) was charged, along with several others, as being part of a conspiracy to deliver cocaine in the Northern District of Alabama. A simple enough allegation. The first indictment claimed that Riggs, and the others, "Beginning sometime in 2011 and continuing through May 16, 2012" conspired to deliver cocaine (Doc. 37). Riggs entered a not-guilty plea.

On July 19, 2012, though, there was a superseding indictment. This new indictment alleged the same time frame for the conspiracy, though (2011-2012) (Doc. 81). Again, Riggs pleaded not guilty.

There was a volley of pretrial motions. Riggs complained about the fact that government agents, without a warrant, and in the dark of the night, crept into the parking lot of Riggs' apartment complex and attached a global positioning satellite device to the underside of Riggs' car. In other motions, Riggs questioned the ability of a drug-sniffing dog to smell marijuana from one hundred yards away from a storage shed; other defendants, including Riggs, challenged the veracity of government agents who claimed in an affidavit that they had obtained cell phone information before the time any court authorization existed for them to obtain the information. The hearing on this motion devolved into a series of stories – and then changed stories – about how the government agents obtained the information in question (See Doc. 416).

On August 22, 2013, though, there was a second superseding indictment. Again, the temporal scope of the conspiracy was alleged to be the years 2011 to 2012 (Doc. 269). Again, Riggs' plea was not guilty.

The case was set for trial on October 29, 2014.

Finally, on September 18, 2014, a little over a month before the trial date, a third superseding indictment was filed (Doc. 419). This time, though, the indictment contained an accusation that from "sometime in 2002 and continuing through May 16, 2012" the defendants conspired to deliver cocaine. In effect, the indictment added nine additional years to the alleged temporal scope of the conspiracy. Riggs objected to the timeliness of the filing of the third superseding indictment. When his objection was overruled, though, Riggs entered a not-guilty plea.

On the morning of the first day of trial, though, the parties informed the court that the three remaining defendants (Mark Cubie, Kelly Riggs, and Ronald Terry) had reached a plea agreement. The government informed the court that this final offer was extended to the defendants the previous day (Sunday) and that the offer must be accepted by all three defendants, or the offer will be withdrawn.

Riggs' plea agreement was signed, and he entered a guilty plea. Paragraph 12 of the plea agreement provides that Riggs, "[H]as been charged in three counts of a nine-count third superseding indictment" (emphasis provided). However, Paragraph 14 of the plea agreement, which sets forth the charge, alleges that "Beginning sometime in 2011 and continuing through May 16, 2012…" the defendant conspired to deliver cocaine. Concerning the weight of the drugs involved, IV of the plea agreement recited that the conspiracy began in 2002. The reader should note that the third superseding indictment alleged that the conspiracy began in 2002, not in 2011. Thus, the plea agreement incorrectly recited the allegations of the third superseding indictment.

The government would argue that the government would recommend a base offense level of 362; however, the plea agreement recited that, "The parties acknowledge and understand that the defendant will not join in this recommendation" (Doc. 467-6). Concerning the factual basis, attachment A to the plea agreement reads as follows:

This investigation began in January 2012 in the Northern District of Alabama. Case agents developed several confidential informants (CIs), and by the end of January, efforts were focused squarely on Mark Cubie. Historical CI information indicated that Cubie was a multi-kilogram cocaine dealer whose source of supply (Lopez) was based in Chicago.

CI-3 made several recorded calls to Cubie and then several controlled contacts, including a buy of one kilogram of cocaine and a money payment of $8,000. On February 2, 2012, after watching Cubie conduct a drug deal, uniformed officers stopped Cubie. He had cocaine, crack, marijuana, cash, and a gun in his vehicle. A GPS was placed on his car, and Cubie was released.

From February 2 until April 26, 2012, surveillance and pen/trap/toll data indicated that Cubie had several stash houses in Birmingham and distributed cocaine to several individuals, including Kelly Riggs, Ronald Q. Terry, Delano Hill, and Edward Cubie. Anthony Burke and Sylvester Pigram assisted Cubie by renting cars, stashing dope, money, and guns, and driving trail cars. The investigation during this period also established that Cubie was traveling to Chicago to meet with Lopez to pick up cocaine and make money deliveries.

On April 26, 20012, case agents began court-authorized monitoring of Cubie's cellular telephone. During the weeks that followed, monitoring, combined with surveillance and pen/trap/toll data, confirmed that Cubie was supplying Riggs, Hill, Edward Cubie, and others and was assisted by Burke, Pigram, and his girlfriend, Machelle Jelks. Cubie typically fronted the drugs to his regular distributors. He used his cellular telephone to arrange drug deliveries and money payments. He and his associates routinely used code words to mask the true meaning of their drug trafficking activities. Court-authorized monitoring also established that Cubie's source of cocaine was in fact, Mr. Lopez. Without identifying it as such, 117 also states that, in the alternative, the government might recommend the "murder cross-reference" contained in U.S.S.G. § 2D1.1(d)(l) and U.S.S.G. § 2A1.2(a).

The evidence shows that the supply was Jose G. Lopez in Chicago. Monitoring and surveillance captured several multi-kilogram transactions and money transfers between Cubie and Lopez. Lopez typically fronted the cocaine to Cubie, usually meeting Cubie at Gurnee Mills Mall in Gurnee, Illinois, or Lopez's business on Western Avenue in Chicago. Usually, once several days passed after each receipt of cocaine, Cubie gathered money in Birmingham from his regular distributors and then traveled to Chicago to pay Lopez and retrieve more cocaine. During the course of the conspiracy, the defendants obtained and distributed at least five kilograms of cocaine.

During Riggs' plea colloquy, the court examined Riggs about what he had done that made him guilty of conspiracy to deliver cocaine. The colloquy went as follows:

THE COURT: What did you do as a member of this conspiracy, if anything?
THE DEFENDANT: Oh, distributor.
THE COURT: A distributor of what?
THE DEFENDANT: Of cocaine.
THE COURT: What kind of cocaine?
THE DEFENDANT: Powder.
THE COURT: When were you distributing cocaine powder?
THE DEFENDANT: Um, '12, 2012.
THE COURT: Is that the only time?
THE DEFENDANT: Yes.
(Doc. 570; Trans. 10-29-013 p. 16.)

After the court accepted Riggs' guilty plea the court ordered a presentence investigation. The PSI was conducted, and a report was filed. Significantly, the PSI report suggested that the court apply the so-called "murder cross-reference" to Riggs due to his alleged involvement in the murder of Earl Benion in 2002. The PSI report did not make a recommendation concerning the weight of the drugs involved in the conspiracy.

The PSI report set off a year-long series of objections and recriminations between the parties. Riggs argued that the Benion homicide occurred nine years before the conspiracy in question was alleged to have existed (Doc. 494-6). The government retorted that the recitation of the charge in 14 of the plea agreement (which states that the conspiracy began in 2011 rather than in 2002) was a "typographical error" because 12 of the plea agreement recites that Riggs was pleading guilty to the third superseding indictment (which alleges that the conspiracy began in 2002). Additionally, the government argued, that Riggs' objection to the weight of the drugs were "mere denials." Finally, it became apparent that the government, into the quantity of cocaine needed for a base offense level of 36, intended to present the testimony of cooperating witnesses whose claim was that they bought cocaine from Riggs in 2003.

It has become clear that Riggs' guilty plea is beyond redemption. As will be outlined in more detail below, the plea was not freely, voluntarily, and intelligently entered because Riggs, in entering the guilty plea, believed he was admitting to being involved in a conspiracy that began in 2011 and continued through 2012. The government, though, plans to urge the court to impose a lengthy prison sentence based upon offense-specific guideline conduct that occurred well before 2011.

Argument

I. The court must permit Riggs to withdraw his guilty plea because it was not knowingly, voluntarily, and intelligently entered.

Everything, from the recitations of the charge in the plea agreement to the factual basis for the plea, suggested that the temporal scope of the conspiracy was the years 2011 and 2012. Thus, it is no wonder that Riggs, in entering his guilty plea, believed that he was admitting to involvement in the conspiracy only during those years. In fact, at the plea hearing, Riggs testified that his only involvement was in the year 2012. Thus, the guilty plea was entered under a reasonable misapprehension over the duration of the conspiracy. This confusion makes a difference, too, because the two years added in the third superseding indictment bring into play for sentencing purposes evidence of grave prior conduct by Riggs. Riggs would not have pleaded guilty had he understood that the government alleged that the conspiracy began in 2002.

Rule 11(d), F. R. Crim. P. provides that after the court has accepted the guilty plea, but before sentencing, the defendant may withdraw the plea if "the defendant can show a fair and just reason for requesting the withdrawal." However, the defendant does not have an unlimited right to withdraw the plea; rather, the burden is on the defendant to demonstrate a fair and just reason for such withdrawal *United States v. Schilling*, 142 F.3d 388, 398 (7th Cir. 1998). The Supreme Court has noted that a plea "operates as a waiver of important rights, and is valid only if done voluntarily, knowingly, and intelligently, 'with sufficient awareness of the relevant circumstances and likely consequences *Bradshaw v. Stumpf*, 545 U.S. 175, 183, 125 S. Ct. 2398, 162 L. Ed. 2d 143 (2005) (quoting *Brady v. United States*, 397 U.S. 742, 748, 90 S. Ct. 1463, 25 L. Ed. 2d 747 (1970)).

Here, Riggs alleges that his plea was not knowingly and intelligently made because, when he entered the plea, he believed that he was admitting to being part of a conspiracy that existed in the years 2011 and 2012. It would be remarkable had Riggs believed anything else.

Although the plea agreement recites that Riggs was pleading guilty to the "third superseding indictment," the recitation of the indictment that is contained in the plea agreement refers to a conspiracy that existed in 2011 and 2012. As if this were not enough, the factual basis for the plea contained in Attachment A sets forth conduct that occurred primarily in 2012. When the court examined Riggs concerning what Riggs did to make him part of the conspiracy, Riggs told the court that he conspired to deliver cocaine in 2012. Finally, the fact that Riggs disputed the weight of the drugs attributable to him for sentencing purposes is set forth plainly in the plea agreement.

The confusion at the guilty plea hearing over the temporal scope of the conspiracy makes a monumental difference. The government seeks to apply the murder cross-reference for the death of Earl Benion. Benion died in 2002 – more than ten years before the originally-alleged existence of the conspiracy. Moreover, concerning the weight of the drugs attributable to Riggs, the government appears to rely upon the testimony of informants who claim to have bought cocaine from Riggs in the summer of 2003 – again, a year before this conspiracy was alleged in the first indictment to have existed.

The difference, according to Riggs, is a deal-breaker. Had he known that the government expected him to admit that this conspiracy existed as early as 2002, he would not have pleaded guilty. As Riggs argued at the hearing on his motion to dismiss the third superseding indictment, he lived in Florida for most of 2002, 2003, and 2004.

There can be little doubt that Riggs was genuinely mistaken about the temporal scope of the conspiracy at the time he pleaded guilty. Riggs' professed confusion over the temporal scope of the conspiracy is hardly the sort of "buyer's regret" – dressed up as ignorance of some minor bit of information – that the court frequently encounters in motions to withdraw guilty pleas. Here, the confusion makes a difference.

Conclusion

For these reasons, it is respectfully requested that the court permit Riggs to withdraw his guilty plea to the third superseding indictment.

KELLY PATRICK RIGGS

UNITED STATES DISTRICT COURT
EASTERN DISTRICT OF WISCONSIN

UNITED STATES OF AMERICA plaintiff	§ § §	Case no.:
v.	§ §	07-cr-123
JANE DOE, defendant	§ § § §	

MOTION TO SUPPRESS EVIDENCE OF WIRE COMMUNICATIONS

Ms. Doe, the above-named defendant, in *Pro se*, hereby moves to suppress evidence of intercepted wire communications allegedly involving Ms. Doe and Jimmie Durant on February 18, 2017 (and any other date) for the reason that probable cause for the issuance of the Title III order for Jimmy Durant's telephone on January 25, 2017, was established through the use of information that the affiant could not have legally had in his possession at the time of the application.

Factual Background

Count Thirteen of the Indictment alleges that on February 18, 2007, the defendant Jane Doe ("Doe") knowingly and intentionally used a communication facility, to wit: a telephone, to commit, cause, or facilitate the commission of an act or acts constituting a drug trafficking crime, to wit; possession with intent to distribute and distribution of cocaine all contrary to 21 U.S.C. §841(a)(l).

Specifically, the complaint alleges on page 34: "On February 18, 2007, at 11:53 p.m., Jane Doe called DURANT And said that "David" called her to ask her about the price for 4 speakers and an amp (4½ ounces of cocaine). DURANT said 28 dollars (2,800 dollars). Doe said she wanted to sell it to David for 32 dollars ($3,200). DURANT told Doe to sell it to David for 28 dollars." p. 35: "On March 3, 2007, at 8:14 a.m., DURANT called Doe and Doe asked DURANT if he was still in Memphis. DURANT said he would be back no later than [sic] Sunday. Doe said she needs to get that (cocaine). Doe asked if Cal (COLEMAN) was straight or whether he'd been going to work (i.e., to sell cocaine). Doe then asked whether DURANT knew anybody that had cocaine available to sell because "Dave" had been constantly bothering her for cocaine. Doe told DURANT she gave Dave some of that 'bubble gum' (cocaine), and he wanted more. DURANT said he did not know." The government's primary evidence of this offense is a recording of a February 18, 2007, telephone call that was intercepted pursuant to a January 25, 2007, authorization to monitor Jimmie Durant's telephone numbers. Beginning in September 2006, the government was investigating drug dealing in Milwaukee and pursuant to Title III began intercepting telephone calls made to numbers listed to Calvin Coleman. It was not until

28

December 6, 2006 (Bates No. 258), though, that Jimmie Durant was named as one of the individuals whose communication might be intercepted (though none of his telephone numbers were targets). In the supporting affidavit for the December 6, 2006, application, Detective Daniel Thompson set forth a chart suggesting that three telephone numbers were listed as "Jimmie Durant" and that these numbers made a certain number of calls to the target number (Coleman). The affidavit alleges that the information in the chart – apparently also including the subscriber names – was obtained from "an analysis of pen register, trap and trace, telephone toll records, subscriber dates, public records, confidential informants and sources, and/or law enforcement surveillance and seizures." In paragraph 37, though, Thompson alleges that "[T]he results of telephone tolls, trap, and trace, and pen register information, have been used in this investigation.

Pen registers, trap and traces, and toll records do not record the identity of the parties to the conversation, cannot identify the nature or substance of the conversation, and cannot differentiate between legitimate calls and calls for criminal purposes." How, then, did Thompson determine that the three numbers were listed to Jimmy Durant?

Later, on January 25, 2007, affidavit (Application 5800; Bates No. 437) filed in support of a Title III application to intercept telephone communications, Thompson alleged, at ¶ 13, that, "[T]elephone records reveal that target telephone #5 is a Nextel cellular telephone subscribed to "Steve Wells" at 3437 W. Wells. St. and target telephone #6 is a Sprint cellular telephone subscribed to DURANT at 2210 N. 29th St." At p. 30 Thompson alleges that, "Telephone records (cell tower locations) indicate that target telephone #6 (DURANT) returned to Milwaukee on January 5, 2007, at 3:27 a.m." On page 34 the affidavit reads, "On January 18, 2007, at 11:07 a.m., target telephone #6 (DURANT) received a 36-second incoming call from 773-817-0174. Telephone records indicate that 773-817-0174 is subscribed to Robert HAMPTON at 13713 S. Stewart Ave., Riverdale, IL." This appears to be information gleaned from subscriber records and/or a pen register and/or cell tower triangulation or a mobile tracking device. On page 42, the affidavit sets forth a chart of calls made to and from target telephones 5 and 6. Thus, it appears that as of January 25, 2007, government agents already had subscriber information and cell tower triangulation information concerning Jimmy Durant and his telephones. Based on Thompson's affidavit, on January 25, 2007, the court granted the application to intercept calls from Durant's two telephone numbers, and Nextel was ordered to provide, among other things, "originating and terminating cellular tower and sector information for calls to and from the target telephones … during the time period of this Order" (Application 5800; Bates No. 494). This was the first authorization for the government to intercept wire communication and obtain cell tower information on Durant's telephones.

Then, on January 30, 2007, the government made an application under 18 U.S.C. 2703(d) to obtain telephone subscriber records concerning Durant's two numbers (460.8561 and 304.4618). This was after Thompson's December 6, 2006, affidavit in which he already claimed to know the identity of the subscriber for the numbers 414.460.8561 and 414.304.4618. The order was granted (Application 6052; Bates 1271). From a review of the discovery materials provided by the government it appears that the first and only application for cell phone tracking information pursuant to 18 U.S.C. §3117 on Jimmie Durant's cell phones, though, was not made until March 23, 2007 – again, after Thompson had already alleged in his January 25, 2007, affidavit that he had subscriber information for Durant's numbers and that Durant's telephone had been operating in Chicago and returned to Milwaukee on January 5, 2007 (No. 07-M-210; Bates No. 1209) 18 U.S.C. § 3117, Mobile tracking devices. It does not appear that the government ever sought subscriber information for any telephone listed to Jane Doe.

Argument

The court must suppress the Title III evidence as to Doe because the relevant application demonstrates that government agents had in their possession subscriber information and location tracking information concerning Jimmy Durant's telephone that they could not have obtained legally.

A. Doe has the standing to challenge communications intercepted on Jimmy Durant's telephone. 18 U.S.C. §2518(10)(a), in turn, provides the means for invoking the sanction:

Any aggrieved person in any trial, hearing, or proceeding in or before any court, department, officer, agency, regulatory body, or other authority of the United States, a State, or a political subdivision thereof, may move to suppress the contents of any intercepted wire or oral communication, or evidence derived therefrom, on the grounds that –

(i) the communication was unlawfully intercepted.

(ii) the order of authorization or approval under which it was intercepted is insufficient on its face; or

(iii) the interception was not made in conformity with the order of authorization or approval. …

Finally, 18 U.S.C. § 2510(11) defines the class of persons entitled to invoke the law. (a) In general. If a court is empowered to issue a warrant or other order for the installation of a mobile tracking device, such order may authorize the use of that device within the jurisdiction of the court, and outside that jurisdiction, if the device is installed in that jurisdiction. (b) Definition. As used in this section, the term "tracking device" means an electronic or mechanical device that permits the tracking of the movement of a person or object. Sanction through the motion to suppress:

"[A]ggrieved person" means a person who was a party to any intercepted wire or oral communication or a person against whom the interception was directed. This suppression remedy, however, can only be invoked in a criminal trial, by the victim of the illegality, to prevent the use of the tainted evidence against him, *United States v. Calandra*, 414 U.S. 338, 347, 354, 94 S. Ct. 613, 619, 622, 38 L.Ed.2d 561 (1974).

Doe was aggrieved by the interception of the February 18, 2007, telephone conversation she allegedly had with Durant.

B. Probable cause for the Title III intercept was established through the use of information that Detective Thompson could not have legally had in his possession at the time of the application.

It is a violation of federal and state law to employ a pen register or trap and trace device without court authorization, 18 U.S.C. § 3121(d); Wis. Stat. § 968.34(1). While the pen register and trap and trace statutes themselves do not codify the exclusionary rule, Title III specifically mandates the exclusion of all direct and derivative evidence obtained as the result of an illegal wiretap, 18 U.S.C. § 2515 & § 251 (1)(a). Where communication is "unlawfully intercepted," the Court must suppress both the contents of the communication and any evidence derived therefrom, 18 U.S.C. § 2518(10)(a)(i); *United States v. Giordano*, 416 U.S. 505, 530-31 (1974). Even relatively technical violations may result in suppression under Title III. See, *e.g.*, *Giordano*, 416 U.S. 505 (suppressing evidence where incorrect DOJ personnel authorized wiretap). The purpose of the suppression remedy in Title III is "not only to protect the privacy of communications but also to ensure that the courts do not become partners to illegal conduct: the evidentiary prohibition was enacted also 'to protect the integrity of the court and administrative proceedings,'" *Gelbard v. United States*, 408 U.S. 41, 51 (1972) (quoted source omitted). Suppression of evidence, in this case, is consistent with the purposes of § 2515 and will serve to have a deterrent effect on the illegal interception of telephone data. Here, the course of events may be determined by reference to the series of affidavits filed with the court. Initially, Jimmy Durant was not listed as a person whose electronic communications would be likely to be intercepted. Suddenly, on December 6, 2006, though, Durant was listed by name in a chart as being associated with certain telephone numbers that were involved with calls to and from target phone number 2 (Coleman). The affidavit merely alleges in general terms that the information set forth in the chart was gleaned from trap-and-trace information, public records, confidential informants, and so forth.

However, as of December 6, 2006, the government had not even applied for subscriber information for Durant. It might be possible that Detective Thompson referred to some "public record" to determine the names associated with the numbers that were calling target telephone number two. This is doubtful,

31

though, since cellular telephone numbers are not listed in any printed media of which this author is aware.

Any doubt, though, that the subscriber information cell tower location information was legally obtained is erased by Thompson's January 25, 2007, affidavit. In it, Thompson alleges that at ¶ 13, "(T)elephone records reveal that target telephone #5 is a Nextel cellular telephone subscribed to 'Steve Wells' at 3437 W. Wells. St. and target telephone #6 is a Sprint cellular telephone subscribed to DURANT at 2210 N. 29th St." On page 30 Thompson alleges that "Telephone records (cell tower locations) indicate that target telephone #6 (DURANT) returned to Milwaukee on January 5, 2007, at 3:27 a.m." On page 34 the affidavit reads, "On January 18, 2007, at 11:07 a.m., target telephone #6 (DURANT) received a 36-second incoming call from 773-817-0174. Telephone records indicate that 773-817-0174 is subscribed to Robert HAMPTON at 13713 S. Stewart Ave., Riverdale, IL." It is simply impossible that Thompson could have this information unless he was referring to subscriber information provided by the cellular telephone company. The government had no authorization to have this information on either January 5, 2007 (the date of the incident) or on January 25, 2007 (the date of the affidavit). There is only one conclusion: Government agents somehow obtained, and were using, cellular telephone subscriber information and tracking information prior to obtaining court approval. One plausible explanation for this situation is that government agents made use of "national security letters" pursuant to 18 USCS § 2709.2. The problem, of course, is that § 2709 prohibits disclosure of information obtained through the use of an NSL and the information can certainly not be used to bootstrap probable cause in a legitimate application for Title III authorization.

Conclusion

For these reasons, it is respectfully requested that the court suppress all Title III evidence of Jane Doe. Respectfully submitted, this 29th day of December 2007.

x._____

Jane Doe, *pro se*
Reg. No. _____
F.C.I. Seagoville
P.O. Box 9000
Seagoville, TX 75159

UNITED STATES DISTRICT COURT
EASTERN DISTRICT OF WISCONSIN

UNITED STATES OF AMERICA plaintiff	§ § §	Case no.:
v.	§ §	06-CR-335
	§	
JOHN H. DOE, *PRO SE* defendant	§ §	

MOTION TO SUPPRESS EXPERT TESTIMONY

Introduction

Based on the counsel's review of the discovery materials provided by the government in this case, the government's case will depend largely upon intercepted and recorded telephone calls between the various alleged participants in this conspiracy. As will be set forth in more detail below, before any recorded telephone call may be played for the jury the government must establish the identity of the parties to the telephone call. Additionally, although witnesses who know "drug code words" used by the group in question may testify as to the meaning of any such code words, no witness may offer an opinion as to what any particular defendant meant when he used any particular word.

Discussion

I. Voice Identification

Rule 901 F.R.E., which governs the requirement of authentication or identification of evidence proffered at trial, provides:

(5) Voice identification. Identification of a voice, whether heard firsthand or through mechanical or electronic transmission or recording, by opinion based upon hearing the voice at any time under the circumstances connecting it with the alleged speaker.

(6) Telephone conversations. Telephone conversations, by evidence that a call was made to the number assigned at the time by the telephone company to a particular person or business, if (A) in the case of a person, circumstances, including self-identification, show the person answering to be the one called or (B) in the case of a business, the call was made to a place of business and the conversation related to business reasonably transacted over the telephone. Significantly, self-identification by a speaker alone is not sufficient authentication. See, *e.g.*, *United States v. Pool*, 660 F.2d 547, 560 (5th Cir. 1981). Where there is self-identification, though, "The authentication may be established by circumstantial evidence such as the similarity between what was discussed by the speakers and what each subsequently did" *United States v. Puerta Restrepo*, 814 F.2d 1236, 1239 (7th Cir. 1987). Thus, before the government may present recordings of intercepted telephone calls and before they may attribute the call to any particular defendant, the following foundation must be established:

The government must establish that the phone call involved a telephone number that is listed to the defendant and that other circumstances, including self-identification, establish that the defendant is the one who answered the call or,

(2) The voice of the caller is identified by a person who has first-hand knowledge of the caller's voice by hearing it on some other occasion.

II. No expert witness may offer an opinion as to what any defendant meant when they used certain words during intercepted telephone calls.

The Seventh Circuit has frequently acknowledged that drug dealers often use "code words" in narcotic transactions in an attempt to conceal their criminal conduct. These "code words," when considered in isolation, might seem unclear or almost nonsensical. The jury, therefore, must analyze them in the context of the totality of the evidence to understand their true meaning. See *United States v. Garcia*, 35 F. 3d 1125, 1127 n.3 (7th Cir. 1994); *United States v. Olson*, 978 F.2d 1472, 1479 n.6 (7th Cir. 1992), cert. denied, 123 L. Ed. 2d 174, 113 S. Ct. 1614 (1993); *United States v. Martinez*, 937 F.2d 299, 306 n.5 (7th Cir. 1991); *United States v. Vega*, 860 F.2d 779, 795 (7th Cir. 1988). In other words, persons who are parties to the conversation may testify as to the meaning of the code words. See, *e.g.*, *United States v. Benitez*, 92 F. 3d 528, 532 (7th Cir. 1996) Contrary to the prosecutor's assertions in this case, though, no case has held that a government agent, who is not a party to an intercepted telephone conversation, may as a matter of course "interpret" the language used by the parties to the conversation. Such testimony is expert opinion evidence because it is based on the purported "Specialized knowledge" of the government agent.

If the code language were a matter of common knowledge, there would be no need to have anyone explain its meaning to the jury. Thus, since such testimony is expert testimony because it involves specialized knowledge, Rule 704(b) F.R.E. comes into play. That section provides that:

No expert witness testifying concerning the mental state or condition of a defendant in a criminal case may state an opinion or inference as to whether the defendant did or did not have the mental state or condition constituting an element of the crime charged or of a defense thereto. Such ultimate issues are matters for the trier of fact alone. Interpreting the words used by a defendant, contrary to the common meaning of the words is nothing if it is not offering an opinion as to the mental state of the defendant while using such words. In a conspiracy case, this amounts to an opinion.

In Benitez, a government informant, Varela, was permitted to testify concerning the meaning of telephone conversations he had with Benitez in which the two discussed buying "horses" for the "Ranch." Varela, though, was a party to the telephone conversation.

Rule 702 FRE provides as follows: "If specialized knowledge will assist the trier of fact to understand the evidence or to determine a fact in issue, a witness qualified as an expert by knowledge, skill, experience, training, or education, may testify thereto in the form of an opinion or otherwise, if (1) the testimony is based upon sufficient facts or data, (2) the testimony is the product of reliable principles and methods, and (3) the witness has applied the principles and methods reliably to the facts of the case.

Put another way, if a person says, "I went to the store," and if we give the words their common meaning, we all may understand that the person is communicating the fact that he went to the store. The defendant's state of mind constitutes an element of the crime charged (*i.e.*, that in saying those words the defendant intended to make an agreement with another to distribute drugs – even though the plain meaning of the words is something else). In *United States v. Lipscomb*, 14 F.3d 1236 (7th Cir. 1994), the Seventh Circuit explained:

[W]e simply cannot ignore the fact that this court and others have routinely assumed that Rule 704(b) imposes an additional limitation, however slight, on the expert testimony of law enforcement officials. To reconcile that fact with our impression that the rule is of more limited scope, we conclude that when a law enforcement official states an opinion about the criminal nature of a defendant's activities, such testimony should not be excluded under Rule 704(b) as long as it is made clear, either by the court expressly or like the examination, that the opinion is based on the expert's knowledge of common criminal practices, and not on some special knowledge of the defendant's mental processes. Relevant in this regard, though not determinative, is the degree to which the expert refers specifically to the "intent" of the defendant, for this may indeed suggest, improperly, that the opinion is based on some special knowledge of the defendant's mental processes.

There is no universal "drug code language" in the same way that there is one Spanish language. Every group of persons involved in the distribution of drugs develops its own code. Other members of the group may testify as to the meaning of the code words. The jury, though, must determine whether on the occasion in question the defendant meant to talk about "paint" or about "cocaine." A case agent is not allowed to tell the jury that, during one particular conversation, the two participants said they needed some paint, but they meant that they needed some cocaine. To be sure, the appellate courts have not flatly banned the testimony of case agents as to the meaning of "drug code" language. Rather, the courts have cautioned that there is a great danger of unfair prejudice in allowing such expert testimony. For example, in *United States v. Dukagjini*, 326 F.3d 45, 53 (2d Cir. 2002) the Second found that, on the other hand, if a person says, "I went to the store" and another witness testifies that what the speaker meant is that he went to buy cocaine, then the witness is testifying as to the mental state of the speaker (*i.e.*, the speaker is saying one thing but means something else).

The Circuit cautioned that [W]e have observed elsewhere when a fact witness or a case agent also Functions as an expert for the government, the government confers upon him 'the aura of special reliability and trustworthiness surrounding expert testimony, which ought to caution its use'" (Internal citations omitted). This aura creates a risk of prejudice, "because the jury may infer that the agent's opinion about the criminal nature of the defendant's activity is based on knowledge of the defendant beyond the evidence at trial," a risk that increases when the witness has supervised the case, *id.* Simply by qualifying as an "expert," the witness attains unmerited credibility when testifying about factual matters from first-hand knowledge. Additionally, when the expert bases his opinion on in-court testimony of fact witnesses, such testimony may improperly bolster that testimony and may "suggest to the jury that a law enforcement specialist…believes the government's witness to be credible and the defendant to be guilty, suggestions we have previously condemned."

Therefore, the appellate courts have instructed the district court, in its role as "gatekeeper," to carefully conduct a *Daubert* analysis when the government proposes to introduce expert testimony concerning drug code language.

A. The government has not provided the defendants with any summary of expert testimony

(G) Expert witnesses. At the defendant's request, the government must give to the defendant a written summary of any testimony that the government intends to use under Rules 702, 703, or 705 of the Federal Rules of Evidence during its case in chief at trial. Here, the government stated on the record that it would follow the "open file policy" under local rules, and this, by rule, amounts to a demand for discovery by the defendant. Thus, the government has an obligation to provide the defense with a Criminal L.R. 16.1 Open File Policy. (a) At the arraignment, the government must state on the record to the presiding judicial officer whether it is following the open file policy as defined in Criminal L.R. 16.1(b). If the government states that it is following the open file policy and the defendant accepts such discovery materials, then the defendant's discovery obligations are under Fed. R. Crim. P. 16(b) arise without further government motion or request, and both parties shall be treated for all purposes in the trial court and on appeal as if each had filed timely written motions requesting all materials required to a summary of any expert testimony it intends to introduce at trial.

There was no notice of expert testimony provided in this case, and therefore, the court should exclude any expert testimony by the government. See Rule 16(d)(2)(C) F. R. Crim. P.

B. The court must conduct a *Daubert* hearing into whether there is a sufficient foundation to permit any case agent to interpret drug code language contained in the recordings of the intercepted calls.

The Notes of the Advisory Committee on 2000 Amendments to Rule 702 explain:

Rule 702 has been amended in response to *Daubert v. Merrell Dow Pharmaceuticals, Inc.*, 509 U.S. 579 [125 L Ed. 2d 469] (1993), and to the many cases applying *Daubert*, including *Kumho Tire Co. v. Carmichael*, [143 L. Ed. 2d 238,] 119 S. Ct. 1167 (1999). In *Daubert,* the Court charged trial judges with the responsibility of acting as gatekeepers to exclude unreliable expert testimony, and the Court in *Kumho* clarified that this gatekeeper function applies to all expert testimony, not just testimony based on science. See also *Kumho*, 119 S. Ct. at 1178 (citing the Committee Note to the proposed amendment to Rule 702, which had been released for public comment before the date of the *Kumho* decision). The amendment affirms the trial court's role as gatekeeper and provides some general standards that the trial court must use to assess the reliability and helpfulness of proffered expert testimony. Consistently with *Kumho*, the Rule as amended provides that all types of expert testimony present questions of admissibility for the trial court in deciding whether the evidence is reliable and helpful. Consequently, the admissibility of all expert testimony is governed by the principles of Rule 104(a). Under that Rule, the proponent has the burden of establishing that the pertinent admissibility requirements are met by a preponderance of the evidence. See *Bourjaily v. United States*, 483 U.S. 171 [97 L. Ed. 2d 144) (1987).

Daubert set forth a non-exclusive checklist for trial courts to use in assessing the reliability of scientific expert testimony. The specific factors explicated by the *Daubert* Court are (1) whether the expert's technique or theory can be or has been tested – that be produced under Fed. R. Crim. P. 16(a)(1)(A), (B), (C), (D), (E) and 16 (b)(1)(A), (B), and (C), and invoking Fed. R. Crim. P. 16(c). That is whether the expert's theory can be challenged in some objective sense, or whether it is instead simply a subjective, conclusory approach that cannot reasonably be assessed for reliability; (2) whether the technique or theory has been subject to peer review and publication; (3) the known or potential rate of error of the technique or theory when applied; (4) the existence and maintenance of standards and controls; and (5) whether the technique or theory has been generally accepted in the scientific community. The Court in *Kumho* held that these factors might also be applicable in assessing the reliability of non-scientific expert testimony, depending upon "the particular circumstances of the particular case at issue" 119 S. Ct. at 1175.

C. So what testimony is allowed?

About "interpreting" the drug code language used in the intercepted telephone calls the court must abide by the following considerations:

(1) Under *Daubert*, there must be a foundation that a drug code language exists within this conspiracy and that the witness interpreting it has first-hand knowledge of the code (*i.e.*, the witness was part of the conspiracy);

(2) If so, then the witness may testify, in general terms, as to the code meaning of certain words within the group in question.

(3) Under Rule 704 F.R.E. and Lipscomb, though, the witness may not offer an opinion as to what an individual defendant meant by using the words during the court of any given telephone call. Rather, under Garcia, et al., the jury must determine the meaning of the words used by the parties to the intercepted telephone call based upon the totality of the evidence in the case; and,

(4) Given the "aura of reliability" that attends to an expert witness the court should be very reluctant to permit a government case agent to interpret the language because, under Rule 403 F.R.E.,

there is a great possibility of unfair prejudice. After all, the jury may believe that the case agent has additional information about the defendant that is not being presented in court.

CONCLUSION

Wherefore, based on the foregoing, the defendant moves this court to issue an order to suppress expert testimony.

Respectfully submitted, on this first day of April 2022.

X_____

UNITED STATES DISTRICT COURT
EASTERN DISTRICT OF WISCONSIN

UNITED STATES OF AMERICA plaintiff	§ § §	Case No
v.	§ §	2:12-CR-297-KOB-JEO
KELLY RIGGS, TIMOTHY BOYD, AND PATRICK COTTON defendants	§ § § § § §	

JOINT BRIEF OF THE DEFENDANTS IN SUPPORT OF PRETRIAL MOTIONS

Introduction

Government agents were working with a confidential informant (CI) during the course of investigating illegal drug trafficking and possession of firearms in the Milwaukee area. As part of that investigation, the agents used the CI to set up an imaginary armed robbery involving the defendants in this case. There is no indication as to how the defendants were chosen to be the subjects of this presentation by the CI.

Under this imaginary scheme, the informant's uncle was to come to Milwaukee with five kilograms of cocaine and perhaps some cash. Specifically, the uncle would be taking the cocaine to a storage facility on Milwaukee's south side. The CI, with the assistance of government investigators, pitched a plan under which the defendants would rob the uncle of his cocaine and his cash when he arrived at the storage facility. Two of these defendants, Riggs and Boyd, were only involved for less than 12 hours. On August 28, 2021, the CI prompted the defendants to come to the storage facility. When they arrived, all were arrested. No robbery took place. No currency changed hands. No cocaine was present.

Kelly Riggs slept through the entire faux robbery

The government indicted the defendants on numerous charges; however, relevant to these motions are the following counts: (1) conspiracy to commit armed robbery where such armed robbery affected interstate commerce; (2) conspiracy to possess cocaine with intent to distribute; (3) attempted armed robbery; (4) attempted possession of cocaine with intent to distribute; and (5) possession of a firearm during the commission of a violent crime.

Argument

I. The indictment must be dismissed because the tactics of law enforcement violate due process.

There comes a point where law enforcement techniques are so repugnant that it violates due process. Here, that point was not only reached it was surpassed. The government used a technique to choose whom it wanted to target. This was not an equal opportunity offer to the public at large. Additionally, unconstrained by reality, the government agents fashioned the lure to be as attractive as possible. In effect, the government's tactics amounted to a search of the defendants' thoughts to see whether they harbored any secret plans to commit a crime such as this. And, finally, the technique places all the power squarely in the hands of the prosecution to decide how serious of a crime will be committed. The net effect is a profoundly unfair prosecution that simply cannot be countenanced by the court.

The Supreme Court has recognized that tactics of law enforcement may be so outrageous as to violate due process. A separate defense based solely upon governmental misconduct may be raised by "even the most hardened criminal." See *United States v. Hodge*, 594 F.2d 1163 (7th Cir. 1979). On this point the Seventh Circuit observed:

The Supreme Court has not yet given any content to the principle that government misconduct may bar prosecution even absent any other deprivation of the defendant's constitutional rights. However, an examination of the post-Hampton cases decided by the courts of appeals indicates that due process grants wide leeway to law enforcement agencies in their investigation of crime. Assuming that no independent constitutional right has been violated, governmental misconduct must be truly outrageous before the due process will prevent the conviction of the defendant. In seeking to detect and punish crime, law enforcement agencies frequently are required to resort to tactics that might be highly offensive in other contexts. Granting that a person is predisposed to commit an offense, we think that it may safely be said that investigative officers and agents may go a long way in concert with the individual in question without being deemed to have acted so outrageously as to violate due process or evoke the exercise by the courts of their supervisory powers to deny to the officers the fruits of their misconduct *United States v. Quinn*, 543 F.2d 640, 648 (8th Cir. 1976). ... Those few cases in which federal courts have recognized this defense have involved misconduct far removed from the facts before us today. See *United States v. Twigg*, 588 F.2d 373 (3rd Cir. 1978) (Government informer contacted defendant about manufacturing narcotics: Government supplied chemicals, glassware, and farmhouse used for manufacturing: informer did lion's share of the manufacturing while defendant's involvement was minimal); *United States v. Archer*, 486 F.2d 670 (2nd Cir. 1973) (federal agents the received court and grand jury by staging sham crime to investigate corruption in state prosecutor's office); *Greene v. United States*, 454 F.2d 783 (9th Cir. 1971) (Government agent-initiated contact with defendants and used veiled threats over an extended period of time to convince them to produce illegal whiskey: supplied ingredients and was the only customer of defendants). *United States v. Kaminski*, 703 F.2d 1004, 1009 (7th Cir. Ill. 1983). As unsavory as many law enforcement tactics may seem, there is a line that cannot be crossed. Although not a bright line, the boundary may nonetheless be discerned.

For example, the line is not crossed when the defendant advertises himself as a professional criminal (usually as an arsonist or as a hitman) and government agents merely pretend to be paying customers– all the while knowing that the services will not be rendered. See, *e.g.*, *Kaminski*, *supra*, 703

F.2d at 1005 where Kaminski, without any prompting, offered his services as a professional arsonist and a government agent merely posed as an interested customer. Another way to recognize the line is by use of the "fly-paper analysis." Sting operations that merely create an opportunity for, and perhaps even attract, members of the general public who are inclined to commit such a crime (albeit an imaginary one) seem to have the approval of the courts. In other words, there is nothing wrong with the government hanging sweet-smelling flypaper (the imaginary crime) to see who in the general public is attracted by it. The best example of this technique is where government agents pose as children seeking a sexual experience with adults who visit internet chat rooms.

Here, though, the law enforcement technique is over the line – going from flypaper to fly-swatter. The government informant, in this case, proposed the crime to the defendants. The defendants never advertised themselves as professional armed robbers who were willing to accept engagements. Rather, the informant selected the defendants and then proposed the crime to them. The informant presented the details of the plan to the defendants and the execution of the plan. As will be outlined in more detail below, then, even though the law enforcement scheme, in this case, does not squarely violate any independent constitutional rights, the totality of the law enforcement conduct fails the smell test. It violates virtually every constitutional principle of fair play. As such, this is one of those few cases where the court is compelled to find that governmental misconduct violates due process.

A. Selective prosecution ("the fly-swatter")

As mentioned above, one hallmark of a permissible sting operation is that it is an equal opportunity enticement. Here, though, it was not an equal opportunity enticement. Rather, the government selected the persons to whom they would make the pitch.

The Fourteenth Amendment prohibits any state from taking action which would "deny to any person within its jurisdiction the equal protection of the laws." This admonition is applicable to the federal government through the Fifth Amendment, *Bolling v. Sharpe*, 347 U.S. 497, 74 S. Ct. 693, 98 L. Ed. 884 (1954); *Washington v. United States*, 130 U.S. App. D.C. 374, 401 F.2d 915, 922 (1968). The promise of Equal protection of the laws is not limited to the enactment of fair and impartial legislation but necessarily extends to the application of these laws. The basic principle was stated long ago in *Yick Wo v. Hopkins*, 118 U.S. 356, 373-374, 6 S. Ct. 1064, 1073, 30 L. Ed. 220 (1886): Though the law itself be fair on its face and impartial in appearance, yet, if it is applied and administered by a public authority with an evil eye and an unequal hand, so as practically to make unjust and illegal discriminations between persons in similar circumstances, material to their rights, the denial of equal justice is still within the prohibition of the Constitution. To show that the government engaged in improper selective prosecution, the defendant "must demonstrate that the federal prosecutorial policy 'had a discriminatory effect and that it was motivated by a discriminatory purpose,'" *United States v. Armstrong*, 517 U.S. 456, 465, 116 S. Ct. 1480, 134 L. Ed. 2d 687 (1996). Again, the tactics of law enforcement here do not fall neatly under existing selective prosecution law. The principle underlying selective prosecution law, though, is seriously offensive. It takes little imagination to conceive of means by which this sort of law enforcement technique might be abused by the government. The government does get to choose whom they prosecute. Thus, there is nothing to stop the government from closely scrutinizing some "enemy of the people" nor from zealously prosecuting him if he commits a crime – but at least they must wait until he commits a crime. Under the tactics used in this case, though, there is nothing to stop the government from targeting "undesirables" to see whether they may be persuaded to commit some imaginary crime. If at first, they balk, then simply make the lure more attractive – after all, every man has his price. The government may choose to rid itself of particularly nettlesome defense lawyers by sending in informants to offer a king's ransom in imaginary drug money as a retainer fee. Why stop there? If a journalist writes an unflattering article about some government official, then sends in the informant to propose a million-dollar fraud scheme and, for good measure, have the snitch tell the journalist that there is "absolutely no way to get caught." If the journalist agrees then there is a "conspiracy."

B. Entrapment ("the lure")

Although the defense of governmental misconduct is wholly separate from the defense of entrapment, a discussion of the principles underlying entrapment is instructive.

Before examining the facts of this case, we should note the peculiar nature of one of these factors: the inducement offered by the Government. As stated previously, predisposition exists prior to contact with the Government. In many cases, however, there is little direct evidence of the defendant's state of mind prior to interaction with Government agents and we must instead rely upon indirect proof available through examination of the defendant's conduct after contact with the agents. Should the defendant initially reject a suggestion that he commit a crime this is indicative of a lack of predisposition.

Conversely, should he initiate contact with the agents in order to commit a crime, this is strong proof of predisposition. The amount of inducement offered by the Government, however, has no such logical correlation with the defendant's predisposition as the Government may offer as much as it wishes to any potential defendant. The amount of inducement gains its relevance through the defendant's reaction to the lure, *Kaminski, supra*, 703 F.2d at 1008.

The tactics used by law enforcement in this case, unconstrained by reality, allowed the agents to make the lure attractive indeed. The uncle was supposed to be coming to Milwaukee with five kilograms of cocaine (*i.e.*, nearly $125,000 worth of drugs) and he was portrayed to be an easy mark because he was coming with only one other person.

C. This is an unreasonable search of an individual's mind (*i.e.*, "thought police" are alive and well)

In a very real sense, the tactics of the government agents, in this case, amount to an unreasonable search of the defendants' minds for evidence of their predisposition to commit a crime of this sort. Certainly, many persons in this country harbor secret plans to commit the perfect crime but who are more or less restrained by the reality that there probably is no perfect crime. But why wait until one of these individuals acts on his or her plan? If only the government could identify the persons who entertain such thoughts, they could be arrested before they act. What better way to discover them than to have secret informers go around pitching "the perfect crime" to selected individuals? If any of these people give expression to their secret thoughts of the perfect crime, then they are then guilty of conspiracy.

D. Separation of powers – this technique vests law enforcement with an unreasonable ability to control the penalty.

Like many well-intentioned plans, the tactics employed by law enforcement, in this case, have unintended consequences that this court ought to examine very closely. How easy it is to profess one's disgust over robbers and drug dealers and, consequently, any plan designed to remove them from society may, at first blush, seem like a good plan. But the founding fathers correctly observed that the greatest danger we face is the concentration of governmental power in any one agency. Here, law enforcement's plan concentrates a vast amount of power in the hands of the prosecutor. Law enforcement decides who will be targeted, how serious the crime will be, and consequently, how severe the penalty will be.

[W]e … have recognized Madison's teaching that the greatest security against tyranny – the accumulation of excessive authority in a single Branch – lies not in a hermetic division among the Branches, but in a carefully crafted system of checked and balanced power within each Branch. "[T]he greatest security," wrote Madison, "against a gradual concentration of the several powers in the same department, consists in giving to those who administer each department, the necessary constitutional means, and personal motives, to resist encroachments of the others," The Federalist No. 51, p. 349 (J. Cooke ed. 1961). Accordingly, as we have noted many times, the Framers "built into the tripartite Federal Government … a self-executing safeguard against the encroachment or aggrandizement of one branch at the expense of the other," *Buckley v. Valeo*, 424 U.S., at 122. See also *INS v. Chadha*, 462 U.S. 919,951 (1983); *Mistretta v. United States*, 488 U.S. 361, 381-382 (1989). If the court approves of the law enforcement technique employed in this case, then the balance of power falls squarely into the hands of the prosecutors. The prosecution will go from prosecuting crimes (of whatever severity) that a defendant decided to commit to deciding the seriousness of the crime that will be pitched to any given defendant. In this way, the Department of Justice decides what the potential penalty will be for any given defendant.

The court should be skeptical of this expansion of governmental power given the ease of prosecuting persons charged with conspiracy to violate the uniformed controlled substances act. Riggs, for example, is being prosecuted even though he showed so little enthusiasm for this faux crime that he slept through the event. A person subject to this law enforcement technique might agree to rob someone of 5 grams of cocaine, only to find him in much greater trouble because the CI suggests to the defendant that the object of the robbery might have several ounces of Heroin. With a sentence (and with no greater danger to the public or evidence of greater criminality by the defendant), the defendant's sentencing exposure is now geometrically increased. Specifically, in this case, the government could have imagined that the uncle would be delivering only several ounces of cocaine but, instead, the agents imagined that it was five kilograms. This is certainly an interesting choice since it just so happens that at five kilograms the law provides for a minimum mandatory prison sentence of ten years (or twenty years if there is a prior drug conviction). It certainly seems as though it is the prosecution that decided what sentence will be imposed on the defendants if they are convicted. Constitutional law teaches that the ends never justify the means. In this scenario, the government chose the ends – all the while using a CI to orchestrate the means employed. If an individual is only a minor nuisance, then, perhaps, the government will only propose that he deliver several grams of cocaine. On the other hand, no crime is too serious to propose against an individual who is a major nuisance. Several of the defendants, in this case, maybe facing life in prison – and it was the prosecution that decided which crimes would be proposed to these defendants.

Conclusion

For all of these reasons, the court should dismiss the indictment against the defendants because the law enforcement technique employed by the government violates due process.

Respectfully submitted on the 22nd day of April 2022.

CHAPTER THREE

FILINGS RELATED TO CRIMINAL APPEALS

This chapter pertains to both direct appeals that should follow your original conviction and any appeal that follows the conviction of new charges after you have already been sentenced to prison. You will likely discover that any appointed attorney will collect his pay for your conviction, pat you on the butt and send you off to prison when you need to appeal.

I have learned that the Criminal Justice Act is far less rewarding to attorneys who encourage appeals over new convictions. And because your attorney will make less money to file an appeal in your case, he or she most likely won't, even when they say they will. Thus, you will likely have to file your own notice of appeal. Even if you trust your attorney, you should file your own notice of appeal just to be on the safe side.

Keep in mind that your attorney is going home to plan his next vacation with his family as you are settling into your new prison cell. Again, file your own notice of appeal. If it duplicates your attorney's filing, the court will correct the docket to reflect that your attorney filed a notice of appeal. If your attorney fails to file the notice, your filing will prompt him or her to do so quickly. I've even witnessed courts that will file a notice for the apathetic attorney to make up for his or her failure.

Don't forget that your notice of appeal in a criminal case must be filed within ten business days or fourteen calendar days of the final judgment – your sentencing date. *This is a strict deadline.* Write the notice of appeal in pencil if you must.

KELLY PATRICK RIGGS

IN THE UNITED STATES DISTRICT COURT
FOR THE NORTHERN DISTRICT OF ALABAMA
SOUTHERN DIVISION

UNITED STATES OF AMERICA plaintiff	§ § §	Case no.:
v.	§ §	2:12-CR-297-KOB-JEO
JOHN DOE defendant	§ § § §	

NOTICE OF APPEAL

Mr. Doe, in *pro se*, hereby gives notice that he appealed this court's judgment and sentence that it imposed on March 6, 2020.

Submitted on March 19, 2020, by:

X_____

JOHN DOE, *pro se*
Reg. No.: _____-___
Federal Correctional Institution
P.O. Box 9000
Seagoville, TX 75159

CERTIFICATE OF SERVICE

I hereby certify that on this 19th day of March 2020, I served this notice on the clerk of this court for filing in the CM/ECF system.

X_____
JOHN DOE, pro se

Reg. No.: _____-___

Federal Correctional Institution

P.O. BOX 9000

Seagoville, TX 75159

The filing of your notice of appeal is just the beginning. An appointed attorney, or even a prepaid private attorney for that matter, will do anything to get out of filing your appeal.

The most common tactic is the filing of an *Anders v. California* brief. This type of brief e that explains to The Court of Appeals that you have no meaningful issues to raise in an appeal. In most cases, this has nothing to do with the merit of your appeal. It only means that your lawyer is looking for the easiest way out of the work required to file a meaningful appeal. An Anders brief is the quickest and least labor-intense avenue to bring your appeal to an end.

The bottom line is that your appointed lawyer is going to receive $6,500 to review your case for appeal. The Anders brief is in a fill-in-the-blanks format on a computer that any office assistant can prepare. That means that the Anders brief is the path of least resistance to collecting the $6,500 paid to the lawyer under The Criminal Justice Act.

This is not the end of the world. Once the clerk at the court of appeals receives the Anders brief, he or she will send you notice of its filing. In that notice will be the option of filing your brief in *pro se*. Do not be afraid to take a chance on this. You have nothing to lose. If you file nothing, you will be denied, so take a chance and express your issues in your *pro se* brief.

The sample brief that follows is an actual appeal brief filed in a United States Court of Appeals. I have changed the names and places but know that the issue is real. Use this example as a format only unless you have the same issue.

No. 16-40364

IN THE UNITED STATES COURT OF APPEALS

FOR THE FIFTH CIRCUIT

UNITED STATES OF AMERICA,

Plaintiff-Appellee,

v.

ALFREDO MONSIVAIS-CORNELIO,

Defendant-Appellant.

Appeal from the United States District Court

for the Southern District of Texas

BRIEF FOR APPELLANT

In accordance with *Anders v. California*, 386 U.S. 738 (1967)

Brett Crow

State Bar of Texas 00923980

6750 West Loop South, Suite 120

Bellaire, Texas 77401

(713) 666-7567

(713) 665-9090 (Fax)

Attorney for the Appellant,

CERTIFICATE OF INTERESTED PERSONS

The undersigned counsel of record certifies that the following listed persons and entities as described in the fourth sentence of Rule 28.2.1 have an interest in the outcome of this case.

1. The Honorable Andy Hanen, United States District Judge.

2. The Honorable Ignacio Torteya, United States Magistrate Judge

3. Alfredo Monsivais-Cornelio, Defendant-Appellant.

4. United States of America, Plaintiff-Appellee.

5. Counsel for Plaintiff-Appellee:

The Assistant United States Attorney Karen Betancourt (trial counsel), and Renata A. Gowie and Richard Berry (appellate counsel).

6. Counsel for Defendant-Appellant:

Assistant Federal Public Defender Sandra Zamora Zayas (trial counsel),

Greg Ahlgren (appellate counsel), David Adler (appellate counsel).

These representations are made so that the judges of this court may evaluate possible disqualification or recusal.

/s/ Brett Crow
Brett Crow

PREAMBLE

This brief is submitted in accordance with Anders v. California, 386 U.S. 738 (1967). Counsel has carefully examined the facts and matters contained in the record on appeal and has researched the law in connection therewith and has concluded that the appeal does not present a non-frivolous legal question. In reaching this conclusion, the counsel has thoroughly read the record and has examined the record for any arguable violations of the Constitution, federal statutes, the Federal Rules of Criminal Procedure, the Federal Rules of Evidence, and the Federal Sentencing Guidelines.

STATEMENT RESPECTING ORAL ARGUMENT

Counsel for the defendant-appellant has moved to withdraw as counsel based on Anders v. California; consequently, oral argument is not requested.

TABLE OF CONTENTS

TABLE OF CITATIONS

<u>CASES</u>

Page

CASES

CONSTITUTIONAL PROVISION

STATUTES AND RULES

TABLE OF CITATIONS - (Cont'd)

STATUTES AND RULES - (Cont'd)

TABLE OF CITATIONS - (Cont'd)

STATEMENT OF JURISDICTION

Jurisdiction of this Court is invoked under 28 U.S.C. §1291, as an appeal from a final judgment of conviction and sentence in the United States District Court for the Southern District of Texas, Houston Division, and under 18 U.S.C. §3742, as an appeal of a sentence imposed under the Sentencing Reform Act of 1984. Notice of appeal was timely filed in accordance with Rule 4(b) of the Federal Rules of Appellate Procedure.

STATEMENT OF THE ISSUES

ISSUE ONE: There is no nonfrivolous issue regarding Monsivais-Cornelia's guilty plea.

ISSUE TWO: There is no nonfrivolous issue regarding Monsivais-Cornelia's sentence.

STATEMENT OF THE CASE

On September 22, 2015, Defendant-Appellant Alfredo Monsivais-Cornelio was charged in a one-count indictment with being an alien who was found present in the United States after removal, in violation of 8 U.S.C. § 1326(a) and (b)(l). ROA.16-40388.13. On November 30, 2015, Mr. Monsivais-Cornelio entered a plea of guilty to the indictment. ROA.16-40388.25-29.

At the guilty plea proceeding, the prosecutor proffered the following as the factual basis for the plea:

On July 17, 2015, Defendant Alfredo Monsivais-Cornelio was found in the Cameron County Jail in Cameron County, Texas, by Immigrations and Customs Enforcement. It was determined that he was an alien and citizen of Mexico who had entered the United States illegally. The defendant had been previously excluded, deported, or removed from the United States on May 11, 2006, after having been convicted of the felony of Alien Unlawfully Found in the United States on May 9, 2006. The defendant had not received the consent of the Attorney General or Secretary of Homeland Security to reapply for admission into the United States when found.

ROA.16-40388.118. Upon questioning by the court, Mr. Monsivais-Cornelio stated that these facts were true. ROA.16-40388.119.

On June 13, 2016, the district court sentenced Mr. Monsivais-Cornelio to serve 24 months in the custody of the Bureau of Prisons, followed by a three-year term of supervised release. The court did not impose a fine and granted the government's motion to remit the special assessment. ROA.16-40388.138-139. Mr. Monsivais-Cornelio filed a timely notice of appeal. ROA.16-40388.32.

Because there are no nonfrivolous issues for appeal of Mr. Monsivais-Cornelia's conviction or sentence, counsel moves to withdraw pursuant to *Anders v. California*, 386 U.S. 738 (1967). All other facts relevant to this appeal are set forth in the Argument section below.

SUMMARY OF THE ARGUMENT

When Monsivais-Cornelio entered his plea of guilty, the court substantially complied with the Federal Rule of Criminal Procedure 11 and ensured that his guilty plea was informed, free, and voluntary. Any arguable deviation from Rule 11's requirements does not amount to a nonfrivolous issue on appeal with regard to Monsivais-Cornelia's conviction.

Likewise, there is no nonfrivolous issue on appeal with regard to Monsivais-Cornelia's sentence. His guideline and criminal history scores were properly calculated, and he was sentenced within the guideline range. Therefore, there is no nonfrivolous issue on appeal regarding Monsivais-Cornelia's sentence.

Accordingly, because there are no nonfrivolous issues on appeal, counsel moves to withdraw, pursuant to *Anders v. California*, 386 U.S. 738 (1967).

ARGUMENT

ISSUE ONE RESTATED: There is no nonfrivolous issue with regard to Mr. Monsivais-Cornelia's guilty plea.

A.   Standard of Review

Whether the requirements of Federal Rule of Criminal Procedure 11 were satisfied is a conclusion of law and is, therefore, reviewable de novo. See *United States v. Cuevas-Andrade*, 232 F.3d 440,443 (5th Cir. 2000) (citing *United States v. Scott*, 987 F.2d 261, 264 (5th Cir.1993)). A district court's finding that there is an adequate factual basis for a plea of guilty, as required by Fed. R. Crim. P. 11(b)(3), is reviewed under the erroneous standard. See *United States v. Rivas*, 85 F.3d 193, 194 (5th Cir. 1996).

However, before this Court will vacate a guilty plea, the Court must find both (1) that the district court varied from the procedures required by Rule 11; and (2) that the variance affected the substantial rights of the defendant. See *United States v. Luciano-Perez*, 274 F.3d 219, 224 (5th Cir. 2001). Where a claim of noncompliance with the requirements of Rule 11 is raised for the first time on appeal, however, it is subject only to review for plain error under Fed. R. Crim. P. 52(b). See *United States v. Dominguez Benitez*, 542 U.S. 74, 79-83 (2004); *United States v. Vann*, 535 U.S. 55, 59 & 62-74 (2002).

B.   There Is No Nonfrivolous Issue with Regard to Mr. Monsivais-Cornelia's Guilty Plea.

A district court may delegate to a magistrate judge the responsibility of conducting a felony guilty plea proceeding. See 28 U.S.C. § 636(b)(3); *United States v. Dees*, 125 F.3d 261, 264-66 (5th Cir. 1997) (holding those plea proceedings conducted by magistrate judges are authorized by statute and comport with Article III of the Constitution). Mr. Monsivais-Cornelio knowingly and voluntarily consented to have his guilty plea hearing conducted by the magistrate judge, ROA.14-40388.75-76, and, in so doing, validly waived his right to have an Article III judge conduct his guilty plea hearing. See *Dees*, 125 F.3d at 266. The magistrate judge's compliance with the requirements of Rule 11 is set forth in the record of this case.

In sum, the district court substantially complied with the requirements of the Fed. R. Crim. P. 11, as outlined above. Any arguable deviation from the requirements of Rule 11 was harmless and certainly not plain error under the circumstances of this case. Thus, there is no nonfrivolous issue under Rule 11 error concerning the taking of Mr. Monsivais-Cornelia's guilty plea. The record shows that his guilty plea was knowingly, understandingly, and voluntarily made, as the district court explicitly found. ROA.16-40388.130. Thus, there is nothing in the record "to show that the district court's error, if any, in finding his guilty plea was knowing and voluntary affected his substantial rights." *United States v. Garcia-Vargas*, 428 Fed. Appx. 386,387 (5th Cir. 2011) (unpublished).

ISSUE TWO RESTATED: There is no nonfrivolous issue with regard to Mr. Monsivais-Cornelia's sentence.

A. Standard of Review

A district court's compliance with the sentencing procedures of Federal Rule of Criminal Procedure 32 is reviewed de novo. See, *e.g.*, *United States v. Myers*, 150 F.3d 459, 465 (5th Cir. 1998). This Court "review[s] the district court's interpretation or application of the Sentencing Guidelines *de novo* and its factual findings for clear error." *United States v. Trujillo*, 502 F.3d 353, 356 (5th Cir. 2007) (footnote and italics omitted). If a defendant fails to object in the district court, this Court reviews the sentence only for plain error. See, *e.g.*, *United States v. Ronquillo*, 508 F.3d 744, 748 (5th Cir. 2007).

After *United States v. Booker*, 543 U.S. 220 (2005), federal courts of appeals reviewed sentences for reasonableness. See *Booker*, 543 U.S. at 261-62. Under the reasonableness review mandated by *Booker*, "[r]egardless of whether the sentence imposed is inside or outside the Guidelines range, the appellate court must review the sentence under an abuse-of-discretion standard," *Gall v. United States*, 552 U.S. 38, 51 (2007). This Court has held that sentences within a properly calculated Guidelines range are entitled to a rebuttable presumption of reasonableness. See *United States v. Alonzo*, 435 F.3d 551, 554 (5th Cir. 2006).

B. There Are No Reversible Errors with Respect to Mr. Monsivais-Cornelio's

1. There Is No Nonfrivolous Issue Arising from the District Court's Sentencing Guideline Calculations.

Using the 2015 edition of the United States Sentencing Guidelines ("USSG"), see ROA.16-40388.153 (1111), the district court correctly calculated Mr. Monsivais-Cornelio's total offense level as shown in the record of this case.

Under the plain language of the Guidelines, the PSR's calculation of Mr. Monsivais-Cornelio's base offense level and application of the two-level reduction for acceptance of responsibility was correct. See USSG §§ 2L1.2(a) & 3E1.1(a). Nor did the district court err in applying a four-level enhancement for a prior conviction of a felony. At his re-arraignment, Mr. Monsivais-Cornelio admitted that he had been removed from the United States on May 11, 2006, ROA.16-40388.119. Earlier in 2006, he had been convicted of being an alien unlawfully found in the United States in violation of 8 U.S.C. § 1326(a). See docket entry 20 in 1:06-CR-00149 in the Southern District of Texas (judgment of conviction) and ROA.16-40388.164-168. As this offense was punishable by up to two years imprisonment, there is no nonfrivolous argument that it was not a prior felony conviction and thus not a basis for the four-level enhancement. And, for this same reason, there is no nonfrivolous argument that the district court erred in finding that the punishment provisions of 8 U.S.C. § 1326(b)(1) applied in the instant proceeding. See ROA.16-40388.137-138 and 160 (¶ 66). The PSR correctly calculated Mr. Monsivais-Cornelia's criminal history score and category by assessing points as follows:

- 2 points for a 2003 DWI with a 2-month sentence;

- 2 points for a 2004 assault with a 2-month sentence;

- 2 points for a 2004 possession of marijuana case with a 3-month sentence;

- 1 point for a 2005 illegal reentry case with a 20-day sentence;

- 2 points for a 2006 alien unlawfully found in the U.S. case with a 104-day sentence: and

- 2 points for a 2015 assault case with a 90-day sentence.

ROA.16-40388.154-156 (¶ 22-27). With eleven criminal history points, the PSR correctly placed Mr. Monsivais-Cornelio in the criminal history category V. See ROA.16-40388.156 (¶ 28); see also USSG Ch.5, Pt. A, Sentencing Table.

A total offense level of ten and a criminal history category of V resulted in a Guideline imprisonment range from 21 to 27 months, ROA.16-40388.160 (¶ 67); see also USSG Ch.5, Pt. A, Sentencing Table.

The PSR correctly noted that, under the Guidelines, supervised release ordinarily should not be imposed upon a deportable alien, ROA.16-40388.161 (¶ 72). The PSR also correctly noted, however, that if the district court chose to impose supervised release, then, pursuant to USSG § 5D1.2(a)(2), the Guideline range for the supervised-release term was from one to three years, ROA.16-40388.161 (¶ 72), with a statutory maximum supervised-release term of three years under 18 U.S.C. § 3583(b)(2), ROA.16-40388.160

2. There Is No Nonfrivolous Procedural Issue Arising from the Imposition of Mr. Monsivais-Cornelia's Sentence.

The district court substantially complied with the relevant procedural requirements of sentencing, as set forth in the case at hand.

Although the district court asked Mr. Monsivais-Cornelio whether he and his counsel had reviewed the PSR together, see ROA.16-40388.135, the district court did not ask the same question with respect to the addendum to the PSR. This error does not present any nonfrivolous issue on appeal, however, because the record does not reflect any prejudice against Mr. Monsivais-Cornelio as a result of this error. See United States v. Esparza-Gonzalez, 268 F.3d 272, 274 (5th Cir. 2001). The district court failed to advise Mr. Monsivais-Cornelio of his right to appeal his conviction and sentence, and his right to do so in forma pauperis, as required by Fed. R. Crim. P. 32(j)(1)(A)-(C). This omission, however, presents no nonfrivolous issue on appeal. Because Mr. Monsivais-Cornelio did, with the assistance of court-appointed counsel, perfect a timely in forma pauperis appeal he cannot present a nonfrivolous argument that the district court's error prejudiced him. See United States v. Tapp, 276 Fed. Appx. 258, 260 (4th Cir. 2007) (unpublished) ("Any failure by the district court to advise Tapp of his right to appeal is harmless as his attorney timely filed a notice of appeal."); see also Peguero v. United States, 526 U.S. 23, 24 (1999) (holding that habeas corpus petitioner could not show prejudice arising from the failure to advise him of his right to appeal where he knew of his right to appeal). With respect to the reasons requirement of 18 U.S.C. § 3553, this Court had held, prior to Booker, that this requirement is generally satisfied when the court indicates the applicable Guideline range and how it is chosen (including by adoption of the PSR in which the Guideline calculations and resulting range are set forth), see United States v. Reyes-Lugo, 238 F.3d 305, 310 (5th Cir. 2001), and the district court adopted the PSR here, ROA.130. Even after Booker, this Court has held that "little explanation is required" when a judge elects to sentence within the Guidelines, United States v. Mares, 402 F.3d 511, 519 (5th Cir. 2005). Here, the district court imposed a prison sentence and supervised release term within the advisory guidelines range. However, even if the court's explanation was not sufficient because Mr. Monsivais-Cornelio did not object to the sufficiency of this explanation, he must show that had the district court provided a more thorough explanation, he would have received a shorter sentence. See *United States v. Mondragon-Santiago*, 564 F.3d 357, 364-65 (5th Cir. 2009). Accordingly, the district court committed no reversible procedural error in sentencing Mr. Monsivais-Cornelio.

3. There Is No Nonfrivolous Substantive Issue with Respect to Mr. Monsivais-Cornelio's Sentence.

This Court presumes on appeal that sentences imposed within a properly calculated advisory Guideline imprisonment range are reasonable. See *Alonzo*, 435 F.3d at 554. Mr. Monsivais- Cornelio cannot overcome that presumption here.

As detailed above, the district court correctly calculated Mr. Monsivais-Cornelio's Guideline imprisonment range and then sentenced him within that range. See ROA.16-40388.172.

Nothing in the record shows that Mr. Monsivais-Cornelia's within-Guideline sentence "does not account for a factor that should receive significant weight, [that] it gives significant weight to an irrelevant or improper factor, or [that] it represents a clear error of judgment in balancing sentencing factors," *United States v. Cooks*, 589 F.3d 173, 186 (5th Cir. 2009) (citation omitted). There is thus no nonfrivolous argument that Mr. Monsivais-Cornelia's prison sentence was substantively unreasonable.

Moreover, there are no nonfrivolous issues with respect to the remaining aspects of Mr. Monsivais-Cornelia's sentence. The three-year term of supervised release that he received was within the correct range provided in the Guidelines for his offense, see USSG § 5D1.2(a)(2), and the district court specifically mentioned that it was imposing the term of supervised release "as an added measure of deterrence," ROA.16-40388.138; see USSG § 5D1.1, comment. (n.5); see also *United States v. Dominguez-Alvarado*, 695 F.3d 324, 330 (5th Cir. 2012). Moreover, the first special condition of supervised release – prohibiting Mr. Monsivais-Cornelio from illegally reentering the United States, see ROA.16-40388.50 – is simply a reiteration of the mandatory condition "that the defendant not commit another Federal...crime during [his] term of supervision." See 18 U.S.C. § 3583(d); USSG § 5D1.3(a)(1), (c)(2); see also *United States v. Torres-Aguilar*, 352 F.3d 934, 937 (5th Cir. 2003). And the second special condition – prohibiting Mr. Monsivais-Cornelio from driving a vehicle or drinking alcoholic beverages while in the United States without the permission of his Probation Officer – is justified by Mr. Monsivais-Cornelio's substance abuse issues, see ROA.16-40388.158 (1143 - 47), and his driving while intoxicated conviction, ROA.16-40388.154 (¶ 22).

Finally, the district court did not impose a fine, and it remitted the $100 special assessment. In sum, this case presents no nonfrivolous issue on appeal.

CONCLUSION

After examining the facts of the case and considering the applicable law, counsel on appeal believes there is no basis for presenting any legally non-frivolous issue.

Respectfully submitted,

/s/ David Crow

David Crow

State Bar of Texas 00923980

6750 West Loop South,

Suite 120

Bellaire, Texas 77401

713-666-7567

713-665-7070 (Fax)

Attorney for Appellant,

Alfredo Monsivais-Cornelio

CERTIFICATE OF SERVICE

I certify that a copy of this brief was served on the AUSA by ECF to AUSA Renata Gowie, on December 14, 2016. In accordance with the Fifth Circuit's Anders Guidelines, I further certify that a copy of the brief for the appellant is being mailed on the same day to Alfredo Monsivais-Cornelio, 43861-179, USP Atlanta, P.O. Box 150160, Atlanta, Georgia, 30315, and that counsel has reasonably attempted to communicate, in a manner and a language understood by the defendant: (i) that counsel has fully examined the record and reviewed the relevant law, and there are no meritorious issues for appeal; (ii) that counsel has therefore moved to withdraw; (iii) that if granted, the motion will result in dismissal of the appeal; but (iv) that the defendant has the right to file a response in English, opposing counsel's motion, within 30 days.

/s/ David Crow

David Crow

CERTIFICATE OF COMPLIANCE

This brief complies with the type-volume limitation of the FED. R. APP. P. 32(a)(7)(B) because it contains 5,012 words, excluding the parts of the brief exempted by FED. R. APP. P. 32(a)(7)(B)(iii).

This brief complies with the typeface requirements of the FED. R. APP. P. 32(a)(S) and the type style requirements of FED. R. APP. P. 32(a)(6) because it has been prepared in a proportionally spaced typeface Corel WordPerfect 12.0 software in Times New Roman 14-point font in text and Times New Roman 12- point font in footnotes.

An electronic copy of this brief has been filed with the court through ECF.

/s/ David Crow

David Crow

KELLY PATRICK RIGGS

IN THE UNITED STATES COURT OF APPEALS
FOR THE ELEVENTH CIRCUIT

CASE NUMBER 18-14124

UNITED STATES OF AMERICA,
PLAINTIFF-APPELLEE,

V.

EMORY SMITH,
DEFENDANT-APPELLANT

ON DIRECT APPEAL FROM THE UNITED STATES DISTRICT COURT FOR THE NORTHERN
DISTRICT OF ALABAMA SOUTHERN DIVISION

INITIAL BRIEF OF THE DEFENDANT-APPELLANT

X_____
EMORY SMITH, *pro se* Reg. No.: _____-___
Federal Correctional Institution
P.O. BOX 9000
Seagoville, TX 75159

POST-CONVICTION RELIEF: THE ADVOCATE

CERTIFICATE OF INTERESTED PERSONS

The case below was *United States v. Emory Smith*, case number 2:12-cr-297-KOB-JEO, in the United States District Court for the Northern District of Alabama, Southern Division. The undersigned pro se litigant certifies that the following listed persons have an interest in the outcome of this case. These representations are made in order so that judges of this Court may evaluate possible disqualification or recusal.

District Judge:	Hon. Sam R. Cummings
Magistrate Judge:	Hon. John E. Ott
Appellant:	Emory Smith
Defense Counsel:	Federal Public Defender for the Northern District of Alabama
	Kevin Butler
	Allison Case
Prosecutors:	U.S. Attorney for the Northern District of Alabama
	Brad Felton
	Staci G. Cornelius
	Daniel Fortune

X_____
Emory Smith, *pro se*

<u>STATEMENT REGARDING ORAL ARGUMENT</u>

An oral argument is not requested.

TABLE OF CONTENTS

TABLE OF AUTHORITIES

FEDERAL STATUTES

RULES

UNITED STATES SENTENCING GUIDELINES

JURISDICTIONAL STATEMENT

The district court had original jurisdiction over this case pursuant to 18 U.S.C.: 3231, and it had jurisdiction to revoke supervised release under 18 U.S.C.: 3606. This Court has appellate jurisdiction under 28 U.S.C.: 1291 and 18 U.S.C.: 3742. The District Court entered written judgment revoking supervised release on November 1, 2018. On November 5, 2018, Mr. Smith filed a timely notice of appeal.

ISSUE PRESENTED FOR REVIEW

Where the case involved no financial crimes and the sentence imposed a ten-year period of supervised release but only minimal restitution, did the district court violate the law by barring Mr. Smith from incurring any new credit charges or opening any additional lines of credit without the prior permission of the probation officer throughout the period of supervised release and regardless of the status of Mr. Smith's restitution payments?

STATEMENT OF THE CASE

On June 11, 2013, Mr. Emory Smith (hereinafter "Smith") was indicted on a one-count indictment for the enticement of a minor, in violation of 18 U.S.C.: 2422(b). In conjunction with his plea agreement, Mr. Smith signed a factual resume admitting that he used a cell phone to entice Jane Doe, then a 16-year-old minor, to engage in illegal sexual activity. According to the factual resume, Mr. Smith and Jane Doe met through their church and exchanged cell phone text messages for several years. When Doe was 16 years old, in September of 2012, Smith convinced Doe by text message to leave her mother's house, go to his residence, and engage in sexual intercourse. Mr. Smith pled guilty, and at his re-arraignment, the Court warned Mr. Smith that his conviction would result in mandatory restitution to the victim.

A presentence report ("PSR") was completed. Mr. Smith's PSR showed no prior criminal convictions. Given Mr. Smith's total offense level of 33 and Criminal History Category of 1, Mr. Smith's guideline range of imprisonment was 135 to 168 months. The PSR also calculated a total of $988.28 in restitution should be paid to Doe for her medical expenses, therapy, and transportation. The PSR showed that Mr. Smith did not have any significant liabilities, and only listed three monthly expenses totaling $754.00. Both parties filed statements adopting the PSR.

At his sentencing hearing, the district judge imposed a sentence of 168 months to be followed by a period of 10 years of supervised release. In its oral pronouncement, the Court ordered several special terms of supervised release, including one mandating Mr. Smith to "refrain from incurring any new credit charges or opening any additional lines of credit without first getting the approval of the probation office." Mr. Smith did not object to the Court's sentence. The written judgment, however, differed from its oral counterpart regarding the borrowing restrictions placed on Mr. Smith. While the oral judgment forbade Mr. Smith from any new borrowing and from obtaining any new lines of credit without the prior approval of his probation officer, for the duration of the ten years, the written judgment imposed such limitations except where "the probation officer makes a determination that the defendant is in compliance with the payment schedule." It is this condition of supervised release that Mr. Smith now challenges.

SUMMARY OF THE ARGUMENT

Special conditions of supervision must deprive the defendant of no more liberty than is reasonably necessary to achieve the goals of deterrence, rehabilitation, and protection of the public. See *United States v. Ferguson*, 369 F.3d 847, 852 (5th Cir. 2004). The imposition of this oral condition of supervision was erroneous because it represents a greater than necessary means to ensure that Mr. Smith meets the financial obligation imposed on him after his imprisonment. The imposition of this condition was plainly erroneous and should be reversed.

ARGUMENT AND AUTHORITIES

1. THE DISTRICT COURT COMMITTED PLAIN ERROR BY ORALLY IMPOSING A CONDITION LIMITING SMITH'S ABILITY TO BORROW MONEY DURING THE ENTIRETY OF HIS TEN-YEAR PERIOD OF SUPERVISED RELEASE, NO MATTER THE STATUS OF HIS RESTITUTION PAYMENT.

A. Standard of Review

This court has previously held that procedural reasonableness claims must be preserved by a specific objection. See *United States v. Whitelaw*, 580 F.3d 256, 259-60 (5th Cir. 2009). Smith did not make an objection at the conclusion of the hearing.

Smith respectfully submits for further review, however, that requiring a reasonableness objection, even a procedural reasonableness objection, in district court fails to acknowledge that reasonableness is a standard of appellate review, not a directive to the district court. See *Rita v. United States*, 551 U.S. 338, 351 (2007). Nonetheless, the current law of the circuit requires objection, and none was lodged. Unpreserved error is reviewed under the plain error standard. See Fed. R. Crim. P. 52(b). The reversible plain error consists of (1 error, (2) that is plain or obvious, (3) that affects substantial rights, and (4) that seriously affects the fairness, integrity, or public reputation of judicial proceedings. See *United States v. Jones*, 527 U.S. 373, 389 (1999).

B. Discussion
1. The court erred.

In this Circuit, an oral sentence prevails over a written sentence from which it varies, *United States v. Shaw*, 920 F. 2D 1225, 1231 (5th Cir. 1991).

A district court has broad discretion in fashioning special conditions of supervised release. See *Ferguson*, 369 F. 3d at 852. Such conditions, however, must be reasonably related to:

(1) the nature and circumstances of the offense and the history and characteristics of the defendant, (2) the need to afford adequate deterrence to criminal conduct, (3) the need to protect the public from further crimes of the defendant, and (4) the need to provide the defendant with needed [educational or vocational training], medical care, or other correctional treatment in the most effective manner, *Ferguson*, 369 F. 3D at 853.

While these criteria "are fairly broad, they do impose a real restriction of the district court's freedom to impose conditions on supervised release," *United States v. Pruden*, 398 F. 3D 241, 248-249 (3rd Cir.2005); *United States v. Jimenez*, No. 06-41678, 2008 U.S. App. LEXIS 9272, at *14 (5th Cir. 2008) (unpublished) (While the court has "wide latitude," its "discretion in imposing special conditions is limited by 18 U.S.C. 3583(d).”); *United States v. T.M.*, 330 F 3d 1235, 1240 (9th Cir. 2003)(cautioning that the discretion to fashion conditions of supervised release “is not unfettered”).

Even if these criteria are satisfied, the court may not impose conditions that “involve a greater deprivation of liberty than is reasonably necessary to achieve statutory goals.” *Ferguson*, 369 F. 3D at 852 (citing *United States v. Paul*, 274 F. 3D 155, 165 (5th Cir. 2001)); *United States v. Scott*, 270 F. 3D 632, 635 (8th Cir. 2001); *United States v. Peterson*, 248 F. 3D 79, 82 (2nd Cir. 2001); *United States v. Brogdon*, 503 F 3d 555, 564 (6th Cir. 2007); *United States v. Prochner*, 417 F. 3D 54, 63 (1st Cir. 2005). A condition of supervised release is “reasonably related to the defendant’s offense or history” only where each interference with the defendant’s liberty is necessary to protect the public. See *Ferguson*, 369 F. 3D at 854; accord *Peterson*, 248 F. 3D at 82-83. The standard governing special conditions is thus “a standard with teeth,” *Pruden*, 398 F. 3D at 249.

For cases in which a defendant is ordered to pay restitution according to a payment schedule, the Sentencing Guidelines recommend a special term of supervised release “prohibiting the defendant from incurring new credit charges or opening additional lines of credit without approval of the probation officer **unless the defendant is in compliance with the payment schedule**.” U.S.S.G.: 5D1.3(d)(2).

Here, the court erred in instituting its oral restriction on Mr. Smith’s borrowing capacity without including an exception for times when Mr. Smith is in compliance with the restitution scheduling order. The court’s oral pronouncement, while inexact in its attempt to follow the language of the written judgment, failed to properly limit the borrowing restrictions in ways intended by both the written judgment and the language in the Sentencing guidelines from which the condition is derived.

A wide-ranging ban on a defendant’s borrowing capacity can be proper in some cases. For example, in *United States v. Murphy*, 48 F. 3D 529 (5th Cir. 1995) (unpublished), this court refused to find plain error in a similar circumstance where the fudge orally imposed a ban on the defendant borrowing or opening lines of credit without the court’s prior approval, in contradiction to the court’s written judgment, *id.* at *1-2. This court upheld this stringent condition in Murphy because its defendant was convicted of embezzlement involving more than $400,000 and evidence showed that he had accepted a large amount of money from his wife that was mostly unaccounted for, *id.* Under such circumstances, the court held that the special conditions reasonably related to the sentencing goals, *id.* at *2.

In contrast to Murphy, Mr. Smith’s case was not a financial crime, and there was no accusation that Mr. Smith improperly used his borrowing capacity to commit the offense of conviction or any prior offense. The PSR contained no evidence that Mr. Smith had previously abused his borrowing capacities, and he had no significant liabilities at the time of the interview.

If the court truly found such a restriction necessary in this case, it should have explained its reasoning. But the court merely provided cursory explanations for its rationale in imposing (1) the general conditions of supervised release and (2) the restitution. These explanations provide no insights into the court's decision to impose the ratcheted-up borrowing capacity restrictions on Mr. Smith.

2. The error was plain.

Two facts demonstrate that the court's oral imposition of this special condition of supervised release was plainly erroneous. First, the court's written judgment demonstrates the court's intention to follow the recommendation of the Sentencing Guidelines. Second, the court failed to explain why it was imposing on Mr. Smith a more restrictive version of the borrowing capacity limitation than that recommended by the Sentencing Guidelines or written into the court's judgment.

The record shows that the court likely intended to only impose a limited restriction on Mr. Smith's borrowing capacity. First, the court appears to have tried to follow the recommendation of the Sentencing Guidelines, which recommend a borrowing-capacity restriction be imposed on persons ordered to pay restitution or fines according to payment schedules. However, the Guidelines recommend this restriction only to the extent that defendants fail to make payments in accordance with the court orders. Inexplicably, the court's oral pronouncement did not include such limiting language.

That this oral condition was plainly imposed in error is also apparent from the discrepancy between the court's oral and written judgment. The court's written judgment reflects the same intent as the Sentencing Guidelines – to curb Mr. Smith's borrowing-capacity limitation to circumstances in which he is not making restitution payments according to schedule. Again, the oral pronouncement does not include such limiting language.

Were the court intending to impose the more stringent condition on Mr. Smith, then the court should have explained why it was imposing this highly restrictive condition on Mr. Smith's situation. This Court has twice found that a district court's failure to offer an adequate explanation where "more is required and d" "easily" constitutes plain error. See Whitelaw, 580 F. 3d at 261-62; *United States v. Mondragon-Santiago*, 564 F. 3D 357, 363-64 (5th Cir. 2009). Though the court offered a perfunctory explanation of its overall intent by imposing the numerous special terms of supervised release, the court's explanation on this point was inadequate and in plain error.

3. The error affected Mr. Smith's substantial rights.

A district court's failure to explain a sentence can affect a defendant's substantial rights in one of two ways – it can impair a party's ability to seek a meaningful appellate review of the sentence, and it can potentially affect the outcome. See *Whitelaw*, 580 F. 3d at 262-64 (discussing both theories and citing *Mondragon-Santiago*, supra; *In re* Sealed Case, 527 F. 3D 188, 193 (D.C. Cir. 2008); *United States v. Lewis*, 424 F.3d 239, 248 (2d Cir. 2005); *United States v. Mendoza*, 543 F. 3D 1186 (10th Cir. 2008)).

This Court rejected the first theory in *Whitelaw*, where a close review of the record "revealed the reasons for Whitelaw's sentences" because it "followed an extensive hearing during which the court heard evidence" and substantial arguments by the government directed specifically at the defendant's claims for leniency, *id.* at 263. But there was no such hearing here, and the district court's explanation for the sentence cannot itself be described as particularly thorough.

Alternatively, and to preserve the matter for further review, Mr. Smith submits that *Whitelaw* is wrongly decided. He respectfully submits that this Court should adopt the reasoning of the Second, Sixth, and D.C. Circuits, which have held that failures to explain impact substantial rights within the meaning of the plain error doctrine. See Sealed Case, 527 D. 3d at 190-93; *Lewis*, 424 F. 3d at 246-49; *United States v. Blackie*, 548 F. 3D 395, 402-04 (6th Cir. 8). There courts have reasoned that failures to explain a sentence affect substantial rights by depriving the defendant of meaningful appellate review (see Sealed Case, 527 F. 3d at 193; *Blackie*, 548 F. 3d at 403; *Lewis*, 424 F. 3d at 247); that these failures impact the public's right to remain informed of the course of judicial proceedings and negatively affect public perception of federal sentencing (see Sealed Case, 527 F. 3d at 193; *Blackie*, 548 F. 3d at 403; *Lewis*, 424 F. 3d at 248); that they may be fairly analogized to "structural errors," where prejudice may be presumed (see *Lewis*, 424 F. 3d at 248-49); and that the requirements of plain error are appropriately relaxed in the review of sentencing errors (see Sealed Case, 527 F.3d at 193; *Lewis*, 424 F.3d at 248).

4. The error affected the fairness, integrity, and public reputation of the judicial proceedings.

The Supreme Court in *Rita* recognized that an adequate explanation of the sentence is critical to promote public confidence in the exercise of judicial authority:

The statute does call for the judge to "state" his "reasons." And that requirement reflects sound judicial practice. Judicial decisions are reasoned decisions. Confidence in a judge's use of reason underlies the public's trust in the judicial institution. A public statement of those reasons helps provide the public with the assurance that creates that trust. *Rita*, 551 U.S., at 356.

Accordingly, the failure to explain this special condition of supervised release seriously affects the public reputation of judicial proceedings, meriting remand.

CONCLUSION

The appellant respectfully requests that the Court strike or modify the terms of supervised release , discussed herein, or, alternatively, that it remands to the district court to adjust them. Finally, Mr. Smith prays for such relief as to which he may be justly entitled.

Respectfully submitted on April 21, 2021, by:

X._____

Emory Smith, *pro se*

Reg. No.: _____-___

P.O. Box 9000

Seagoville, TX 75159

CERTIFICATE OF SERVICE

Mr. Smith certifies that on April 21, 2021, he filed this brief by depositing it in the prison legal mailing system as available to inmates, and that the United States Attorney's office has been served via U.S. Mail at their last known address.

Respectfully submitted, by:

X._____

Emory Smith, *pro se*

CHAPTER FOUR

FILINGS FOR COMPASSIONATE RELEASE IN FEDERAL COURT

Section 3582(c)(1)(A) of Title 18 of the United States Code is well known among federal prisoners as the Compassionate Release Statute. This statute authorizes a court to reduce a defendant's term of imprisonment for "extraordinary and compelling reasons." The First Step Act of 2018 amended section 3582(c)(1)(A) to allow a defendant to file a motion seeking compassionate release directly in federal court after satisfying an administrative exhaustion requirement. Before the First Step Act, the statute permitted only the Director of the Federal Bureau of Prisons ("BOP") to file that motion on the defendant's behalf. We all know how that works out.

The compassionate release landscape rapidly evolved in the year 2020, with two notable developments. First, motions for compassionate release dramatically increased in the second half of 2020 as COVID-19 inundated federal prisons. The Commission chose to study the fiscal year 2020 timeframe in part to compare the time periods before and after the emergence of COVID-19. Second, the Commission lost a voting quorum shortly after the enactment of the First Step Act, preventing any possible amendment of the compassionate release policy statement of §181.13. Because §181.13 and its commentary reflect the pre-First Step Act procedural requirement that a reduction may be granted only upon motion of the Director of the BOP pursuant to 18 U.S.C. § 3582(c)(1)(A), most circuit courts have concluded that §181.13 was not "applicable" to offender-filed motions. As a result, district courts in those circuits began to independently identify "extraordinary and compelling reasons" under section 3582(c)(1)(A).

Nonetheless, most grants of compassionate release were based on a reason specifically described in the policy statement or a reason comparable to those specifically described reasons, like, for example, the health risks associated with COVID-19. All right, with all the legal crap out of the way, I'll explain what this means to you as a Jailhouse Lawyer.

Let me start by telling you a little about my experience with the First Step Act while I was in prison. When the Act was first passed in 2018, I took the bull by the horns, seeing it as a new way for potential relief for some people. I started with all the benefits gained for early release for programming. Then, I discovered that the prison I was locked up in was the hardest hit in the country by COVID-19. This spawned an idea. I had determined that the new outbreak was a threat to the health of the elderly and infirmed prisoners around me. That's when I decided to explore The First Step Act's new change to the Compassionate Release statute.

When I learned that an inmate could file his own motion for Compassionate Release, I got started for everyone who had underlying health problems. What you will find in this chapter is all the stock forms you will need to file for anyone you feel is at risk. I even include one of my winning cases.

Here, I have provided you with the fill-in-the-blank motion required to get the ball rolling. You'll find the medical forms that have all the questions that need to be answered for the court and a proposed release plan. This part is important, so don't forget to fill it out. I also added, for your convenience and clarity, the stock form used by The Federal Public Defenders Office.

After I left prison, once I was released early under the provisions of The First Step Act, I went to a halfway house in Mississippi. Once there, I was contacted by a prisoner who was still at the prison in which I was last incarcerated. He needed help filing for compassionate release. I agreed to help him through his family. I developed the case and encouraged them to hire an attorney I had come to know as an honorable man. Under his direction, I formed the first motion, which you will find in this chapter, and sent it to him via email. He refined my motion and filed it with the Federal Court. What follows is the order from the court releasing him to his family. What I want you to know is that this same motion can be filed *pro se* and still gain a wide range of relief. This is your time now: Take a chance and make it happen. Just do something.

UNITED STATES DISTRICT COURT
FOR THE
_____ DISTRICT_____

UNITED STATES OF AMERICA plaintiff	§ § §	Case No.: _____ *(Write the number of your criminal case)*
v.	§ § §	
_____ *(Write your full name here)* defendant, *pro se* prisoner	§ § § §	

MOTION FOR SENTENCE REDUCTION UNDER
18 U.S.C. § 3582(c)(1)(A) (Compassionate Release)

NOTICE

The public can access electronic court files. Federal Rule of Criminal Procedure 49.1 addresses the privacy and security concerns resulting from public access to electronic court files. Under this rule, papers filed with the court should not contain: an individual's full social security number or full birth date; the full name of a person known to be a minor; or a complete financial account number. A filing may include only: the last four digits of a social security number; the year of an individual's birth; a minor's initials; and the last four digits of a financial account number.

Does this motion include a request that any documents attached to this motion be filed under seal? (Documents filed under seal are not available to the public.)

☐ Yes

☐ No

If you answered yes, please list the documents in section IV of this form.

I. SENTENCE INFORMATION

Date of sentencing:

Term of imprisonment imposed:

Approximate time served to date:

Projected release date:

Length of Term of Supervised Release:

Have you filed an appeal in your case?

☐ Yes

☐ No

Are you subject to an order of deportation or an ICE detainer?

☐ Yes

☐ No

II. EXHAUSTION OF ADMINISTRATIVE REMEDIES

18 U.S.C. § 3582(c)(1)(A) allows you to file this motion (1) after you have fully exhausted all administrative rights to appeal a failure of the Bureau of Prisons to bring a motion on your behalf, or (2) 30 days after the warden of your facility received your request that the warden makes a motion on your behalf, whichever is earlier.[1]

Please include copies of any written correspondence to and from the Bureau of Prisons related to your motion, including your written request to the Warden and records of any denial from the Bureau of Prisons.

Have you personally submitted your request for compassionate release to the Warden of the institution where you are incarcerated?

☐ Yes, I submitted a request for compassionate release to the warden on

☐ No, I did not submit a request for compassionate release to the warden.

If no, explain why not:

Was your request denied by the Warden?

☐ Yes, my request was denied by the warden on (date):_____

☐ No, I did not receive a response yet.

III. GROUNDS FOR RELEASE

Please use the checkboxes below to state the grounds for your request for compassionate release. Please select all grounds that apply to you. You may attach additional sheets if necessary to further describe the reasons supporting your motion. You may also attach any relevant exhibits. Exhibits may include medical records if your request is based on a medical condition or a statement from a family member or sponsor.

---

[1] *The requirements for this compassionate release motion being filed with the court differ from the requirements that you would use to submit a compassionate release request to the Bureau of Prisons. This form should only be used for a compassionate release motion made to the court. If you are submitting a compassionate release request to the Bureau of Prisons, please review and follow the Bureau of Prisons program statement.*

A. Are you 70 years old or older?

☐ Yes.

☐ No.

If you answered "No," go to Section B below. You do not need to fill out Section A.

If you answered "Yes," you may be eligible for release under 18 U.S.C. § 3582(c)(1)(A)(ii) if you meet two additional criteria. Please answer the following questions so the Court can determine if you are eligible for release under this section of the statute.

Have you served 30 years or more of imprisonment pursuant to a sentence imposed under 18 U.S.C. § 3559(c) for the offense or offenses for which you are imprisoned?

☐ Yes.

☐ No.

Has the Director of the Bureau of Prisons determined that you are not a danger to the safety of any other person or the community?

☐ Yes.

☐ No.

Do you believe there are other extraordinary and compelling reasons for your release?

☐ Yes.

☐ No.

If you answered "Yes," please check all boxes that apply so the Court can determine whether you are eligible for release under 18 U.S.C. § 3582(c)(1)(A)(i).

☐ I have been diagnosed with a terminal illness.

☐ I have a serious physical or medical condition; a serious functional or cognitive impairment; or deteriorating physical or mental health because of the aging process that substantially diminishes my ability to provide self-care within the environment of a correctional facility, and I am not expected to recover from this condition.

☐ I am 65 years old or older and I am experiencing a serious deterioration in physical or mental health because of the aging process.

☐ The caregiver of my minor child or children has died or become incapacitated and I am the only available caregiver for my child or children.

☐ My spouse or registered partner has become incapacitated, and I am the only available caregiver for my spouse or registered partner.

☐ There are other extraordinary and compelling reasons for my release.

Please explain below the basis for your request. If there is additional information regarding any of these issues that you would like the Court to consider but which is confidential, you may include that information on a separate page, attach the page to this motion, and, in section IV below, request that that attachment be sealed.

ATTACHMENTS AND REQUEST TO SEAL

Please list any documents you are attaching to this motion. A proposed release plan is included as an attachment. You are encouraged but not required to complete the proposed release plan. A cover page for the submission of medical records and additional medical information is also included as an attachment to this motion. Again, you are not required to provide medical records and additional medical information. For each document, you are attaching to this motion, state whether you request that it be filed under seal because it includes confidential information.

Document	Attached?		Request to seal?	
Proposed Release Plan	☐ Yes	☐ No	☐ Yes	☐ No
Additional medical information	☐ Yes	☐ No	☐ Yes	☐ No
_____	☐ Yes	☐ No	☐ Yes	☐ No
_____	☐ Yes	☐ No	☐ Yes	☐ No

V. **REQUEST FOR APPOINTMENT OF COUNSEL**

I do not have an attorney and I request an attorney be appointed to help me.

☐   Yes.

☐   No.

VI. **MOVANT'S DECLARATION AND SIGNATURE**

For the reasons stated in this motion, I move the court for a reduction in sentence (compassionate release) under 18 U.S.C. § 3582(c)(1)(A). I declare under penalty of perjury that the facts stated in this motion are true and correct.

_____   _____
Date   Signature

_____
Name

_____
Bureau of Prisons Register#

_____
Bureau of Prisons Facility

_____
Institution's Address

ATTACHMENT TO MOTION FOR COMPASSIONATE RELEASE

UNITED STATES DISTRICT COURT
FOR THE
_____ DISTRICT_____

UNITED STATES OF AMERICA plaintiff	§ § §	Case No.: _____ *(Write the number of your criminal case)*
v.	§ § §	
_____ *(Write your full name here)* defendant, *pro se* prisoner	§ § §	

MEDICAL RECORDS AND ADDITIONAL MEDICAL INFORMATION
In Support of Motion for Sentence Reduction Under 18 U.S.C. § 3582(c)(1)(A)

NOTICE

The public can access electronic court files. Federal Rule of Criminal Procedure 49.1 addresses the privacy and security concerns resulting from public access to electronic court files. Under this rule, papers filed with the court should not contain: an individual's full social security number or full birth date; the full name of a person known to be a minor; or a complete financial account number. A filing may include only: the last four digits of a social security number; the year of an individual's birth; a minor's initials; and the last four digits of a financial account number.

If you attach documents to this form that you believe should not be publicly available, you may request permission from the court to file those documents under s al. If the request is granted, the documents will be placed in the electronic court files but will not be available to the public.

Do you request that the attachments to this document be filed under seal?

☐ Yes.

☐ No.

ATTACHMENT TO MOTION FOR COMPASSIONATE RELEASE

UNITED STATES DISTRICT COURT
FOR THE
_____ DISTRICT_____

UNITED STATES OF AMERICA plaintiff	§ § §	Case No.: _____
	§	*(Write the number of your criminal case)*
v.	§	
	§	
	§	
_____	§	
(Write your full name here)	§	
defendant, *pro se* prisoner	§	

PROPOSED RELEASE PLAN
In Support of Motion for Sentence Reduction Under 18 U.S.C. § 3582(c)(1)(A)

If you provide information in this document that you believe should not be publicly available, you may request permission from the court to file the document under seal. If the request is granted, the document will be placed in the electronic court files but will not be available to the public.

Do you request that this document be filed under seal?

☐ Yes.

☐ No.

PROPOSED RELEASE PLAN

To the extent the following information is available to you, please include the information requested below. This information will assist the U.S. Probation and Pretrial Services Office to prepare for your release if your motion is granted.

A. Housing and Employment

Provide the full address where you intend to reside if you are released from prison:

_____

Provide the name and phone number of the property owner or renter of the address where you will reside if you are released from prison:

_____

Provide the names (if under the age of 18, please use their initials only), ages, and relationships to you of any other residents living at the above-listed address

_____

If you have employment secured, provide the name and address of your employer, and describe your job duties:

_____

List any additional housing or employment resources available to you:

_____

B. Medical needs

Will you require ongoing medical care if you are released from prison?

☐ Yes.

☐ No.

Will you have access to health insurance if released?

☐ Yes.

☐ No.

If yes, provide the name of your insurance company and the last four digits of the policy number. If no, how do you plan to pay for your medical care?

_____

If no, are you willing to apply for government medical services (Medicaid/Medicare)?

☐ Yes.

☐ No.

Do you have copies of your medical records documenting the condition(s) for which you are seeking release?

☐ Yes.

☐ No.

If yes, please include them with your motion. If no, where are the records located?

Are you currently prescribed medication in the facility where you are incarcerated?

☐ Yes.

☐ No.

If yes, list all prescribed medication, dosage, and frequency:

Do you require durable medical equipment (*e.g.*, wheelchair, walker, oxygen, prosthetic limbs, hospital bed)?

☐ Yes.

☐ No.

If yes, list equipment:

Do you require assistance with self-care such as bathing, walking, toileting?

☐ Yes.

☐ No.

If yes, please list the required assistance and how it will be provided:

Do you require assisted living?

☐ Yes.

☐ No.

If yes, please provide the address of the anticipated home or facility and the source of funding to pay for it.

Are the people you are proposing to reside with aware of your medical needs?

□ Yes.

□ No.

Do you have other community support that can assist with your medical needs?

□ Yes.

□ No.

Provide their names, ages, and relationship to you. If the person is under the age of 18, please use their initials only:

Will you have transportation to and from your medical appointments?

□ Yes.

□ No.

Describe the method of transportation:

SIGNATURE

I declare under penalty of perjury that the facts stated in this attachment are true and correct.

_____   _____
Date   Signature

_____
Name

_____
Bureau of Prisons Register#

_____
Bureau of Prisons Facility

_____
Institution's Address

MEDICAL RECORDS AND ADDITIONAL MEDICAL INFORMATION

To the extent you have medical records or additional medical information that support your motion for compassionate release, please attach those records or that information to this document.

SIGNATURE

I declare under penalty of perjury that the facts stated in this attachment are true and correct.

_____   _____
Date   Signature

_____
Name

_____
Bureau of Prisons Register#

_____
Bureau of Prisons Facility

_____
Institution's Address

IN THE UNITED STATES DISTRICT COURT
SOUTHERN DISTRICT OF MISSISSIPPI
EASTERN DIVISION

UNITED STATES OF AMERICA plaintiff	§ § § §	Case no.: X: XX-XX-XXX-XXX-XXX
v.	§ §	
XXXXXXXX defendant	§ § §	

MOTION FOR COMPASSIONATE RELEASE

TO THE HONORABLE KEITH STARRETT, UNITED STATES DISTRICT JUDGE FOR THE SOUTHERN DISTRICT OF MISSISSIPPI, EASTERN DIVISION:

Now comes Xxxxxxxx, register number xxxxxxxx, pursuant to 18 U.S.C. Section 3582(c)(1)(A)(i), Section 1B1.13 of the US Sentencing Guidelines, BOP program statement 5050.50 and 28 CFR Section 571.61 and through his counsel seeks this Court to grant him compassionate release from FPC Xxxxxxxx Federal Prison to time served or home confinement.

Upon his conviction on xxxxxxxx, Xxxxxxxx was taken into federal custody. Thereafter, he was sentenced to serve xxx months in custody for _____. He is xx years old; his release date is xxxxxxxxx, and he has served ___% of his sentence. Further, he has recently been diagnosed with _____. Thus, in addition to his advanced age and _____, his _____ also places him in the most vulnerable group for susceptibility to the coronavirus and serious medical complications from that disease.

Counsel has requested compassionate release from the Warden at FPC _____. See the letter and enclosures attached as Exhibit 1. Although thirty days have not elapsed from this request, this Court can act without waiting for the thirty days to elapse since the BOP will not be able to respond to his request within that time, *cf. FDIC v. Scott*, 125 F.3d 254, 258 (5th Cir. 1997)[when an exhaustion step is futile, the Court may waive the requirement].[1] Further, under this Court's supervisory powers the Court may formulate procedural rules not specifically required by the Constitution to implement a remedy for recognized rights, *United States v. Santana*, 6 F.3d 1, 10 (1st Cir. 1993). The President of the United States has declared a state of emergency because of the threat of the coronavirus to the lives of those in federal prison and is considering releasing persons such as Xxxxxxxx. Thus, this Court may act before thirty days from Xxxxxxxx's request of the BOP to file this motion has elapsed.

Xxxxxxxx is a person with regard to whom the compassionate release is appropriate. Counsel was in the process of obtaining his BOP medical records to craft this motion for compassionate release when the coronavirus broke out. The See Response to Request for Medical Records from BOP is attached as Exhibit 2. The coronavirus is known to cause serious health complications for the elderly. Xxxxxxxx is____-year-old man with underlying medical issues. He is _____. He also has _____, and it was also recently discovered that Xxxxxxxx has _____. See the medical record attached in cumulative Exhibit 1. If he is not released from the facility, the virus and his underlying medical issues put him at risk of contracting the disease and suffering serious health complications. Contracting the coronavirus in prison might be a death sentence for Xxxxxxxx.

Should he be left in the facility, he will remain in a vulnerable situation. A case of coronavirus has been diagnosed for a person at the _____.[2] In another federal facility housing immigration detainees, an ICE employee tested positive on March 19, 2020, for coronavirus.[3] The coronavirus is a particular threat to prison populations because of the circumstances of confinement and the inmates' proximity to each other, https://www.businessinsider.com/trump-consider-coronavirus-executiveorder-federal-prisons2020-3. In the District of Oregon, federal Chief Judge Mario Hernandez varied downward from a sentence of imprisonment in two cases to a sentence of home confinement, because of the pandemic. The New Jersey Supreme Court Chief Justice entered an order on March 23, 2020; with the agreement of country prosecutors, the Attorney General, and Public Defenders; for the commutation or suspension of sentences to release approximately 1000 low-risk persons serving jail sentences, https://www.njcourts.gov/pressrel/2020/pr032320a.pdf?c=IRD.

The International Association of Chiefs of Police told ABC News that police are scaling back arrests for low-level offenses to limit officer exposure. Sheriff David Mahoney, with the National Sheriffs' Association, is working with local, state, and federal partners "to decrease the number of people who are physically arrested and brought to jail," https://abcnews.go.com/US/coronavirus-outbreak-changing-uscriminal-justice-system/story?id=69757440.

For persons in custody in prisons, President Trump is considering issuing an Executive Order to release elderly inmates in federal prisons, https://www.businessinsider.com/trump-consider-coronavirus-executiveorder-federal-prisons2020-3. One of the reasons for this is that the elderly constitute a high-risk group for contracting coronavirus and a high-risk group for serious complications from the virus.

In addition, persons with underlying health conditions, regardless of their age, are in a high-risk group for serious complications from the coronavirus. Xxxxxxxx has such underlying health conditions: ._____.

This request is also being made according to BOP program statement 5050.50, elderly inmates who meet the following criteria should be released.

Age 65 and older

A. Suffer from chronic or serious medical conditions related to the aging process

B. Experiencing deteriorating mental or physical health that substantially diminishes their ability to function in a correctional facility

C. Conventional treatment promises no substantial improvement to their mental or physical condition

D. Have served at least 50% of their sentence

A. Age 65 or Older

Xxxxxxxx is a[n] ___-year-old man.

B. Suffer from chronic or serious medical conditions related to the aging process and conventional treatment will not improve his condition

After his incarceration, Xxxxxxxx experienced _____. Soon thereafter, he developed a tremor and dizziness. As a result, he is _____. This limits his mobility and ability to engage in full self-care. This also makes him vulnerable in custody. In addition, of more recent concern is the _____. He already has _____, which he treats with _____. His conditions are age-related and will not improve. These conditions also place him at high risk for serious medical complications were he to contract the coronavirus.

C. Xxxxxxxx's current deteriorating physical health diminishes his ability to function in the facility

He is _____ and, thus, his self-care is limited. This requires him to self-isolate. However, this is not a practical reality in the prison setting. Further, the scope of care available to him during incarceration will be more limited than that available in the community. His mobility challenges present daily difficulties for him and the institution's staff. And he may be a risk of manipulation by other inmates based on his physical vulnerability.

D. Served at least 50% of his sentence

Xxxxxxxx was taken into federal custody on _____. Thereafter, he was sentenced to serve xxx months in custody for _____. At his sentencing, the trial court found that he was at a very low risk to recidivate and that he did not need a lengthy prison sentence. This Court also found that he was not a risk of flight. To date, he has served _____ days. Xxxxxxxx has served approximately _____ months out of his _____ month sentence.

The BOP website states that his current release date is _____. Therefore, at this time, he has served ___% of his sentence. Xxxxxxx was deemed to have no risk of reoffending at the time he was sentenced and is at no risk of reoffending now. He is _____ and _____ is of diminishing health. He poses no risk to the safety of the community.

Because Xxxxxxxx is xx years old, is suffering from underlying health conditions that place him at greater risk from the coronavirus, because he suffers from deteriorating medical conditions that will not improve, and because the coronavirus presents a national emergency; we respectfully request that this Court grant his release to time served or a sentence of home confinement.

Respectfully submitted,

x._____

---

[1] *The First Step Act allows counsel to request release directly from the Court after making the request of the Bureau of Prisons to the Warden of the facility imprisoning Xxxxxxxx*

[2] *Cite proof of virus in your client's location here_____*

[3] *https://www.themarshallproject.org/2020/03/19/first-ice-employee-tests-positive-for-coronavirus*

IN THE UNITED STATES DISTRICT COURT
FOR THE NORTHERN DISTRICT OF KANSAS

UNITED STATES OF AMERICA plaintiff	§ § §	Case no.:
	§	2:06-CR-20056-001-KHV
v.	§ §	
SAVINO DAVILA defendant	§ § §	

MOTION FOR SENTENCE REDUCTION PURSUANT TO 18 U.S.C.: 3582(c)(1)(A)(i)

Comes now Defendant Savino Davila, (hereinafter "Davila") by and through the assistance of counsel, Greg Klebanoff, to move this court to reduce his sentence to a term of time served based on extraordinary circumstances. Davila's reasons for seeking relief under what has become known as the "Compassionate Release" statute, after the passing of the First Step Act's new authorization, are as compelling as the novel and global coronavirus pandemic that now plagues our country's prisons. Davila's unique and specific extraordinary circumstances are due to his personal and often debilitating diabetes, the widespread infection of the COVID-19 virus at FCI Seagoville, the prison's ability to continue his treatment for diabetes due to the prison medical staff being overwhelmed with other infected prisoners, and the potentially deadly effect the Coronavirus have on prisoners who are immune-deficient, such as Mr. Davila. Thus, because Davila's circumstances meet the "extraordinary and compelling reasons" standard set out in 18 U.S.C.: 3582(c)(1)(A)(i) he asks this court to reduce his sentence to time served.

THE COURT'S JURISDICTION TO GRANT THE REQUESTED RELIEF

1) 18 U.S.C.: 3582(c)(1)(A)(i) in the relevant part states that this Court is empowered to reduce a defendant's sentence when "extraordinary and compelling reasons warrant such a reduction."

2) Under the First Step Act (hereinafter "FSA") Congress revised 18 U.S.C.: 3582(C)(1)(a) to empower the District Courts – rather than the Director of the Federal Bureau of Prisons (hereinafter "BOP") – to determine what circumstances constitute "extraordinary and compelling reasons" for a sentence reduction, in conjunction with the factors set forth in 18 U.S.C.: 3553(a).

3) That 28 U.S.C.: 944(t) delegated authority to the United States Sentencing Commission (hereinafter "Sentencing Commission") to promulgate general policy statements regarding sentencing modification provisions in 3582(c)(1)(A), describing what "should be considered extraordinary and

compelling reasons for the sentencing reduction, including the criteria to be applied and a list of specific examples."

4) The Sentencing Commission complied with this directive in drafting USSG: 1B1.13 and its accompanying commentary.

5) 1B1.13 states in relevant parts, that upon motion of the Director of the BOP, under 18 U.S.C.: 3582(c)(1)(A), the court may reduce a defendant's sentence if, after considering 18 U.S.C. 3553(a)'s factors, the court determines that "(1)(A) Extraordinary and compelling reasons warrant the reduction..."

6) The Commentary to 1B1.13 then gives four categories of "reasons" that would meet the extraordinary and compelling standard, those being: A. The medical condition of the defendant, B. Age of 65 or over, C. Family circumstances, and "D. As determined by the Director of the BOP, there exists in the defendant's case an extraordinary and compelling reason other than, or in combination with, the reasons in subdivision (A) through (C)."

7) Subdivision (D) hereinabove is a "catch-all provision" and it is this subdivision upon which Davila bases his motion. 1B1.13's Commentary is outdated and does not track the revisions Congress made to 3582 under the FSA.

8) It was the clear intent of Congress to empower the District Courts to make determinations as to what constituted "extraordinary and compelling" under the so-called catch-all provision, and specifically to remove this determination from the BOP's purview. The Commentary is outdated and in need of revision, but since the Sentencing Commission cannot now even convene a quorum due to the lack of members, it is within the province of the District Court to effectuate the will of Congress, particularly where said intent is clear and unambiguous. See Davila's accompanying Brief in Support for recent decisions which support this view.

9) That a Request to modify and reduce a sentence pursuant to 18 U.S.C.: 3582(c)(1)(A) was filed with Warden K. Zook by Davila on July 3, 2020.

10) That Warden Zook denied Davila's request on July 14, 2020.

11) Davila has continued to follow all available administrative remedies available to him under the specific circumstances in his particular situation of total lockdown and lack of prison staff.

12) Warden Zook has yet to file a motion for a sentence reduction, on behalf of Mr. Davila, and the thirty (30) days specified by the FSA expired on August 3, 2020.

RELEVANT FACTS AND PROCEDURAL HISTORY

On March 31, 2006, an indictment was returned, charging Davila with conspiracy to possess and distribute cocaine, cocaine base, and marijuana in violation of 21 U.S.C.: 841(A)(1) and 846. Davila was arrested on April 12, 2006. On October 23, 2007, Davila entered a plea of guilty pursuant to a plea agreement (Doc. 326). On December 19, 2008, Davila was sentenced to 360 months with 5 years of supervised release to follow. On February 9, 2015, Davila was granted a reduction in sentence pursuant to 18 U.S.C.: 3582(c)(2) following the Sentencing Guidelines amendment 782.

Mr. Davila contends that he could be released pursuant to 3582(c)(1)(A)(i) because he, as a chronic care inmate, faces a high risk of death or serious injury from a COVID-19 infection, FCI Seagoville has been unable to control the outbreak at its facilities while maintaining a minimum level of care and medical services for the bulk of its chronic care inmates, and the BOP and FCI Seagoville officials have been unable to take other significant actions within its control to meaningfully reduce the prison population beyond scheduled releases (after full service of sentences) at FCI Seagoville.

Mr. Davila's circumstances are indeed extraordinary and compelling because the current conditions at FCI Seagoville prevent him from receiving adequate medical care for his chronic care condition (diabetes) and his condition leaves him in an immune-deficient condition that is highly susceptible to a COVID-19 infection and death. In the recent decision of *United State v. Rupert*, case no.: 10-cr-40009-JES-JAG, U.S.D.C., C.D. of Illinois, which is persuasive yet not controlling, the Court opined that "'The mere presence of COVID-19 in a particular prison cannot justify compassionate release – if it could, every inmate in the prison could obtain release.' See, *e.g.*, *United States v. Melgarejo*, No. 12-cr-20050, at ECF Doc. 41 at p.5 (C.D. Ill. May 12, 2020). Rather, a prisoner [may] satisfy the extraordinary and compelling reasons requirement by showing that his particular institution is facing a serious outbreak of COVID-19 infections, the institution is unable to successfully contain the outbreak, and his health condition places him at significant risk of complication should he contract the virus,'" *id.* at 5-6. [You may want to explain Mr. Davila's circumstances in a little more detail here.]

MR. DAVILA HAS BEEN ENGAGED IN PRODUCTIVE ACTIVITIES THAT PROMOTE SELF-REHABILITATION AND IS NOT A DANGER. TO ANYONE IN THE COMMUNITY.

Mr. Davila will not pose a danger to himself or his community if he is released. A principle that is lost on most prisoners is their own need for personal change. Mr. Davila, however, is quite different from most prisoners. Over the years he has spent incarcerated, Mr. Davila realized his need for self-rehabilitation and has now become a living, breathing example to others around him. After being committed to serve a long sentence in the Bureau of Prisons, Mr. Davila came to a life-changing realization. He knew that he had to take advantage of the training that was offered by the BOP to become the person that his family and his community need him to be.

Mr. Davila started his life's quest at the education department of the prison to which he is assigned. He began his personal development by engaging in vocational training, personal development, and business management classes. He has been enrolled in Cedar Valley College as a full-time student since the Fall of 2018. He is pursuing an Advanced Level certificate in the applied trades program of HVAC-Heating Ventilation and Air Conditioning from the University's Career Technical Education (Vocational) division at the Federal Correctional Institution in Seagoville, Texas. He is expected to advance to the next level of his training after classes resume. Classes are currently suspended due to the COVID-19 outbreak at the Texas prison. Additionally, Davila provides the following list of programs as 3553(a) factors he feels are relevant to his motion. They all have to do with rehabilitative efforts while he has been in prison:

> Adult Ed Learning
> VT Heating and Air Conditioning
> Stress Management
> Small Business Marketing Tech
> Writing a Business Plan
> Eat for Health/Fit for Life
> Federal Deposit Insurance
> Reading Is Fundamental
> Parenting From the Inside
> Parenting Reentry Plan
> Real Estate Class
> Technical Analysis Class
> Admission and Orientation
> Release Requirements
> RPP #1; HLTH SRVC Infectious Disease
> RPP Orientation; CORE 5
> Extreme Cardio
> Adv CDL Truck
> Business MGT
> Beginning Yoga
> (See the included Inmate Education DATA Transcript for more details.)

Mr. Davila's efforts are not mere window dressing. They represent proof of his extraordinary efforts to rehabilitate himself as well as to assist fellow prisoners in doing the same. In *Pepper v. United States*, 562 U.S. 476, 490-93 (2011) The Supreme Court addressed the admissibility of a defendant's post-conviction rehabilitative efforts in the context of a resentencing hearing subsequent to a successful appeal. Although this motion does not follow a successful appeal, it is similar to resentencing because the First Step Act now authorizes defendants to file their own motions for sentence reductions. Thus, it is clear that post-conviction carceral rehabilitative efforts, after the passing of the FSA, are indeed admissible in the context of a 3582 action. This means that what the court said about their applicability to certain 3553(a) factors is relevant here. "In addition, evidence of post-sentencing rehabilitation may be highly relevant to several of the 3553(a) factors that Congress has expressly instructed district courts to consider at sentencing. For example, evidence of post-sentencing rehabilitation may also be plainly relevant to 'the history and characteristics of the defendant,' 3553(a)(1). Such evidence may also be pertinent to 'the need for the sentence imposed the general purposes of sentencing set forth in 3553(a)(2) – in particular, to 'afford adequate deterrence to criminal conduct,' 'protect the public from further crimes of the defendant,' and 'provide the defendant with needed education or vocational training ... or other correctional treatment in the most effective manner.' ... Post Sentencing rehabilitation may also critically inform a sentencing judge's overarching duty under 3553(a) to 'impose a sentence sufficient, but not greater than necessary to comply with the sentencing purposes set forth in 3553(a)(2)."

IF RELEASED TODAY, MR. DAVILA WOULD IMPLEMENT HIS PRE-ESTABLISHED RELEASE PLAN.

Mr. Davila realizes that one of the most critical elements of anti-recidivism is pre-planning. His study of this single element has shown that a high percentage of people who return to prison are those who simply fail to plan. Recent statistics, produced by Mr. Davila's own personal observations at Seagoville F.C.I., have revealed that most prisoners who return to prison do so because of a failure to follow conditions of supervised release as opposed to new criminal conduct or new indictments. Almost all failures to follow conditions of supervised release, that have been identified by Mr. Davila were preventable with a reasonable amount of pre-planning.

Davila has and continues to plan for his eventual release. One of the most important aspects of any prisoner's Release Plan is whether that particular prisoner will still pose a threat to the people of his community by continuing to engage in criminal activity. Over the last fifteen years, Mr. Davila has engaged in educational programs so that he may understand how and why it is important to avoid engaging in criminal activity that will lead to recidivism. His own personal commitment to his family, friends, and community, is to leave prison a better man than he was at his sentencing when this court last considered Mr. Davila's history and characteristics.

Mr. Davila has worked hard to become a new person, someone whom his family, friends, and community can be proud of, someone who will be a productive member of society, and someone who is far removed from being a threat. Unfortunately, and notwithstanding his efforts to rehabilitate, the COVID-19 outbreak has added a new dynamic to any reasonable threat assessment of Mr. Davila's potential release. Today this court, and Mr. Davila as well, must give due consideration to the threat of continued infection that Mr. Davila's potential release could impose upon his community. Thus, Mr. Davila has amended his Proposed Release Plan to include the following:

(I) TRAVEL – Due to the overwhelming effect that the COVID-19 pandemic has had on the United States Prison system, Mr. Davila has established a proposed travel plan in the event of his release. Mr. Davila's cousin, Abryn Neal, lives in Dallas, Texas, and is willing to provide Mr. Davila with transportation from the prison gates to the airport in the Dallas Fort Worth Metro area. Once Mr. Neal ensures that Mr. Davila is safe aboard his flight the responsibility of travel then shifts to Lana and Michael Gaston, who will be waiting at a prearranged airport to provide transportation to their home.

(II) HOME – Mr. Davila plans to reside with his aunt and uncle, Lana, and Michael Gaston, who reside in Summerville, SC. Mr. Davila chose to reside with his aunt and Uncle upon release for many reasons. But some of the most important are the continual influence and mentorship that his uncle, Michael Gaston, will have on Mr. Davila's continued growth; the space that their home will provide for the necessary quarantine period after Mr. Davila's release, and Mr. Davila's desire to continue his education at Trident Technical College. The most important aspect of residing with his aunt and uncle, however, is their ability to provide the space and care necessary for a productive quarantine period.

The Gaston home is a single-family home consisting of 2,823 square feet of living space and was built in 2011. It has two levels, four bedrooms, and three bathrooms. Their current plan is that Mr. Davila will occupy the upper level which has its own living space, bathroom, and laundry facilities. He will be cared for by his aunt Lana Gaston. The family has also included an alternate caregiver – Jann Henderson – as a replacement in the event that any unforeseen circumstances were to arise unexpectedly, during Mr. Davila's fourteen-day quarantine period. With the assistance and cooperation of the specified caregivers, Mr. Davila will be sequestered in a single bedroom and bathroom on the upper level of the home. Mr. Davila's family have pledged their assistance to meet Mr. Davila's additional needs such as laundry, meal preparation, and transport for medical care as may be needed to control his diabetes.

(III) MEDICAL – Upon release Mr. Davila's current medical needs to control his diabetes will remain a paramount issue in his life. Thus, his family has pre-planned to obtain all needed medical treatment at Roper St. Francis Berkeley Hospital. The hospital is fortified with a full-service medical center that employs an experienced medical staff. At only three miles from the Gaston home, all nonemergency medical transportation will be supplied by Mr. Davila's appointed caregiver, which will be alternated as necessary. The care that can be provided by the specified medical center far surpasses the current abilities of the medical staff currently employed at Seagoville F.C.I. prison.

(IV) INITIAL FINANCIAL SUPPORT – In the first 14 days after release, Mr. Davila's financial needs will be minimal. Because he will be at Gaston's home, Mr. Davila's initial financial needs will be met by his family.

(V) EMPLOYMENT – Mr. Davila's release plan stands out from other prisoners because of his extraordinary family and community support, along with its phase-in employment plan. In his first 14 days from release, Mr. Davila will be in quarantine. This means that he will be physically separated from other people to ensure there is no chance to spread the COVID-19 infection. But, with the use of a telephone and an internet-ready computer, Mr. Davila will be submitting applications to companies that are known to hire ex-offenders. After the expiration of his quarantine, Mr. Davila will be immediately employed by a local Labor Force, at which he will be able to engage in productive employment with consideration to his abilities with his diabetes in mind. This initial employment is engineered to be a temporary position that will provide for Mr. Davila's necessary support until he is able to secure more permanent employment.

In the long-term planning phase, Mr. Davila has and will continue to apply for employment with companies such as Trane, Carrier, and others that could make use of his education and training in the HVAC system installation industry. These companies and others like them routinely hire ex-felons, and Mr. Davila has engineered his prison programming portfolio with the purpose of obtaining the skills and experience that these companies require of their employees. As mentioned earlier, herein, Mr. Davila has prepared himself for re-entry with long-term employment in mind.

(VI) COMMUNITY VOLUNTEER – There can be no doubt that this Court is aware that a pledge to do volunteer work has become cliché in most cases – used by almost all prisoners who want to get out of prison. Mr. Davila is also aware of this shameful fact. He knows that he and this Court have heard these noble promises only to be disappointed when the defendant does return to prison. But Mr. Davila takes his pledge a step further. His passion, to continue the mentorship he started in prison, is so strong in his heart that he is willing to offer his pledge as a condition of his supervised release. This Court should also know that Mr. Davila's passion is not because he wishes to accelerate his release, but because no matter when he is ultimately released, he has a personal burden to repay his community for the harm he caused by his previous lifestyle.

Upon release, no matter when that may be, Mr. Davila pledges his active service as a volunteer to Playmaker Threads, a not-for-profit agency. The agency anticipates that Mr. Davila will serve as their

Brand Ambassador, working remotely from Summerville, South Caroline. [Greg, I'm forwarding some background and contact information for this agency for your review. Feel free to contact them for additional information.]

CONCLUSION

IN THE UNITED STATES DISTRICT COURT
FOR THE NORTHERN DISTRICT OF KANSAS

UNITED STATES OF AMERICA plaintiff	§ § §	Case no.:
	§ §	2:06-CR-20056-001-KHV
v.	§ §	
SAVINO DAVILA defendant	§ §	

MOTION FOR COMPASSIONATE RELEASE UNDER 18 U.S.C. 18 3582

By Greg Klebanoff

COMES NOW the Defendant, Savino Davila, by and through the assistance of counsel, Greg Klebanoff, with his Motion for Compassionate Release Under 18 U.S.C. § 3582(c)(1)(A), and he states and avers as follows – to wit:

INITIAL STATEMENT OF RELIEF SOUGHT

The defendant's reasons for seeking relief under what has become known as the "Compassionate Release" statute are as real and urgent as the coronavirus pandemic currently bedeviling our nation's prison system prisons. Davila's "extraordinary and compelling" circumstances are the fact that he has diabetes, the widespread infection rate of COVID-19 at FCI Seagoville, the prison's inability to provide him adequate treatment due to the overwhelming effect of the pandemic upon the prison's medical staff, and the virus' potentially deadly effect upon diabetic inmates. Davila contends these circumstances meet the "extraordinary and compelling" standard delineated in 18 U.S.C. § 3582(c)(1)(A)(i) and thus he asks this Court to reduce his sentence to time served.

JURISDICTIONAL STATEMENT

1.   Jurisdiction is invoked under 18 U.S.C. § 3582(c)(1)(A)(i), which permits the sentencing court to reduce the term of imprisonment if, after consideration of the factors set forth in § 3553 (a), it finds "extraordinary and compelling reasons warrant[ing] such a reduction," *id.*

2.   For over three decades the BOP had virtually unfettered discretion to refuse such motions. The landscape fundamentally changed when the president signed the First Step Act of 2018 into law. That act amended § 3582(c)(1)(A)(i), allowing the defense to initiate a request for compassionate release when a defendant has exhausted his administrative rights to appeal, failure of the BOP to bring a motion on the defendant's behalf or the lapse of 30 days from the receipt of such a request by the warden of the defendant's facility, First Step Act of 2018 § 603 (b).

3.   That 28 U.S.C. § 944(t) delegates authority to the United States Sentencing Commission to promulgate general policy statements regarding sentencing modification provisions in § 3582(c)(1)(A), - describing what "should be considered extraordinary and compelling reasons for the sentencing reduction, including the criteria to be applied and a list of specific examples," *id.*

4.   Commentary to § 1B1.13 delineates four categories of "reasons" that satisfy the extraordinary and compelling standard-namely: (a) Medical condition of a defendant; (b) Age of a defendant 65 or over; (c) Family circumstances; and (d) "other reasons."

5.   The "other reasons" identified in subdivision (d) are a "catch-all provision."

6.   Davila bases his motion on his medical condition of pre-diabetes, the COVID-19 outbreak, and the institution's resulting inability to provide medical care, as well as his being procedurally barred from objecting to his presentence report due to ineffective assistance of counsel.

7.   Thus, this Court may determine as to what constitutes "extraordinary and compelling" reasons under 18 U.S.C. § 3582.

8.   That a Request to modify and reduce the sentence pursuant to 18 U.S.C. § 3582(c)(1)(A) was filed with Warden K. Zook by Davila on July 3, 2020.

9.   That Warden Zook denied Davila's request on July 14, 2020.

10.   That Davila has continued to follow all available administrative remedies available to him under the specific circumstances in his particular situation of total lockdown and lack of prison staff.

11.   That the specific contents of Davila's request are irrelevant to whether he has exhausted his administrative remedies, *United States v. Resnick*, No. 14-CR-810-CM, 2020 WL 1651508 (S.D.N.Y. Apr. 2, 2020) (rejecting government's argument that, since defendant's original request to BOP did not include COVID-19 argument the defendant must re-exhaust).

12.   Warden Zook has yet to file a motion for a sentence reduction, on behalf of Mr. Davila, and the thirty (30) days specified by the FSA expired on August 3, 2020, making this motion ripe.

IN THE UNITED STATES DISTRICT COURT
FOR THE NORTHERN DISTRICT OF KANSAS

UNITED STATES OF AMERICA plaintiff	§ § §	Case no.:
	§	2:06-CR-20056-001-KHV
v.	§ §	
SAVINO DAVILA defendant	§ § §	

MEMORANDUM IN SUPPORT OF MOTION FOR COMPASSIONATE RELIEF RELEASE UNDER 18 U.S.C. 18 3582

By Greg Klebanoff

Defendant, Savino Davila, respectfully moves this Court for an Order reducing his sentence to time served based on the "extraordinary and compelling reasons" discussed herein, pursuant to 18 U.S.C. § 3582(c)(1)(A). In light of the COVID-19 pandemic, upon which his motion is partially based, Davila requests that this motion be handled sans oral argument and on an expedited basis to save his life or prevent debilitating illness.

INTRODUCTION

Savino Davila is currently incardinated in FCI Seagoville, a low-security federal prison located in the Dallas/Fort Worth metropolitan area. He is on his fifteenth year of a 30-year sentence for conspiracy to distribute cocaine, cocaine base, and marijuana. This July he requested that the warden reduce his sentence pursuant to 18 U.S.C. § 3582(c)(1)(A). When the warden failed to file a motion for sentence reduction within 30 days, he retained counsel to file on his own behalf.

Whatever the merits of the warden's decision not to act on the relief Davila requested, it is manifestly erroneous in light of Davila's increased exposure to COVID-19 in FCI Seagoville – a veritable Petri dish of viral pathogens – his pre-diabetes, the institution's inability to provide him adequate treatment when its health care facilities are already stretched to the limit, and the increased risks COVID-19 poses to pre-diabetics. Davila was not given a death sentence for his non-violent drug offense, nor does he deserve one.

Following the lead of courts and boards of corrections across the country, this Court both can and should reduce Davila's sentence to time served to save him from death or debilitating illness.

FACTUAL BACKGROUND

In October 2007 Davila plead guilty to one count of conspiracy to deliver cocaine base, cocaine, and marijuana of a twenty-eight-count indictment. The government charged that between April 2003 and March 2006 he was involved in an operation responsible for delivering at least 50 grams of cocaine base, 5 kilograms of cocaine, and 100 kilograms of marijuana in Kansas and Missouri.

As the Court will recall, at Davila's sentencing hearing defense counsel Bruce Houdek argued vigorously that the defendant was entitled to a motion for a downward departure from the sentencing guidelines on the grounds that he had provided substantial assistance to the government in Kansas City, Missouri homicide investigation. The government conceded that Davila provided information on the homicide but declined to make the motion on the grounds that it was not then known whether the information would be helpful and because the Defendant apparently indicated he would testify against his codefendants but ultimately refused to do so. Counsel Houdek felt strongly enough about the matter that he asked the Court to continue the sentencing hearing so he could formally request the Court to move for the downward departure. The Court denied Houdek's request on the grounds that sentencing had already been continued several times and more than a year had already lapsed since Davila entered his plea.

Moreover, it came out in the sentencing hearing that Counsel Houdek had apparently put so much time into working on trying to get his client a downward departure that he neglected to file any formal objections to Davila's presentence report. For these reasons, Davila, through no fault of his own, was procedurally barred from pursuing two potentially fruitful strategies for reducing his sentence.

At sentencing the government contended – and the court found – that Davila had been a leader in the drug conspiracy he pleaded guilty to and granted the government's motion for a firearm enhancement on the grounds that two guns were found in the defendant's home at the time of his arrest. Davila's offense level was set at 40 and his criminal history was III, giving him a presumptive sentence of 360 months to life. He was sentenced at the bottom of the scale to 360 months, which in 2015 was reduced to 292 months.

ARGUMENT

When congress delegated responsibility for what counts as "extraordinary and compelling reasons" to the U.S. Sentencing Commission (28 U.S.C. § 994 (t)), it essentially said that anything could be considered, handing down only one limitation on said authority – namely, that "[r]ehabilitation of the defendant *alone* [emphasis added] shall not be considered an extraordinary and compelling reason," 28 U.S.C § 994(t). The inclusion of the word "alone," however, indicates that rehabilitation can be considered relevant in tandem with other factors. Davila submits that he should receive an early release under the statute because (1) he had exhibited evidence of rehabilitation; (2) he was procedurally barred from filing objections to his presentence report that could result in a reduced sentence; and (3) he has pre-diabetes in an FCI facility ill-equipped to address it during the COVID-19 outbreak.

Davila is eligible for release under 18 U.S.C. § 3582(c)(1)(A) because, as an inmate with pre-diabetes, he faces an increased risk of death or debilitating harm should he contract COVID-19. Moreover, FCI Seagoville has been unable to control the outbreak of COVID-19 in its facilities while maintaining a minimum level of care and medical services for the bulk of its chronic care inmates. Additionally, the BOP and FCI Seagoville officials have been unable to take other significant actions within their control to meaningfully reduce the prison population beyond the scheduled releases of inmates at FCI Seagoville.

Davila's circumstances are extraordinary and compelling because the current conditions at FCI Seagoville prevent him from receiving adequate medical care for his pre-diabetes, which leaves him in an immune-deficient condition highly susceptible to a COVID-19 infection. In *United States v. Rupert*, 10-cr-40009-JES-JAG, U.S.D.C. (C.D. Ill. May 21, 2020), another federal district ruled that while the presence of COVID-19 in a given prison could not in itself meet the extraordinary and compelling standard justifying release, the standard could nonetheless be met by proof of the following: (1) that a particular prison is facing a serious COVID-19 outbreak; (2) that the institution is unable to contain the outbreak; and (3) that the prisoner is already afflicted with a health condition that places him at increased risk should he contract the virus, *id.* at 5-6.

Davila suffers from pre-diabetes, and diabetes has been identified by the Centers for Disease Control as a factor increasing the risk of severe injury to persons of any age from COVID-19. See CDC, Coronavirus Disease 2019 (COVID-19): People with Certain Medical Conditions, August 14, 2020, https://www.cdc.gov/coronavirus/2019-ncov/need-extra-precautions/pcople-with-medical-conditions.html. In addition, FCI Seagoville, where Davila is incarcerated, has been hit especially hard by COVID-19. As of August 18, 2020, 1,334 federal inmates and 596 BOP staff at Seagoville have tested positive of which 114 inmates and one staff member have died. See Walter Pavlo, A Look Inside a Federal Prison With COVID-19: FCI Seagoville, Forbes, August 19, 2020, https://www.forbes.com/sites/walterpavlo/2020/08/19/a-look-inside-a-federal-prison-with-COVID-19-fci-seagoville/#51b18efd7cdb. As of August 8, 2020, in FCI Seagoville more than 1,300 inmates out of 1,750 – a stunning three out of every four inmates – had tested positive for COVID-19 and three had died. See Casey Tolan, Nelli Black, and Drew Griffin, Inside the Federal Prison where Three out of Every Four Inmates Have Tested Positive for Coronavirus, CNN, August 8, 2020, https://www.cnn.com/2020/08/08/us/federal-prison-coronavirus-outbreakinvs/index.html. Though the situation at FCI Seagoville is especially bad, COVID-19 is wreaking havoc on the prison system as a whole and the situation has only gotten worse since August. On December 18, 2020, the Associated Press reported that one in five federal inmates have tested positive for COVID-19. See Beth Schwartzapfel, Katie Park, and Andrew DeMillo, 1 in 5 Prisoners in the US has had COVID-19, 1,700 Have Died, December 18, 2020, Associated Press, https://apnews.com/article/pandemics-race-and-ethnicity-prisons-united-states-coronavirus-pandemic-0bef0673013aa579551db5ad61b885e0. While COVID-19 vaccines are expected in the federal prison system on the week of December 19th, the Bureau of Prisons announced a policy that it will be first be given to staff and only made available to inmates when additional doses are available. See Clare Hymes, Federal Prisons to Prioritize Staffers for COVID-19 Vaccine, December 17, 2020, CBS News, https://www.msn.com/en-us/news/us/federal-prisons-to-prioritize-staffers-for-covid-19-vaccine/ar-BB1bZBy2?ocid=uxbndlbing.

DAVILA HAS BEEN ENGAGED IN PRODUCTIVE ACTIVITIES THAT PROMOTE SELF-REHABILITATION AND IS NOT A DANGER TO ANYONE IN THE COMMUNITY.

Davila will not pose a danger to himself or his community if he is released. While many prisoners disregard the need for changing their outlooks on life if they are to function as productive members of society, Davila is cut from a different cloth. During his incarceration, he recognized his need for rehabilitation and is now a living, breathing example to those around him.

Davila started this process as soon as he arrived in prison and started down the road to rehabilitation by taking advantage of any program, he thought might help him. He has been enrolled in Cedar Valley College as a full-time student since the Fall of 2018. He is pursuing an Advanced Level certificate in the applied trades program of HVAC Heating Ventilation and Air Conditioning from the University's Career Technical Education (Vocational) division at FCI Seagoville. He is expected to advance to the next level of his training after classes resume. While classes are currently suspended due to COVID-19, Davila looks forward to resuming his education as soon as possible. Moreover, he has completed the following courses and programs:

1. Adult Ed Learning;
2. VT Heating and Air Conditioning;
3. Stress Management;
4. Small Business Marketing Tech;
5. Writing a Business Plan;
6. Eat for Health/Fit for Life;
7. Federal Deposit Insurance;

8. Reading Is Fundamental;

9. Parenting From the Inside;

10. Parenting Reentry Plan;

11. Real Estate Class;

12. Technical Analysis Class;

13. Admission and Orientation;

14. Release Requirements;

15. RPP #1; HLTH SRVC Infectious Disease;

16. RPP Orientation; CORE 5;

17. Extreme Cardio;

18. Adv CDL Truck;

19. Business MGT; and

20. Beginning Yoga

(See the included Inmate Education DATA Transcript for more details.)

These efforts are not mere window dressing; rather they represent cogent evidence of Davila's efforts to rehabilitate himself, as well as to assist fellow prisoners in the same endeavor. In *Pepper v. United States*, 562 U.S. 476, 490-93 (2011) the Supreme Court of the United States ruled that evidence of post-sentence rehabilitation could be considered when resentencing a defendant whose prior sentence was set aside in an appeal. Though Davila's sentence has not been set aside, *Pepper* is a relevant authority in the instant case because it stands for the proposition that evidence of rehabilitation is properly weighed by a court in its consideration of how long a criminal defendant should remain in prison.

In *Pepper,* the court approved a 40-point downward departure in a defendant's score under the Federal Sentencing Guidelines – resulting in a 75% reduction in his presumptive sentence – based on the defendant's substantial assistance to the government and evidence of post-sentencing rehabilitation, *id.* 476-77. Pepper "testified at his resentencing hearing that he was no longer a drug addict, having completed a 500-hour drug treatment program while in prison; that he was enrolled in community college and had achieved very good grades" and was working part-time, *id.* Pepper's evidence of post-sentence rehabilitation is strikingly similar to Davila's.

Accordingly, Davila asks that the court consider evidence of his rehabilitation in deciding whether to grant his prayer for relief.

IF RELEASED TODAY, DAVILA WOULD IMPLEMENT HIS
PRE-ESTABLISHED RELEASE PLAN.

Davila realizes that one of the most critical elements of preventing recidivism is foresight and planning. Those who fail to plan return to prison, often from failure to follow conditions of supervised release as much as new criminal conduct. Davila has identified a great many such failures and has maliciously planned his own release to prevent them from happening to him.

He has worked hard to become a new person, someone whom his family, friends, and community can respect. Unfortunately, and notwithstanding his efforts to rehabilitate, the COVID-19 outbreak has added a new dynamic to any reasonable threat assessment of Mr. Davila's potential release. Today this court, and Mr. Davila as well, must give due consideration to the threat of continued infection that Mr. Davila's potential release could impose upon his community. Thus, Mr. Davila has amended his Proposed Release Plan to include the following:

I.   TRAVEL – Due to the overwhelming effect that the COVID-19 pandemic has had on the United States Prison system, Davila has established a proposed travel plan in the event of his release. Davila's cousin, Abryn Neal, lives in Dallas, Texas, and is willing to provide Davila with transportation from the prison gates to the airport in the Dallas Fort Worth Metro area. Once Mr. Neal ensures that Davila is safe aboard his flight, the responsibility of travel then shifts to Lana and Michael Gaston, who will be waiting at a prearranged airport to provide transportation to their home.

II.   HOME – Mr. Davila plans to reside with his aunt and uncle, Lana and Michael Gaston, who reside in Summerville, SC. Davila chose to reside with his aunt and uncle upon release for many reasons. But some of the most important are the continual influence and mentorship that his uncle, Michael Gaston, will have on Davila's continued growth, the space that their home will provide for the necessary quarantine period after Davila's release, and his desire to continue his education at Trident Technical College. The most important aspect of residing with his aunt and uncle, however, is their ability to provide the space and care necessary for a productive quarantine period.

The Gaston home is a single-family home that contains 2,823 square feet of living space and was built in 2011. It has two levels, four bedrooms, and three bathrooms. Their current plan is that Mr. Davila will occupy the upper level which has its own living space, bathroom, and laundry facilities. He will be cared for by his aunt, Lana Gaston. The family has also included an alternate caregiver – Jann Henderson – as a replacement in the event that any unforeseen circumstances were to arise unexpectedly, during Mr. Davila's fourteen-day quarantine period. With the assistance and cooperation of the specified caregivers, Davila will be sequestered in a single bedroom and bathroom on the upper level of the home. Davila's family has pledged their assistance to meet Davila's additional needs such as laundry, meal preparation, and transport for medical care as may be needed to control his diabetes.

III   MEDICAL – Upon release, Mr. Davila's current medical needs to control his pre-diabetes will remain a paramount issue in his life. Thus, his family has pre-planned to obtain all needed medical treatment at Roper St. Francis Berkeley Hospital. The hospital is fortified with a full-service medical center that employs an experienced medical staff. At only three miles from the Gaston home, all non-emergency medical transportation will be supplied by Mr. Davila's appointed caregiver, which will be alternated as necessary. The care that can be provided by the specified medical center far surpasses the current abilities of the medical staff currently employed at Seagoville FCI prison.

IV.   INITIAL FINANCIAL SUPPORT – In the first 14 days after release, Mr. Davila's financial needs will be minimal. Because he will be at Gaston's home, Mr. Davila's initial financial needs will be met by his family.

V.   EMPLOYMENT – Mr. Davila's release plan stands out from other prisoners because of his extraordinary family and community support, along with its phase-in employment plan. In his first 14 days from release, Davila will be in quarantine. This means that he will be physically separated from other people to ensure there is no chance to spread the COVID-19 infection. But, with the use of a telephone and an internet-ready computer, Mr. Davila will be submitting applications to companies that are known to hire ex-offenders. After the expiration of his quarantine, Mr. Davila will be immediately employed by a local Labor Force, at which he will be able to engage in productive employment with consideration to his abilities with his diabetes in mind. This initial employment is engineered to be a temporary position that will provide for Mr. Davila's necessary support until he is able to secure more permanent employment.

In the long-term planning phase, Mr. Davila has and will continue to apply for employment with companies such as Trane, Carrier, and others that could make use of his education and training in the HVAC system installation industry. These companies and others like them routinely hire ex-felons and Mr. Davila has engineered his prison programming portfolio with the purpose of obtaining the skills and experience that these companies require of their employees. As mentioned earlier, herein, Mr. Davila has prepared himself for re-entry with long-term employment in mind.

COMMUNITY VOLUNTEER – While a pledge to do volunteer work has become something of a cliché – trotted out by virtually all who want to get out of prison – Davila is sincere in his intention to make good on it. He knows this Court has heard these noble promises only to be disappointed when the defendant fails to make good on his promise and winds up back in prison. Davila takes his pledge a step further and is willing to offer his pledge as a condition of his supervised release. This Court should also know that Davila's passion is not because he wishes to accelerate his release, but because no matter when he is ultimately released, he has a personal burden to repay his community for the harm he caused by his previous lifestyle.

Upon release, no matter when that may be, Davila pledges his active service as a volunteer to Playmaker Threads, a not-for-profit agency. The agency anticipates that Davila will serve as their Brand Ambassador working remotely from Summerville, South Carolina.

CONCLUSION

For all the foregoing reasons, Davila respectfully requests that the Court take this opportunity to grant a reduction in his sentence based on extraordinary and compelling reasons and reduce his sentence to time served.

Date:

IN THE UNITED STATES DISTRICT COURT
FOR THE NORTHERN DISTRICT OF KANSAS

UNITED STATES OF AMERICA plaintiff	§ § §	CRIMINAL ACTION
	§	No. 06-20056-01-KHV
v.	§ §	
SAVINO DAVILA defendant	§ § §	

MEMORANDUM AND ORDER

On June 27, 2011, the Court sentenced the defendant to 360 months in prison. On February 9, 2015, under 18 U.S.C. § 3582(c)(2) and sentencing Amendment 782, the Court reduced the defendant's sentence to 292 months. This matter is before the Court on the defendant's Motion for Compassionate Release Under 18 U.S.C. § 3.582(Doc. #884) filed on December 6, 2021. The government opposes the defendant's motion. See Government's Response to Defendant's Motion for Compassionate Release (Doc. #888) filed December 23, 2021. For reasons stated below, the Court sustains the defendant's motion.

FACTUAL BACKGROUND

Defendant currently is confined at FCI Seagoville, a Bureau of Prisons ("BOP") facility in Seagoville, Texas. As of January 31, 2022, 1,079 inmates and 94 staff members at FCI Seagoville had tested positive for coronavirus disease 2019("COVID-19"). See COVID-19 Cases, https://www.bop.gov coronavirus (last visited Jan. 31, 2022). Seven inmates at the facility have died from COVID-19. See *id.* Some 931 of the remaining 1,072 inmates and 75 of the 94 staff members who tested positive have recovered. See *id.*

Defendant states that because of pre-diabetes, he is at high risk of severe illness or death if he contracts COVID-19. With good time credit, the defendant's projected release date is January 5, 2027. Defendant asks the Court to grant compassionate release based on his health condition, ineffective assistance of counsel at sentencing, and post-sentencing rehabilitation. See Motion for Compassionate Release Under 18 U.S.C. § 3582 (Doc. #884) at 4.

ANALYSIS

A federal district court may modify a defendant's sentence only where Congress has expressly authorized it to do so. See 18 U.S.C. § 3582(b)-(c); *United States v. Blackwell*, 81 F.3d 945, 947 (10th Cir. 1996). Congress has set forth only three limited circumstances in which a court may modify a sentence: (1) upon motion of the BOP Director or defendant under Section 3582(c)(1)(A); (2) when "expressly permitted by statute or by Rule 35" of the Federal Rules of Criminal Procedure; and (3) when the defendant has been sentenced "based on a sentencing range that has subsequently been lowered by the Sentencing Commission." See 18 U.S.C. § 3582(c).

The Court may order compassionate release for "extraordinary and compelling reasons." See 18 U.S.C. § 3582(c)(1)(A)(i). The Court may entertain requests for compassionate release only upon a motion of the BOP or of the defendant after he submits a request to BOP and the earlier of (1) when he "fully exhaust[s] all administrative rights to appeal" or (2) "the lapse of 30 days from the receipt of such a request by the warden of the defendant's facility." See 18 U.S.C. § 3582(c)(1)(A). Here, the government has not raised the issue of exhaustion. Thus, the government effectively concedes that the defendant has satisfied the exhaustion prerequisite to filing a motion for compassionate release.

The Court may grant compassionate release if the defendant establishes that (1) extraordinary and compelling reasons warrant a reduced sentence, (2) a reduced sentence is consistent with the applicable Sentencing Commission policy statement, and (3e Section 3553(a) factors warrant a reduced sentence. See 18 U.S.C. § 3582(c)(l)(A); *United States v. Maumau*, 993 F.3d 821, 831 (10th Cir. 2021); *United States v. McGee*, 992 F.3d 1035, 1042-43 (10th Cir. 2021). The Sentencing Commission has not issued an "applicable" policy statement for motions for compassionate release filed by defendants. See *Maumau*, 993 F.3d at 837; *McGee*, 992 F.3d at 1050. Unless and until the Sentencing Commission issues such a policy statement, the second requirement does not apply. See *United States v. Warren*, No. 11-20040-01-WPJ, 2021 WL 1575226, at *2 (D. Kan. Apr. 22, 2021); see also *United States v. Jones*, 980 F.3d 1098, 1111 (6th Cir. 2020) (where an incarcerated person files a motion in district court may skip step two of § 3582(c)(1)(A) inquiry and has full discretion to define "extraordinary and compelling" without consulting policy statement at U.S.S.G. § 1B1.13). Accordingly, the Court evaluates only the first and third requirements.

I.   Extraordinary and Compelling Reasons for Release

The Court has the discretion to independently determine whether the defendant has shown "extraordinary and compelling reasons" that warrant a release. See *McGee*, 992 F.3d at 1044, 1048. In the context of compassionate release, "extraordinary" means "exceptional to a very marked extent." *United States v. Baydoun*, No. 16-20057, 2020 WL 4282189, at *2 (E.D. Mich. July 27. 2020) (quoting "extraordinary," *Webster's Third International Dictionary, Unabridged* (2020)). "Compelling" means "tending to convince by the forcefulness of evidence," *id*. The Court also considers how the Sentencing Commission has defined extraordinary and compelling reasons for BOP motions. See *United States v.*

Carr 851 F. App'x 848, 853 (10th Cir. 2021) (district court has the discretion to consider the definition extraordinary and compelling reasons in Section 1B1.13 application notes). For BOP motions, the Sentencing Commission has identified four reasons that may constitute grounds for compassionate release: (1) the defendant's medical condition; (2) the defendant's age; (3) the defendant's family circumstances; and catchall category for an "extraordinary and compelling reason other than, or in combination with," the first three categories. See U.S.S.G. § 1B1.13, Reduction in Term of Imprisonment Under 18 U.S.C. § 3582(c)(1)(A) (Policy Statement), cmt.1 (Nov. 2018). In addition, the policy statement requires that before granting relief, the Court must find that defendant "is not a danger to the safety of any other person or to the community." See U.S.S.G. § 1B1.13(2) (citing 18 U.S.C. § 3142(g)).

Here, the defendant seeks compassionate release based on his health condition, ineffective assistance of counsel at sentencing, and post-sentencing rehabilitation. As to the defendant's pre-diabetes, the government concedes that the defendant "may have established extraordinary and compelling reasons pursuant [to] CDC and/or DOJ guidelines allowing for compassionate release." Government's Response to Defendant's Motion for Compassionate Release (Doc. #888) at 15. Even so, the government argues that because the defendant recovered from a COVID-19 infection in June of 2020 and he refuses to be vaccinated, his medical condition does not establish extraordinary and compelling reasons for release. See *id.* at 17. The Court need not address whether the defendant's pre-diabetes by itself warrant a reduced sentence because he has established that his medical condition and successful rehabilitation together establish extraordinary and compelling reasons for release.

A defendant can show that his rehabilitation and other factors collectively establish extraordinary and compelling reasons for release.[1] See *United States v. Foreman*, No. 02-CR-135-TCK, 2021 WL 2143819, at *7 (N.D. Okla. May 26, 2021) (personal rehabilitation, lack of criminal history, and the disparity between the defendant's sentence and those sentences for similar crimes after First Step Act constitute extraordinary and compelling reasons for relief); *United States v. Marks*, 455 F. Supp. 3d 17, 26 (W.D.N.Y. 2020) (combination of defendant's rehabilitation and changes to "stacking" provisions of 18 U.S.C. § 924(c) establish extraordinary and compelling reasons for sentence reduction), appeal withdrawn, No. 20-1404, 2021 WL 1688774 (2d Cir. Jan. 5, 2021).

Here, the defendant's rehabilitative efforts have been remarkable. Since his incarceration, the defendant has had no disciplinary infractions. By all accounts, he has been a model inmate. He has participated in a variety of classes, work assignments, recreational activities, and volunteer activities. Defendant has submitted letters of recommendation from eight BOP employees or contractors who either supervise or interact with him on a routine basis. Defendant's work supervisor of seven years in food services expresses that he "always" has a positive attitude, has grown in love and kindness to others, and would be a great candidate for early release. A BOP officer, who states that he believes the defendant is not a danger to the public and would be a great candidate for release, notes that in some eight years, he has never seen the defendant act disrespectfully to staff or inmates. An instructor notes that the defendant was one of the top students in a heating, ventilation, and air conditioning vocational training program. A BOP Recreation Specialist for more than 32 years, who believes that the defendant would be an "awesome candidate for early release," notes that the defendant has volunteered in the Recreation Department for the past seven years, his work is outstanding, he has an eagerness to go above and beyond what he is assigned to do, and he exhibits model behavior. Defendant's unit counselor states that the defendant's interaction with both staff and inmates is "always" positive and uplifting. Another food services supervisor recommends the defendant for early release and notes that he is "always" respectful to staff and inmates. The government's response does not address the defendant's eight letters of recommendation or offer any argument to refute his successful rehabilitation efforts.

In nearly three decades of reviewing post-conviction requests from federal inmates in a variety of contexts, the Court cannot recall that prison personnel have ever expressed such enthusiastic and broad support for an inmate's release. In these circumstances, the defendant's current medical condition, the COVID-19 pandemic, and his remarkable rehabilitative efforts collectively establish extraordinary and compelling reasons for release.[2]

II   Section 3553(a) Factors

Next, the Court must determine whether a sentence reduction is warranted, and the extent of any reduction, under the applicable factors set forth in 18 U.S.C. § 3553(a). See 18 U.S.C. § 3582(c)(1)(A). The Court considers the nature and circumstances of the offense, the defendant's personal history and characteristics, the purposes of sentencing including the need to protect the public from further crimes

---

[1] *Rehabilitation alone cannot constitute an extraordinary and compelling reason for relief. See 28 U.S.C. § 994(t) (while Sentencing Commission shall issue policy statements on what constitutes reasons for sentence reduction, "[r]ehabilitation of the defendant alone shall not be considered an extraordinary and compelling reason").*

of the defendant, any threat to public safety, and the need to avoid unwanted sentence disparities among defendants with similar records who are convicted of similar conduct. See 18 U.S.C. § 3553(a).

The government argues that after balancing Section 3553(a) factors, the Court should deny release. The defendant committed a significant drug trafficking offense and had a history of criminal offenses. Indeed, as the government notes, the defendant's criminal history started at age 11 and includes attempted indecent liberties, disorderly conduct, theft, assault, and possession of cocaine – all by the age of 16. Defendant certainly had a troubled criminal past from age 11 through his conviction in this case at age 30. That troubled past makes the defendant's rehabilitation efforts, described above, all the more remarkable. The government acknowledges that the defendant does not appear to pose a direct danger to society upon release. He already has served approximately 189 months in prison (the equivalent of 222 months with good time credit, or approximately 76 percent of his original sentence). When combined with a special term of supervised release that includes three months of home confinement, a reduced sentence under Section 3582(c)(1)(A) is consistent with the seriousness of the offense, the need for deterrence, and the need to protect the public.

In light of the defendant's current medical condition, the COVID-19 pandemic, his remarkable rehabilitative efforts, and the applicable factors under 18 U.S.C. § 3553(a), the Court finds that a sentence of time served with a special term of supervised release including home confinement of three months is sufficient, but not greater than necessary, to reflect the seriousness of the offense, afford adequate deterrence, protect the public, and provide defendant needed treatment in the most effective manner. See 18 U.S.C. § 3553(a)(2)(A)-(D). Accordingly, the Court reduces the defendant's sentence of 292 months in prison to time served with a special term of supervised release of three months to start immediately on his release. During the special term of supervised release, defendant shall remain at his place of residence except for employment; education; religious services; medical, substance abuse, or mental health treatment; attorney visits; court appearances; court-ordered obligations; or other activities as pre-approved by the U.S. Probation Officer. During the special term of supervised release, defendant shall also follow all location monitoring procedures specified by the probation officer and must contribute toward the cost, to the extent he is financially able to do so, as directed by the court and/or

---

[2] *Defendant also argues that counsel provided ineffective assistance of counsel at sentencing. The Court need not address this argument because defendant's medical condition and rehabilitation are sufficient to establish extraordinary and compelling reasons for release.*

the probation officer. Defendant shall remain subject to his standard term of supervised release of five years, which will begin immediately after the expiration of the special term of supervised release.

IT IS THEREFORE ORDERED that defendant's Motion for Compassionate Release Under 18 U.S.C. § 3582 (Doc. #884) filed December 6, 2021, is SUSTAINED. The Court reduces the defendant's sentence of 292 months in prison to TIME SERVED. Defendant shall immediately begin a special term of supervised release of three months. All terms and conditions that apply to defendant's standard term of supervised release (as set forth in the Amended Judgment in A Criminal Case (Doc. #798) filed June 28, 2011, at 3) shall apply to defendant's special term of supervised release. In addition, during the special term of supervised release, defendant shall remain at his place of residence except for employment; education; religious services; medical, substance abuse, or mental health treatment; attorney visits; court appearances; court-ordered obligations; or other activities as pre-approved by the U.S. Probation Officer. During the special term of supervised release, the defendant shall also follow all location monitoring procedures specified by the probation officer and must contribute toward the cost, to the extent he is financially able to do so, as directed by the court and/or the probation officer. During the first 14 days of his special term of supervised release, the defendant shall self-quarantine. After the special term of supervised release expires, the defendant will begin his standard term of supervised release of five years.

Except as modified above, all other terms and conditions of the Amended Judgment in a Criminal Case (Doc. #798) filed June 28, 2011 shall remain in effect.

Dated this 2nd day of February 2022 at Kansas City, Kansas.

s/ Kathryn H. Vratil
KATHRYN H. VRATIL
United States District Judge

CHAPTER FIVE

SPECIFIC MOTION FOR SENTENCE REDUCTION

Motions for sentence reductions hold a special place in my heart. This is the kind of thing that I cut my teeth on. As a matter of fact, Guidelines Amendment 782 – the drugs minus two decisions – was the first widespread reason for my notoriety as a jailhouse lawyer. After working on hundreds of cases and winning most, I discovered that Amendment 782 was not the first Amendment that allowed a reduction of a sentence, though it is a very important one. So here are the facts about Amendment 782 that I learned through my work as an advocate:

On July 18, 2014, the United States Sentencing Commission unanimously voted to make a serious amendment to the federal sentencing guidelines retroactive. The amendment was a significant change to the drug quantity table in §2D1.1.

Generally, the "Drugs Minus Two" amendment reduces the base offense level by two points in most federal drug cases. Going forward, a person's federal sentencing guidelines will be calculated with the benefit of these reduced offense levels for the drug quantities involved in the case.

Before making this amendment retroactive, the Sentencing Commission received thousands of letters and conducted hearings. There were proposals from a variety of different organizations to limit the application of this amendment. One proposal would have limited the amendment to inmates who had qualified for "safety valve" treatment at the time of sentencing. Another proposal would have limited the amendment to defendants who had no history of violence and did not use any firearms in connection with their offense. Another proposal would have required the Sentencing Commission to consider the person's criminal history before determining whether the reduction would apply.

The Sentencing Commission decided not to limit the application of this new amendment in any of these ways. Almost every inmate who was at the time serving a federal sentence for a drug crime was entitled to a reduction under this "Drugs Minus Two" amendment. According to the Sentencing Commission, there were approximately 48,000 people who qualified for a sentence reduction under the new amendment. For those who were successful in their petitions, the Sentencing Commission estimates that the average sentence reduction would have been about two years. The Commission was wrong; in the average case, we were seeing a three-year to a six-year reduction in the sentence.

The real question was how to go about getting this reduction under the new guideline amendment.

This is the question I answer in this section. As I said, there were other Amendments that were passed with the intent to reduce a federal drug sentence. Unfortunately, there are still hundreds of prisoners who have yet to take full advantage of their rights under these changes. This is where *you* come in as an advocate. It's your purpose and opportunity to reach out with this information and help everyone you can. In this chapter, I provide you with all the relevant changes and the motions and briefs you need to get this done.

Please take advantage of everything I give you here. You won't regret it.

KELLY PATRICK RIGGS

UNITED STATES DISTRICT COURT
WESTERN DISTRICT OF MICHIGAN

UNITED STATES OF AMERICA §
plaintiff §   File No._____

v. §   Hon. _____
  §
  §
_____ §
defendant §

MOTION FOR MODIFICATION OR REDUCTION OF SENTENCE
PURSUANT TO 18 U.S.C. § 3582(c)(2)

I hereby request a modification or reduction of my sentence pursuant to 18 U.S.C. § 3582(c)(2) and Amendments 706 and 711 to the United States Sentencing Guidelines, which made a reduction in the base offense level for crack-cocaine offenses retroactive as of March 3, 2008, and in support of my motion state as follows:

1. I am serving a term of imprisonment.

2. My sentence was based, at least in part, on crack cocaine. _____ (Yes or No)

3. I was sentenced in the Western District of Michigan on _____ (date) to a term of _____ months in prison. My total offense level was _____ and my criminal history category was _____.

4. My projected release date is _____.

5. I hereby request a court-appointed attorney. _____ (Yes or No)
If yes, please complete the attached Financial Affidavit.
(Note: appointment of counsel is discretionary with the Court)

WITH THE EXCEPTION OF THE FINANCIAL AFFIDAVIT, PLEASE DO NOT SUBMIT OR ATTACH ANY OTHER MATERIALS AT THIS TIME OR YOUR MOTION WILL BE REJECTED AND RETURNED.

Signature of Petitioner: _____ Date: _____

Print or Type Name: _____ Register #: _____

Current Address: _____

120

UNITED STATES DISTRICT COURT
WESTERN DISTRICT OF MICHIGAN

UNITED STATES OF AMERICA plaintiff	§ § §	File No._____
	§	Hon. _____
v.	§ §	
	§	
_____	§	
defendant	§	

MOTION FOR MODIFICATION OR REDUCTION OF SENTENCE PURSUANT TO 18 U.S.C. § 3582(C)(2) (GUIDELINE AMENDMENT NO. 750)

I hereby request a modification or reduction of my sentence pursuant to 18 U.S.C. § 3582(c)(2) and Amendment 750 to the United States Sentencing Guidelines, which made a reduction in the base offense level for crack-cocaine offenses retroactive as of November 1, 2011, and in support of my motion state as follows:

1. I am serving a term of imprisonment.

2. My sentence was based, at least in part, on crack cocaine. _____ (Yes or No)

3. I was sentenced in the Western District of Michigan on _____ (date) to a term of _____ months in prison. My total offense level was _____ and my criminal history category was _____.

4. My projected release date is _____.

5. I hereby request a court-appointed attorney. _____ (Yes or No)
   If yes, please complete the attached Financial Affidavit.
   (Note: appointment of counsel is discretionary with the Court)

WITH THE EXCEPTION OF THE FINANCIAL AFFIDAVIT, PLEASE DO NOT SUBMIT OR ATTACH ANY OTHER MATERIALS AT THIS TIME OR YOUR MOTION WILL BE REJECTED AND RETURNED.

Signature of Petitioner: _____ Date: _____

Print or Type Name: _____ Register #: _____

Current Address: _____

KELLY PATRICK RIGGS

UNITED STATES DISTRICT COURT
WESTERN DISTRICT OF MICHIGAN

UNITED STATES OF AMERICA §
plaintiff §
§ File No._____
§
v. § Hon. _____
§
§
_____ §
defendant §

MOTION FOR MODIFICATION OR REDUCTION OF SENTENCE PURSUANT TO
18 U.S.C. § 3582(C)(2) (GUIDELINE AMENDMENT NO. 782)

I hereby request a modification or reduction of my sentence pursuant to 18 U.S.C. § 3582(c)(2) and

Amendment 782 to the United States Sentencing Guidelines, which made a reduction in the base

offense level for drug offenses retroactive as of November 1, 2014, and in support of my motion state as

follows:

1. I am serving a term of imprisonment.

2. My sentence was based, at least in part, on a drug quantity. _____ (Yes or No)

3. I was sentenced in the Western District of Michigan on _____ (date) to a term of

   _____ months in prison. My total offense level was _____ and my criminal history

   category was _____.

4. My projected release date is _____. I understand that the Amendment does not authorize

   the release of any defendant before November 1, 2015.

5. I hereby request a court-appointed attorney. _____ (Yes or No)
   If yes, please complete the attached Financial Affidavit.
   (Note: appointment of counsel is discretionary with the Court)

**WITH THE EXCEPTION OF THE FINANCIAL AFFIDAVIT, PLEASE DO NOT SUBMIT OR
ATTACH ANY OTHER MATERIALS AT THIS TIME OR YOUR MOTION WILL BE
REJECTED AND RETURNED.**

Signature of Petitioner: _____ Date: _____

Print or Type Name: _____ Register #: _____

Current Address: _____

122

UNITED STATES DISTRICT COURT
FOR THE NORTHERN DISTRICT OF TEXAS
DALLAS DIVISION

UNITED STATES OF AMERICA plaintiff	§ § §	No. 3:97-CR-263-M(02)
v.	§ §	
MARSHA SMITH defendant	§ § §	

DEFENDANT'S BRIEF IN SUPPORT FOR
SENTENCE REDUCTION UNDER 18 U.S.C. § 3582(C)(2)

"[T]he problems associated with the 100-to-1 drug quantity ratio are so urgent and compelling that this amendment is promulgated as an interim measure to alleviate some of those problems. The Commission, however, views the amendment only as an interim solution to some of the problems associated with the 100-to-1 drug quantity ratio. It is neither a permanent nor a complete solution to those problems."

* * * * *

"The Commission believes that there is no justification for the current statutory penalty scheme for powder and crack cocaine offenses. The Commission remains committed, however, to its recommendation in 2002 that any statutory ratio is to be no more than 20-to-1."

TABLE OF CONTENTS

TABLE OF AUTHORITIES

FEDERAL CASES

STATUTES

1. Amendment 706

This Court may modify a defendant's term of imprisonment once it has been imposed when the United States Sentencing Commission makes an amendment to the Guidelines retroactive, and the amended guideline was part of the basis of the defendant's guideline range.

The court may not modify a term of imprisonment once it has been imposed except that –

(2) in the case of a defendant who has been sentenced to a term of imprisonment based on a sentencing range that has subsequently been lowered by the Sentencing Commission pursuant to 28 U.S.C. 994(o), upon motion of the defendant or the Director of the Bureau of Prisons, or on its own motion, the court may reduce the term of imprisonment, after considering the factors set forth in [18 U.S.C. §] 3553(a) to the extent that they are applicable if such a reduction is consistent with applicable policy statements issued by the Sentencing Commission.

18 U.S.C. § 3582(c)(2).

On November 1, 2007, Amendment 706 altered the drug quantity table set forth in USSG § 2D1.1, lowering the base offense level for offenses involving "cocaine base" (crack cocaine) by two levels. On December 7, 2007, the Sentencing Commission approved making Amendment 706 retroactive by listing it in USSG: 1B1.10(c)'s list of retroactive amendments with an effective date of March 3, 2008. Because Amendment 706 has been made retroactive and the defendant's sentence was based on the pre-Amendment 706 drug quantity table, 18 U.S.C. § 3582(c) allows this Court to review and reduce, as warranted by the factors set forth in 18 U.S.C. § 3553(a), the defendant's sentence.

In revisiting the defendant's sentence, the guidelines, their commentary, and the commission's policy statements remain advisory. When sentencing (or, as here, effectively re-sentencing) a defendant, this Court "may not presume that the Guidelines range is reasonable." Rather, this Court must treat the Guidelines "as one factor among several" that 18 U.S.C. § 3553(a) mandates it considers, albeit the "initial" one that it should use as a "starting point." Once this Court correctly calculates the sentence that the Guidelines recommend, the Court must then "make an individualized assessment," considering the remaining factors sets forth in § 3553(a). Because the Guidelines merely reflect a "wholesale" view of "rough[ly] approximat[ing]...sentences that might achieve § 3553(a)'s objectives," *Booker* and § 3553(a) require this Court to tailor an individualized sentence "at retail" that actually does achieve § 3553(a)'s objectives in the case before it. Consequently, this Court must "filter the Guidelines' general advice through § 3553(a)'s list of factors." When the Guidelines' "rough approximation" conflicts with this Court's view of the sentence warranted by other § 3553(a) factors, this Court may disregard the sentence recommended Guideline sentence in favor of one is tailored to the circumstances of the particular defendant.

This Court has the discretion to find that the Guidelines' "rough approximation" of an appropriate sentence would result in a sentence "greater than necessary" because the Court has the discretion to disagree with the Sentencing Commission's policy judgments – *especially those animating the drug quantity table set forth in* USSG § 2D1.1. This Court, "may determine…that, in a particular case, a within-Guidelines sentence is 'greater than necessary to serve the objectives of sentencing" the individual defendant, by "consider[ing] the disparity between the Guidelines' treatment of crack and powder cocaine offenses." Indeed, as the government readily conceded in Kimbrough, since "the Guidelines 'are now advisory...courts may vary [from the Guidelines ranges] based solely on policy considerations, including disagreements with the Guidelines.'"

2. United States v. Hicks

In *United States v. Hicks*, the Ninth Circuit acknowledged that *Booker* vested sentencing judges with the discretion to disagree with not only a specific sentencing guideline but with the Sentencing Commission's policy statements as well. It did so, moreover, in the context of a proceeding to reduce a sentence under 18 U.S.C. 3582(c). The Court observed that§ 3582(c)(2) "allows the district court to re-calculate the defendant's sentencing range using the newly-reduced Guideline, and then determine an appropriate sentence in accordance with § 3553(a) factors." "Booker's clear language," the Court further noted, "makes the [re-calculated] range advisory." The Court explained:

> Booker explicitly stated that "as by now should be clear, [a] mandatory system is no longer an open choice," *Booker*, 543 U.S. at 263. … Although the Court acknowledged that Congress had intended to create a mandatory Guidelines system, *Booker* stressed that this was not an option: "[W]e repeat, given today's constitutional holding, [a mandatory Guideline regime] is not a choice that remains open [W]e have concluded that today's holding is fundamentally inconsistent with the judge-based sentencing system that Congress enacted into law," *id.* at 265. The Court never qualified this statement, and never suggested, explicitly or implicitly, that the mandatory Guideline regime survived in any context.

> In fact, the Court emphasized that the Guidelines could not be construed as mandatory in one context and advisory in another. … [T]he Court dismissed this notion, stating, "we do not see how it is possible to leave the Guidelines as binding in other cases. … [W]e believe that Congress would not have authorized a mandatory system in some cases and a non-mandatory system in others, given the administrative complexities that such a system would create," *id.* at 266. … In short, *Booker* expressly rejected the idea that the Guidelines might be advisory in certain contexts and not in others, and Congress has done nothing to undermine this conclusion.

Accordingly, "Because a 'mandatory system is no longer an open choice,' … district courts are necessarily endowed with the discretion to depart from the Guidelines when issuing new sentences under § 3582(c)(2)." "Mandatory Guidelines," the Ninth Circuit concluded, "no longer exist, in this context or any other." That being so, the final clause of § 3582(c)(2) – limiting a reduction to one that is "consistent with applicable policy statements issued by the Sentencing Commission" – must be read to require no more than an application of the Guidelines in an advisory, rather than a mandatory fashion.

The Ninth Circuit further considered what effect the Sentencing Commission's policy statements should have in a § 3582(c)(2) proceeding after *Booker*. Addressing whether the policy statements set forth USSG § 1B1.10 (Nov. 2000) preclude a district court from "go[ing] below the Guidelines' minimum when modifying a sentence under§ 3582(c)(2)," the Ninth Circuit held they did not, and – important here – that even if they did, they "must be void" under *Booker*.

The pre-*Booker* version of USSG § 1B1.10 that the Court confronted in Hicks provided that "the court should consider the term of imprisonment that it would have imposed had the amendment[s] to the guidelines listed in subsection (c) been in effect at the time the defendant was sentenced[.]" An application note added that "the court shall substitute only the amendments listed in subsection (c) for the corresponding guideline provisions that were applied when the defendant was sentenced. All other guideline application decisions remain unaffected." background commentary remarked that reductions of retroactive Guideline amendments were "discretionary" and did "not otherwise affect the lawfulness of a previously imposed sentence, [did] not authorize a reduction in any other component of the sentence, and [did] not entitle a defendant to a reduced term of imprisonment as a matter of right."

In holding that these policy statements did not preclude a court from treating the re-calculated guideline range as advisory, the Court emphasized that§ 1B1.10(b) "state[d] only that the court 'should consider the term of imprisonment that it could have imposed …' and not that it may only impose that sentence." The Court similarly observed that "just because Hicks is not entitled to a sentence reduction as a matter of right does not mean that he may not be entitled to one as a matter of discretion."

3. USSG § 1B1.10

The Sentencing Commission's recent amendment of § 1B1.10, which went into effect on March 3, 2008, attempts to make the Guidelines mandatory in a § 3582(c)(2) proceeding and to preclude a district court from departing below the minimum of the re-calculated guideline range. Among other things, the new version of § 1B1.10 suggests that "[a] reduction in the defendant's term of imprisonment is not consistent with this policy statement and therefore is not authorized under 18 U.S.C. § 3582(c)(2) if … an amendment listed in subsection (c) does not have the effect of lowering the defendant's applicable guideline range." It opines that "proceedings under 18 U.S.C. § 3582(c)(2) and this policy statement do not constitute a full resentencing of the defendant." It amends the use of "should" – which the Ninth Circuit relied upon in *Hicks* – to "shall," in USSG § 1B1.10(b)

The provision that the district court shall substitute only the retroactive amendment for the corresponding guideline provisions that were applied to the defendant, which was and still is set forth in USSG § 1B1.10 app. n. 2, is redundantly incorporated directly into § 1B1.10(b)(l) but modified to expressly state that the district court "shall leave all other guideline application decisions unaffected." The amended policy statement advises that "the court shall not reduce the defendant's term of imprisonment under 18 U.S.C. § 3582(c)(2) and this policy statement to a term that is less than the minimum of the amended guideline range[.]" And it unequivocally states that "[i]n no event may the reduced term of imprisonment be less than the term of imprisonment that the defendant has already served."

The Sentencing Commission's commentary on § 1B1.10 goes even further. Evidently, the Commission was not content with simply capping a reduction at the low end of the re-calculated guideline range. Instead, it seeks to impose a one-way ratchet that works only in favor of the government. One application note seeks to preclude applying a retroactive amendment if it does not reduce the defendant's guideline range when operating alone. Another application note attempts to limit this Court's consideration of § 3553(a)'s non-guideline factors. Other application notes allow this Court to consider "the nature and seriousness of the danger to any person or the community that may be posed by a reduction in the defendant's term of imprisonment," and "post-sentencing conduct of the defendant that occurred after imposition of the original term of imprisonment." Both of these things, however, can only be considered in determining whether "a reduction is warranted" in the first place and "the extent of such a reduction … within" the re-calculated guideline range. In other words, these application notes would attempt to limit this Court's consideration of § 3553(a)'s non-guideline factors and allow it to either deny giving the reduction at all or elevate the new sentence above the low-low end of the re-calculated guideline range. The examples of how the Commission envisions § 1B1.10 operating in a § 3582(c)(2) proceeding set forth in Application Note 3 make it clear that it believes evidence should be introduced only to deny a reduction altogether or to persuade the Court to impose a sentence that is not at the low-end of the re-calculated guideline range.

As has been noted, this Court is not bound by USSG § 181.10 or its commentary. Presciently, the Ninth Circuit observed in *Hicks*:

> *Booker* makes clear that the Guidelines are no longer mandatory in any context. … *Booker* was not a mere statutory change that can be set aside …; rather, it provides a constitutional standard that courts may not ignore by treating the Guidelines ranges as mandatory in any context. Thus, to the extent that the policy statements are inconsistent with Booker by requiring that the Guidelines be treated as mandatory, the policy statements must give way.

While the government may claim that this portion of *Hicks* is "*dicta*" that need not be followed, the defendant submits that it is "considered *dicta*," which the Ninth Circuit's reasoning in *Hicks* fully supports, and which this Court should heed.

But in any event, the Ninth Circuit's view in Hicks accords with the Supreme Court's observation in *Neal v. United States* that "the Commission does not have the authority to amend [a] statute" that the Supreme Court has previously construed, so as to say or allow something that the Supreme Court's construction of the statute precludes. The statute as construed by the courts "controls" if it conflicts with a provision of the Guidelines. The Commission cannot effectively overrule or otherwise limit *Booker* by way of amending USSG § 1B1.10. Nor, for that matter, can the Commission overrule or limit judicial decisions such as *Hicks, Gall, Kimbrough,* or *Rita.* Accordingly, to the extent that USSG § 1B1.10 (Mar. 2008) would render any provision, commentary, or policy statements of the Guidelines binding and mandatory on this Court, then it must give way under *Booker* or any of its progeny. Similarly, to the extent that § 1B1.10 attempts to overrule or limit the Ninth Circuit's construction of § 3582(c)(2), it is § 1B1.10, and not *Hicks* that must give way.

And there are good reasons not to heed § 181.10's advice. For one thing, the amendments to § 1B1.10 and its application notes inject an unexplained internal inconsistency into § 1B1.10. Making an amendment retroactive by listing it in § 1B1.10(c) represents the Sentencing Commission's view that reducing a defendant's sentence by the amount warranted by the retroactive change fulfills the purposes of sentencing: "The listing of an amendment in subsection (c) reflects policy determinations by the Commission that a reduced guideline range is sufficient to achieve the purposes of sentencing[.]" Yet the amendments to § 1B1.10 and its 46 application notes discussed above put into effect a quite different "policy determination." First, it presumes that a reduction does not necessarily achieve the purposes of sentencing, and it concludes that a reduction would only do so if neither the public's safety nor post-sentencing conduct suggests otherwise.

Moreover, like the pre-Amendment 706 drug quantity table's 100:1 crack/powder ratio, § 1B1.10 is not based on any determination made from empirical data or national experience. As such, it does "not exemplify the Commission's exercise of its characteristic institutional role." Among other things, the amended § 1B1.10 was not the product of consultation with authorities or representatives of the Federal criminal justice system. It has not been subject to congressional review, nor the notice and public comment that attend to the guidelines.

Section 1B1.10 also attempts to cut off the purposes of sentencing set forth in § 3553(a)(2). Rather than establish a sentencing policy that strives to "permit individualized sentences" and that "reflects, to the extent practicable, advancement in knowledge of human behavior as it relates to the criminal justice process," § 1B1.10 attempts to prohibit this Court's consideration of such things. In sum, the Sentencing Commission's authority to promulgate a policy statement – without consulting experts, without notice and public comment, and without congressional review – must be exercised in accordance with the Commission's statutory duties, its purpose, and the statutory purposes of sentencing. Amended § 1B1.10, however, does not assure that the purposes of sentencing set forth in § 3553(a) are met, nor does it accord with the Commission's statutory duties and purpose. As *Kimbrough* teaches, this Court may reject § 1B1.10 for precisely these reasons.

4. The Bad Math

There are also good reasons to reject not only the pre-Amendment 706 drug quantity table but the new, post-Amendment 706 drug quantity table as well. While the new drug quantity table appears to have been adopted after the Commission had studied the matter more thoroughly than when it adopted the old table, it still incorporates widely disparate ratios. It is difficult, if not impossible, to comprehend how the new crack/powder ratios "provide certainty and fairness" or how it "avoid[s] unwarranted sentencing disparities." Nor has the Commission provided any sort of empirical or experiential basis to justify varying the crack/powder ratio based on the amount of drugs involved in the offense. Rather, the new ratios are random, arbitrary, and without a rational basis. Adopting a partial remedy to a known problem is one thing, but adopting an irrational, partial remedy is quite another. When the Sentencing Commission promulgates a provision that is based on "unsound judgment," such as the arbitrary crack/powder ratios animating USSG § 2D1.1's new drug quantity table, this Court may exercise its discretion to reject that provision of the Guidelines.

There is yet another reason to reject the new drug quantity table: it is based on bad math. While the Sentencing Commission amended the base offense levels for cocaine base, it did not amend the base offense levels for marihuana. As a result, applying the new table in cases that require converting an amount of cocaine base into an amount of marihuana creates inequalities between similarly situated defendants, the very thing the conversion process purports to remedy. Under this new table, the conversion ratios vary wildly by offense level.

As a result, a defendant may be propelled into a higher base offense level simply by the operation of the conversion ratio. In cases where conversion into an equivalent amount of marihuana is involved, the new drug quantity table thus advises treating defendants differently for no apparent reason beyond fiat. This Court need not and should not follow such automated advice.

As the tables clearly demonstrate, the various crack-to-powder ratios create sharp disparities and inequalities in the advisory guideline range available for a particular offense. Applying the various ratios to Ms. Smith reveals the following guideline ranges:

5. Marsha Smith - The Person Behind the Statistic

Ms. Smith is before this Court as a 37-year-old African American woman who entered the Bureau of Prisons at the age of 26 years old when she was arrested on August 5, 1997. It appears she has served 128 months of a 190-month sentence – a sentence which the United States Sentencing Commission now recognizes there is no justification for. According to the Bureau of Prisons website, she is currently set to be released a little over three years from now, on August 24, 2011.

Marsha Smith was born in Clovis, New Mexico to the union of A.J. and Betty Shepard. She had a good and happy childhood growing up with an intact family. Ms. Smith was a good basketball player and graduated from Levelland High School in Levelland, Texas, in 1990. Ms. Smith's mother described her daughter as well-respected in the community when she was growing up and helped at home by raising her younger brothers, Michael Shepard, and Benny Joe Shepard.

Upon graduation from high school, Ms. Smith attended the American Business School for one semester in 1992. Although she attended for only one semester, it was there she learned to perform clerical work and how to type and operate computers. With these skills, she landed several jobs following her graduation, including jobs as a receptionist with First Image Management Company, Babich and Associates, and Affiliated Computer Services.

Ms. Smith was at the beginning of launching a successful career, but her life came crashing down when she met and fell in love with Phillip Foote in March 1997. Phillip Foote was using a false name and introduced himself as Miguel Johnson. After a brief stint of dating, she allowed Phillip Foote to move in with her. While Phillip Foote was living at Ms. Smith's apartment, he began dealing crack cocaine and storing it in the apartment. Upon execution of a search warrant of the apartment, law enforcement officials found crack cocaine in a drawer underneath the stove and both powder and crack cocaine in the car Phillip Foote was driving. Phillip Foote admitted that the drugs were his.

Ms. Smith was charged with the same crimes as Phillip Foote and the jury convicted both Mr. Foote and Ms. Smith on all four counts of the indictment. This was so even though investigative reports revealed there was no indication Ms. Smith was directly or indirectly involved in the drug transaction. At sentencing, Ms. Smith received a mandatory guideline-driven sentence of 190 months, while Phillip Foote received 215 months.

Marsha Smith's past ten years have been difficult. From behind bars, she has watched the passing of two of her grandparents, and her father has entered a nursing home. "He's hoping that she gets out soon so that he can see her, put his arms around her."

During her time in prison, she has tried to make the best of her situation. Ms. Smith has completed many of the classes offered by the Bureau of Prisons, including 1) overall wellness; 2) advanced ceramics; 3) comprehensive legal research, and 4) career planning techniques. Furthermore, she has maintained a steady job with UNICOR prison industries throughout her entire incarceration, which provided her with enough money to pay off the $5,000.00 fine ordered by the Court at her sentencing.

At the time of Ms. Smith's sentencing, she was categorized as having a criminal history category of I. Indeed, Ms. Smith never had a previous arrest, much less a conviction. According to the data published by the United States Sentencing Commission, those people with a criminal history category of I have only an 11% chance of recidivism. Ms. Smith does not pose a "significant public safety risk" nor is she among the "most serious and violent offenders in the federal system" that United States Attorney General Michael B. Mukasey sought to frighten the American public about in his testimony before the United States Congress.

CONCLUSION

At a minimum, this Court should re-calculate and reduce Ms. Smith's guideline range by two levels in accordance with Amendment 706. However, Ms. Smith urges the Court to look deeper and take into account any relevant disparities – such as the disparity that results from applying the arbitrary ratios in the new drug quantity table or the increased disparity between that recalculated guideline range and the range that results from applying the career offender guideline – this Court should exercise its discretion under *Booker* and § 3553(a) and reduce the defendant's sentence to one that is "no greater than necessary" to fulfill the purposes of sentencing. The Sentencing Commission and the government would have this Court mechanistically reduce Ms. Smith's range by two levels only if the case falls within the narrow range of cases in which those two levels themselves added time to her term of imprisonment. Such an act is one "that could [be] performed by a machine; it is not a judicial assessment of the individual before the court." Section 3582(c)(2), by mandating that this Court impose a new sentence in accordance with 3553(a), requires this Court to individualize the new sentence it imposes on the defendant. It does not reduce this Court to being a mere calculator. Accordingly, Ms. Smith requests that she be sentenced to time served. Society has extracted enough from Ms. Smith, and she should be given the opportunity to reintegrate into society, instead of languishing in a minimum-security prison for another three years. "She's been in there for so long … for so long."

CHAPTER SIX

PROCEDURES FOR FILING A HABEAS CORPUS PETITION
UNDER 28 U.S.C.: 2254

For all of you out there who have been reading my books on post-conviction relief and ineffective assistance of counsel, you know that I have always written from my own experiences and my own practice of writing for others. This chapter is no different. This chapter is not the last chapter of this book, but it is the last one being written. This one has become very personal for me because of the passion I witnessed another advocate have for the case. As in many cases, this man is innocent of the conduct and the charged offense.

When I was released from prison, I continued to serve federal prisoners as a writer and advocate. I still, to this day, fight for those who cannot fight for themselves. But in addition to that, and because of this case, I decided to add proceedings for Alabama State prisoners in this book.

This all started because of my work. In addition to writing books and federal cases, I took a job with a nonprofit organization called Cullman Reentry Addiction Assistance. This is a transitional home for men, where I serve as the Assistant Director. My duties include preparing prisoners and their families for parole hearings and providing a home and job plan for the parolee.

In mid-October of 2021, I was at work live streaming the Sunday Church service that we provide for our residents. This was an odd day for me because I don't usually work Sundays. At the same time, another legal advocate from the Lovelady Center in Birmingham, Alabama decided not to attend a church service. She, Ms. Susan McDonald, was working on a case that was very close to her heart. Susan was preparing the case for the Alabama Parole Board. The man she was helping was Jerry Wayne Wiggins, and in preparation for his parole hearing, she needed to establish a job and home plan. Susan called our office phone that Sunday morning with the intention of leaving a message. Of course, I missed the call. For no known reason, I called the number back and got no answer. She, in turn, called me back, and we finally connected.

In our first conversation, Susan began by explaining her needs for a home and job plan. But, in the same conversation, she began telling me that Jerry was innocent of the offense. It's not a good subject to raise in a parole hearing. As we continued speaking, I explained to her who I was and what I did with The Federal Innocence Project. After confirming my status with a few internet searches, Susan developed a new vigor for Jerry's case. She continued through the parole hearing, and Jerry was denied. We then began the research on Jerry's case.

As always, I accept little that I am told about a case until I can confirm the facts. What I did not know was that Susan had been studying Jerry's case for more than a year. She took me right to the place in the record that proved all of Jerry's claims, even though neither of them really knew how to frame the claims. In the end, she showed me in the record where Jerry was provided ineffective assistance of counsel and where the State of Alabama violated the Brady Rule.

Because of this case, I have learned that state prisoners need a bit more information made available to them, to give them direction in establishing a claim for post-conviction relief.

Understanding whom a 2254 Federal Habeas Corpus petition is for is an important point. It is for a person who is in custody under a state court judgment and who may challenge his or her conviction in federal court on the ground that there was a violation of his or her federal constitutional rights. It is called a 2254 petition because of the statute governing federal habeas petitions challenging state court judgments, which is 28 U.S.C. section 2254.

What you will find in this chapter is the information needed to understand the ins and outs of the law, the 2254 statute, and all its governing rules. In addition, you will find tips for filing and following procedures. I also include a petition that was filed in the Northern District of Alabama on behalf of an Alabama State prisoner.

28 U.S. CODE § 2254 – STATE CUSTODY; REMEDIES IN FEDERAL COURTS

(a) The Supreme Court, a Justice thereof, a circuit judge, or a district court shall entertain an application for a writ of habeas corpus on behalf of a person in custody pursuant to the judgment of a State court only on the ground that he is in custody in violation of the Constitution or laws or treaties of the United States.

(b)

    (1) An application for a writ of habeas corpus on behalf of a person in custody pursuant to the judgment of a State court shall not be granted unless it appears that –

    (A) the applicant has exhausted the remedies available in the courts of the State; or

    (B)

        (i) there is an absence of available State corrective process; or

        (ii) circumstances exist that render such a process ineffective to protect the rights of the applicant.

    (2) An application for a writ of habeas corpus may be denied on the merits, notwithstanding the failure of the applicant to exhaust the remedies available in the courts of the State.

    (3) A State shall not be deemed to have waived the exhaustion requirement or be estopped from reliance upon the requirement unless the State, through counsel, expressly waives the requirement.

(c) An applicant shall not be deemed to have exhausted the remedies available in the courts of the State, within the meaning of this section, if he has the right under the law of the State to raise, by any available procedure, the question presented.

(d) An application for a writ of habeas corpus on behalf of a person in custody pursuant to the judgment of a State court shall not be granted with respect to any claim that was adjudicated on the merits in State court proceedings unless the adjudication of the claim –

    (1) resulted in a decision that was contrary to, or involved an unreasonable application of, clearly established Federal law, as determined by the Supreme Court of the United States; or

    (2) resulted in a decision that was based on an unreasonable determination of the facts in light of the evidence presented in the State court proceeding.

(e)

    (1) In a proceeding instituted by an application for a writ of habeas corpus by a person in custody pursuant to the judgment of a State court, a determination of a factual issue made by a State court shall be presumed to be correct. The applicant shall have the burden of rebutting the presumption of correctness by clear and convincing evidence.

    (2) If the applicant has failed to develop the factual basis of a claim in State court proceedings, the court shall not hold an evidentiary hearing on the claim unless the applicant shows that –

    (A) the claim relies on –

      (i) a new rule of constitutional law, made retroactive to cases on collateral review by the Supreme Court, that was previously unavailable; or

      (ii) a factual predicate that could not have been previously discovered through the exercise of due diligence; and

   (B) the facts underlying the claim would be sufficient to establish by clear and convincing evidence that but for constitutional error, no reasonable factfinder would have found the applicant guilty of the underlying offense.

(f) If the applicant challenges the sufficiency of the evidence adduced in such State court proceeding to support the State court's determination of a factual issue made therein, the applicant, if able, shall produce that part of the record pertinent to a determination of the sufficiency of the evidence to support such determination. If the applicant, because of indigency or other reason is unable to produce such part of the record, then the State shall produce such part of the record and the Federal court shall direct the State to do so by order directed to an appropriate State official. If the State cannot provide such a pertinent part of the record, then the court shall determine under the existing facts and circumstances what weight shall be given to the State court's factual determination.

(g) A copy of the official records of the State court, duly certified by the clerk of such court to be a true and correct copy of a finding, judicial opinion, or other reliable written indicia showing such a factual determination by the State court shall be admissible in the Federal court proceeding.

(h) Except as provided in section 408 of the Controlled Substance Act, in all proceedings brought under this section, and any subsequent proceedings on review, the court may appoint counsel for an applicant who is or becomes financially unable to afford counsel, except as provided by a rule promulgated by the Supreme Court pursuant to statutory authority. Appointment of counsel under this section shall be governed by section 3006A of title 18.

(i) The ineffectiveness or incompetence of counsel during Federal or State collateral post-conviction proceedings shall not be a ground for relief in a proceeding arising under section 2254.

RULES GOVERNING SECTION 2254 CASES
IN THE UNITED STATES DISTRICT COURTS

Rule 1. Scope

(a) Cases Involving a Petition under 28 U.S.C. § 2254. These rules govern a petition for a writ of habeas corpus filed in a United States district court under 28 U.S.C. § 2254 by:

   (1) a person in custody under a state-court judgment who seeks a determination that the custody violates the Constitution, laws, or treaties of the United States; and

   (2) a person in custody under a state-court or federal court judgment who seeks a determination that future custody under a state-court judgment would violate the Constitution, laws, or treaties of the United States.

(b) Other Cases. The district court may apply any or all these rules to a habeas corpus petition not covered by Rule l(a).

Rule 2. The Petition

(a) Current Custody; Naming the Respondent. If the petitioner is currently in custody under a state-court judgment, the petition must name as respondent the state officer who has custody.

(b) Future Custody; Naming the Respondents and Specifying the Judgment. If the petitioner is not yet in custody- but may be subject to future custody – under the state-court judgment being contested, the petition must name as respondents both the officer who has current custody and the attorney general of the state where the judgment was entered. The petition must ask for relief from the state-court judgment being contested.

(c) Form. The petition must:

   (1) specify all the grounds for relief available to the petitioner;

   (2) state the facts supporting each ground;

   (3) state the relief requested;

   (4) be printed, typewritten, or legibly handwritten; and

   (5) be signed under penalty of perjury by the petitioner or by a person authorized to sign it for the petitioner under 28 U.S.C. § 2242.

(d) Standard Form. The petition must substantially follow either the form appended to these rules or a form prescribed by a local district-court rule. The clerk must make forms available to petitioners without charge.

(e) Separate Petitions for Judgments of Separate Courts. A petitioner who seeks relief from judgments of more than one state court must file a separate petition covering the judgment or judgments of each court.

Rule 3. Filing the Petition; Inmate Filing

(a) Where to File; Copies; Filing Fee. An original and two copies of the petition must be filed with the clerk and must be accompanied by:

   (1) the applicable filing fee, or

(2) a motion for leave to proceed in forma pauperis, the affidavit required by 28 U.S.C. § 1915, and a certificate from the warden or other appropriate officer of the place of confinement showing the amount of money or securities that the petitioner has in any account in the institution.

(b) Filing. The clerk must file the petition and enter it on the docket.

(c) Time to File. The time for filing a petition is governed by 28 U.S.C. § 2244(d).

(d) Inmate Filing. A paper filed by an inmate confined in an institution is timely if deposited in the institution's internal mailing system on or before the last day for filing. If an institution has a system designed for legal mail, the inmate must use that system to receive the benefit of this rule. Timely filing may be shown by a declaration in compliance with 28 U.S.C. § 1746 or by a notarized statement, either of which must set forth the date of deposit and state that first-class postage has been prepaid.

Rule 4. Preliminary Review; Serving the Petition and Order

The clerk must promptly forward the petition to a judge under the court's assignment procedure, and the judge must promptly examine it. If it plainly appears from the petition and any attached exhibits that the petitioner is not entitled to relief in the district court, the judge must dismiss the petition and direct the clerk to notify the petitioner. If the petition is not dismissed, the judge must order the respondent to file an answer, motion, or other response within a fixed time, or to take other action the judge may order. In every case, the clerk must serve a copy of the petition and any order on the respondent and on the attorney general or other appropriate officer of the state involved.

Rule 5. The Answer and the Reply

(a) When required. The respondent is not required to answer the petition unless a judge so orders.

(b) Contents: Addressing the Allegations; Stating a Bar. The answer must address the allegations in the petition. In addition, it must state whether any claim in the petition is barred by a failure to exhaust state remedies, a procedural bar, non-retroactivity, or a statute of limitations.

(c) Contents: Transcripts. The answer must also indicate what transcripts (of pretrial, trial, sentencing, or post-conviction proceedings) are available, when they can be furnished, and what proceedings have been recorded but not transcribed. The respondent must attach to the answer parts of the transcript that the respondent considers relevant. The judge may order that the respondent furnish other parts of existing transcripts or that parts of un-transcribed recordings be transcribed and furnished. If a transcript cannot be obtained, the respondent may submit a narrative summary of the evidence.

(d) Contents: Briefs on Appeal and Opinions. The respondent must also file with the answer a copy of:

(1) any brief that the petitioner submitted in an appellate court contesting the conviction or sentence or contesting an adverse judgment or order in a post-conviction proceeding.

(2) any brief that the prosecution submitted in an appellate court relating to the conviction or sentence; and

(3) the opinions and dispositive orders of the appellate court relating to the conviction or the sentence.

(e) Reply. The petitioner may file a reply to the respondent's answer or other pleadings. The judge must set the time to file unless the time is already set by local rules.

Rule 6. Discovery

(a) Leave of Court Required. A judge may, for good cause, authorize a party to conduct discovery under the Federal Rules of Civil Procedure and may limit the extent of discovery. If necessary for effective discovery, the judge must appoint an attorney for a petitioner who qualifies to have counsel appointed under 18 U.S.C. § 3006A.

(b) Requesting Discovery. A party requesting discovery must provide reasons for the request. The request must also include any proposed interrogatories and requests for admission and must specify any requested documents.

(c) Deposition Expenses. If the respondent is granted leave to take a deposition, the judge may require the respondent to pay the travel expenses, subsistence expenses, and fees of the petitioner's attorney to attend the deposition.

Rule 7. Expanding the Record

(a) In General. If the petition is not dismissed, the judge may direct the parties to expand the record by submitting additional materials relating to the petition. The judge may require that these materials be authenticated.

(b) Types of Materials. The materials that may be required include letters predating the filing of the petition, documents, exhibits, and answers under oath to written interrogatories propounded by the judge. Affidavits may also be submitted and considered as part of the record.

(c) Review by the Opposing Party. The judge must give the party against whom the additional materials are offered an opportunity to admit or deny their correctness.

Rule 8. Evidentiary Hearing

(a) Determining Whether to Hold a Hearing. If the petition is not dismissed, the judge must review the answer, any transcripts and records of state-court proceedings, and any materials submitted under Rule 7 to determine whether an evidentiary hearing is warranted.

(b) Reference to a Magistrate Judge. A judge may, under 28 U.S.C. § 636(b), refer the petition to a magistrate judge to conduct hearings and to file proposed findings of fact and recommendations for disposition. When they are filed, the clerk must promptly serve copies of the proposed findings and recommendations to all parties. Within 14 days after being served, a party may file objections as provided by local court rules. The judge must determine de nova any proposed finding or recommendation to which an objection is made. The judge may accept, reject, or modify any proposed finding or recommendation.

(c) Appointing Counsel; Time of Hearing. If an evidentiary hearing is warranted, the judge must appoint an attorney to represent a petitioner who qualifies to have counsel appointed under 18 U.S.C. § 3006A. The judge must conduct the hearing as soon as practicable after giving the attorneys adequate time to investigate and prepare. These rules do not limit the appointment of counsel under§ 3006A at any stage of the proceeding.

Rule 9. Second or Successive Petitions

Before presenting a second or successive petition, the petitioner must obtain an order from the appropriate court of appeals authorizing the district court to consider the petition as required by 28 U.S.C. § 2244(b)(3) and (4).

Rule 10. Powers of a Magistrate Judge

A magistrate judge may perform the duties of a district judge under these rules, as authorized under 28 U.S.C. § 636.

Rule 11. Certificate of Appealability; Time to Appeal

(a) Certificate of Appealability. The district court must issue or deny a certificate of appealability when it enters a final order adverse to the applicant. Before entering the final order, the court may direct the parties to submit arguments on whether a certificate should issue. If the court issues a certificate, the court must state the specific issue or issues that satisfy the showing required by 28 U.S.C. § 2253(c)(2). If the court denies a certificate, the parties may not appeal the denial but may seek a certificate from the court of appeals under the Federal Rule of Appellate Procedure 22. A motion to reconsider a denial does not extend the time to appeal.

(b) Time to Appeal. Federal Rule of Appellate Procedure 4(a) governs the time to appeal an order entered under these rules. A timely notice of appeal must be filed even if the district court issues a certificate of appealability.

Rule 12. Applicability of the Federal Rules of Civil Procedure

The Federal Rules of Civil Procedure, to the extent that they are not inconsistent with any statutory provisions or these rules, may be applied to a proceeding under these rules.

BASIC GUIDE TO FILING FOR HABEAS CORPUS IN A FEDERAL COURT PURSUANT TO 28 U.S.C. 2254 INTRODUCTION

This Guide is intended to help you understand the procedures that you must follow if you represent yourself in a Federal Court. You cannot rely on this Guide alone, however, because it does not address every situation that might arise in your case. Moreover, this Guide does not offer any information about the specific issues in your personal case. This Guide is not legal advice. I encourage you to review this Guide together with Title 28 of the United States Code ("U.S.C.") sections (§§) 2241-2254; the Rules Governing Section 2254 Cases in the United States District Courts; the Federal Rules of Civil Procedure; and the Court's Local Rules.

If you are a prisoner, the United States Code should be available in your prison law library. The Federal Rules of Civil Procedure appear at the end of Title 28 of the United States Code. The Rules Governing Section 2254 Cases appear immediately after 28 U.S.C. § 2254 in the United States Code. If your prison law library does not have the most recent version of this Court's Local Rules, they can be obtained from the Clerk's Office by request. Each of these resources is also available online. This Guide is organized in the sequence that a habeas petition proceeds through the Court and is written in a question-and-answer format.

SECTION ONE: GENERAL INFORMATION

What is the Clerk's Office?

The Clerk's Office maintains the Court's records. Most of your interactions with the Court will be through the Clerk's Office, where you will file the documents that will be reviewed by the judge. The Clerk's Office cannot give you legal advice or tell you when a judge might make a decision in your case, but the Clerk's Office can tell you whether a particular document has been filed and can provide copies of documents in the court record at a cost.

What does it mean to file documents with the Clerk's Office?

The Clerk's Office receives documents on behalf of the Court and maintains a record of the documents received. By filing a document with the Clerk's Office, you ensure that the document becomes part of the official record in your case. This record allows both you and the judges to be certain of what documents have been presented in a case. You may file any document, including a habeas petition, either by mailing the document to the Clerk's Office or by personally delivering the document to the Clerk's Office during business hours. After receiving your documents, the Clerk's Office will record (or "docket") your papers and send them to the judge assigned to your case. Any documents you file with the Court in a habeas matter will also be served on the party opposing your habeas petition.

How do I contact the Clerk's Office?

You may contact the Clerk's Office at the appropriate address and phone number. If you are a prisoner, you will find a listing of court addresses and phone numbers in the directory found in most law libraries.

What is a magistrate judge?

A federal magistrate judge is a judicial officer who has some, but not all, of the powers of a district judge appointed under Article III of the United States Constitution. Magistrate judges may (among other things) set deadlines, enter orders on scheduling, and issue Reports and Recommendations regarding whether your habeas petition should be granted or denied. You may object to any portion of a Report and Recommendation entered by a magistrate judge in your case, and your objection will be reviewed by a district judge. The local court rules of your jurisdiction will explain more about the role of magistrate judges.

SECTION TWO: THE BASICS

What is a petition for a writ of habeas corpus?

A petition for a writ of habeas corpus is a request for the Court to review the legality of your detention. Section 2241 of Title 28 of the United States Code (28 U.S.C. § 2241) permits courts to issue writs of habeas corpus where a prisoner establishes that he is in custody in violation of the Constitution or laws or treaties of the United States. Habeas corpus petitions filed by state prisoners held pursuant to a state-court judgment are subject to several restrictions, many of which may be found in 28 U.S.C. § 2244 and 28 U.S.C. § 2254. Because of the importance of these restrictions, habeas petitions filed by state prisoners held pursuant to a state-court judgment are often referred to as "petitions governed by§ 2254," or as "§ 2254 petitions."

Who may file a habeas petition?

There are several conditions discussed in the following questions that you must meet to properly file a habeas petition.

Do you meet the "in custody" requirement?

A petitioner cannot seek a writ of habeas corpus unless he is being held "in custody" at the time that the habeas corpus petition is filed. The "in custody" requirement sometimes, though not always, is met if the petitioner is on probation, parole, or supervised release. Detention at a jail or prison also constitutes being "in custody" for purposes of § 2241 and § 2254. By filing a habeas petition, you are challenging the legality of that custody.

Did you exhaust alternative remedies before filing your petition?

A petitioner generally must exhaust alternative remedies before filing a habeas petition. For state prisoners, this will likely mean first presenting your claims to the state courts, including the state supreme court, before seeking federal habeas relief.

What type of relief is available if a petition is granted?

A habeas petition is appropriate for challenging the fact that you are in custody or for challenging the length of time for which you have been committed to custody. If your habeas petition is granted, your term in custody will be invalidated to the extent that the custody is found to be unlawful. Monetary damages are not available in a habeas corpus action. You may not challenge the conditions of your confinement in a habeas action.

Is there a limitation period for filing a habeas petition?

Yes, if you are a state prisoner challenging the validity of a state-court judgment. Habeas corpus petitions governed by § 2254 are subject to a one-year limitations period. In most cases, the one-year limitation period will begin to run after the judgment you seek to challenge becomes final. Judgment will become final upon denial of a writ of certiorari by the Supreme Court of the United States or, if you do not file a petition for a writ of certiorari, ninety days after the final ruling on direct appeal.

If your claim depends upon a new rule of constitutional law that applies retroactively, or if you were impeded by state action from filing a habeas petition, or if your habeas petition relies upon a factual predicate that could not with due diligence have been discovered earlier, the limitations window for that claim may begin at a different date. See 28 U.S.C. § 2244(d). If you are a prisoner representing yourself, your habeas petition is deemed to be "filed" as of the date that it is properly placed in the prison mail system. Should you properly file a petition for post-conviction relief in the state courts, the limitations window will be paused or "tolled" during the time that the petition remains pending in the state courts. Your federal limitations window will begin to run again after you have exhausted all appeals within the state courts or after the time for filing an appeal in the state courts has expired. The rules governing the timeliness of habeas petitions under§ 2254 are both strict and technical. Failure to file your habeas petition in a timely fashion will likely result in summary denial of your petition.

May I amend my habeas petition after I file it?

Maybe: After the respondent has answered your petition, you must receive permission from the court to file an amended petition. If you want to amend your petition, you will need to follow the procedures for amendments found in Federal Rule of Civil Procedure 15(a) and any applicable Local Rule. Note that any claims added to an amended petition, like those in the original petition, must be both timely and fully exhausted in the state courts.

May I file a second habeas petition challenging my state-court conviction?

If your § 2254 petition is deemed to be "second or successive," you must receive authorization from the United States Court of Appeals for the Eighth Circuit before proceeding with your habeas claims in a Federal District Court. The Federal Circuit Courts are permitted to authorize only certain kinds of claims for review in a second or successive habeas petition. See 28 U.S.C. § 2244(b)(2). If you received a ruling on the merits of an initial habeas petition challenging your conviction, any subsequent habeas petition attacking the same conviction will likely be found to be second or successive. That said, not all habeas petitions filed second in time are "second or successive" within the meaning of the relevant statute. For example, if your first habeas petition was denied without prejudice for failure to exhaust available state court remedies, you may file a new petition again, raising those claims after they have become exhausted without first receiving authorization from the Circuit Court in your jurisdiction.

SECTION THREE: HOW TO START A § 2254 PROCEEDING

What are the requirements to start a§ 2254 proceeding?

To start a § 2254 proceeding in a Federal District Court, you must do the following:

- Complete the habeas petition itself, either by using the Court's form "Petition for Relief from a Conviction or Sentence by a Person in State Custody" or by writing your own document. You may also submit any exhibits you believe to be relevant.

- Complete a civil cover sheet (if available).

- Pay the $5.00 filing fee or, if you cannot pay the fee, complete an application to Proceed in District Court Without Prepaying Fees or Costs ("IFP application"); and

- Mail the documents and fee to the Clerk's Office of the Federal Court in your jurisdiction. Keep a copy of all documents for your own records.

How do I complete the habeas corpus petition form?

You are not required to use the Court's standard habeas form, but that document will assist you in providing the information needed to decide your petition. Failure to include the necessary information could result in delay or dismissal of your proceedings. Your habeas petition and all other documents prepared by you for the Court should be typed or legibly handwritten, preferably in black ink.

Can I file one habeas petition for judgments from multiple courts?

No. A petitioner who seeks relief from judgments entered in more than one court must file a separate petition covering the judgment(s) of each court. See Rule 2 of the Rules Governing § 2254 Cases.

Whom should I name as the respondent on the habeas corpus petition?

The proper respondent in a proceeding governed by § 2254 is the warden or the custodian of the facility where you are held. See Rule 2(a) of the Rules Governing § 2254 Cases. The naming of an incorrect respondent generally will not, by itself, result in the dismissal of the habeas petition.

How should I answer Question 12 (grounds for relief) on the habeas corpus petition?

For each ground for relief, you should state the legal basis under which your claim arises. That basis must be founded in federal law, such as a constitutional provision, United States Supreme Court case, federal law, or treaty of the United States. The claim must be a claim that you have already raised in each level of the state courts. The petition should include a brief description of the factual circumstances that are relevant to the claim.

May I file attachments with my petition?

If you have documents that support your petition, you may attach copies of the documents to the petition as exhibits. The purpose of an exhibit is to present proof or clarification of an allegation in your petition. If you decide to attach exhibits to your petition, then you should explain or otherwise make clear why you are attaching each exhibit to the petition. You should label each separate exhibit and, if possible, number the pages of each exhibit.

May I file a memorandum of law with my petition?

Yes. A memorandum of law sometimes called a brief, is a document where you explain your legal arguments. You should only include arguments that support the claims raised in the petition. Prose litigants may write their memoranda legibly by hand or type their memoranda on standard 8.5 x 11-inch paper. The memorandum should include page numbers. Most Court's Local Rules limit memoranda to 12,000 words unless advance permission to file a longer memorandum is sought and received from the judge.

Do I need to notarize the petition?

No, but you are required to sign all documents (except exhibits) filed with the Court, including your petition. By signing a document, you are attesting that the statements in your document are true to the best of your knowledge. Knowingly making a false material declaration under oath (perjury) can be punished by fine or imprisonment. See 18 U.S.C. § 1623. Notarization of court documents, however, is almost always unnecessary.

What is a civil cover sheet?

The civil cover sheet is a form provided by the Clerk's Office and is used to gather information about the nature of your lawsuit. You must file a civil cover sheet when you file your petition.

How do I pay the $5.00 filing fee?

You may submit your $5.00 filing fee by check from your prison trust account and mail it to the Clerk's Office address provided in the law library. Checks are payable to the "Clerk, U.S. District Court."

What if I cannot afford the filing fee?

If you cannot afford the $5.00 filing fee, you may apply to proceed without prepaying the fee by completing and filing the AO239 form "Application to Proceed in District Court Without Prepaying Fees or Costs." This document is also referred to as an application to proceed in forma pauperis, or "IFP application" for short. If your application is granted, you will not be required to pay the $5.00 filing fee. See 28 U.S.C. § 1915. You will be notified of the judge's decision regarding your IFP application by mail.

Do I need to serve a copy of my petition?

No. You do not need to serve the respondent a copy of your petition. The respondent will be notified of your petition when it is received and filed by the Court.

May I request an appointment of counsel?

Yes. Be aware, though, that there is no statutory or constitutional right to counsel in habeas corpus actions. If you file a motion to appoint counsel, you should explain the particular reasons that you believe the appointment of counsel is necessary or appropriate in your case.

What other documents should I file at the start of my case?

The only documents required to initiate a habeas action are the habeas petition itself and the IFP application (or $5.00 filing fee). You may, but need not, file any other documents that you believe would be helpful to the Court in deciding your petition.

How can I find out when my petition was received by the Clerk's Office?

You may request in writing that the Clerk notify you when your petition was received and filed.

SECTION FOUR: INITIAL REVIEW

What is an initial review?

Your habeas petition and IFP application (if one is submitted) will be reviewed by a judge or magistrate judge upon filing. The judge will dismiss the petition if it is clear that you are not entitled to relief. This initial review process may take several weeks.

How will I know the results of the initial review?

If your petition is permitted to go forward, an order will be entered requiring the respondent to answer the petition. You will receive a copy of this order. If your petition is deficient, either an order of dismissal or a Report and Recommendation recommending dismissal will be entered. You will receive a copy of these documents also. The Court's initial review is limited to the petition itself, attached exhibits, and other materials already part of the judicial record. Should the respondent be required to answer the petition, a review of the record may reveal grounds for dismissal that are not plainly apparent from the petition and exhibits.

SECTION FIVE: THE HABEAS PROCEEDINGS

How will the Court get the state-court record in my case?

If the judge orders the respondent to file an answer, the respondent must supply the Court with a copy of those portions of the state court record that the respondent believes are relevant to the petition. See Rule 5, Rules Governing § 2254 Cases. For example, if the habeas corpus petition challenges only the legality of the sentencing, then the respondent may supply the Court with only the sentencing records, rather than the entire transcript of the trial. The respondent will not supply you with a copy of your state-court record. If the respondent does not lodge all portions of the state-court record that you deem relevant to a determination of the claims, you can file a motion to expand the record under Rule 7 of the Rules Governing § 2254 cases. The Court may sometimes ask the respondent to supply additional documents from the state court as well.

May I reply to the respondent's answer?

Yes. The Court's scheduling order will set a deadline for the filing of a reply brief.

Is discovery allowed?

Sometimes, you must request permission from the Court before conducting discovery. See Rule 6 of the Rules Governing Section 2254 Cases. Habeas petitions are usually resolved without formal discovery.

Will there be an evidentiary hearing?

Probably not. The written record is usually enough for the Court to resolve the habeas petition, and federal courts are greatly restricted from receiving or considering evidence that is not part of the state court record. See 28 U.S.C. § 2254(e)(2).

Will there be any hearing before the judge decides my case?

Perhaps. The judges presiding over the case will determine whether an oral argument by the parties is necessary.

How do I object to an adverse Report and Recommendation?

If a magistrate judge issues a Report and Recommendation in your case and you disagree with the recommendation, the Local Court Rule provides that you have 14 days to file an objection. Your objection will be reviewed by the district judge assigned to the case. Your objection to the Report and Recommendation must be specific and relate to the magistrate judge's proposed findings and recommendations; new arguments are not permitted at this stage. Your objection may be no more than 3,500 words in length. See Local Rules. If you file an objection, the respondent is permitted to respond to your objection within 14 days after your objection is filed. Upon receiving your objection, the district judge assigned to the case will review the record and make a decision.

SECTION SIX: JUDGMENT AND APPEAL

What do I need to do to file an appeal?

Judgment will be entered after your case has become final. You will receive a copy of the judgment after it is entered, along with instructions on how to pursue an appeal with the United States Court of Appeals. An appeal may only be made after judgment has been entered in your case. The time for filing an appeal starts from the date that the judgment is entered on the docket. Habeas corpus petitioners proceeding under § 2254 also must receive a certificate of appealability in order to pursue their claims before the appellate court. The district court will grant or deny a certificate of appealability when it enters the final order in your case that is averse to you. See Rule 11 of the Rules Governing§ 2254 Cases. If the district court grants you a certificate of appealability, then you may proceed and file a notice of appeal. If the district court judge denies you a certificate of appealability, then you may still file a notice of appeal, but the claims that you seek to raise on appeal will not be heard and decided unless the Court of Appeals grants you a certificate of appealability after your notice of appeal has been filed. See Rule 22(b) of the Federal Rules of Appellate Procedure. The district court will specify the claims to which the certificate of appealability applies.

How do I file an appeal?

First, you must file a notice of appeal. A sample notice of appeal is included in a previous chapter of this book. Second, you must pay the $505.00 filing fee for the appeal. As with the filing fee in the district court, if you cannot afford to pay this fee, you can apply to proceed without prepaying the fee by completing the AO239 form "Application to Proceed in District Court Without Prepaying Fees or Costs." Even though you are seeking IFP status on appeal, you should file this application in the district court. If your application is granted, you will not be required to pay the $505.00 filing fee. If the district judge denies your motion to proceed with IFP on appeal, you may ask the Appeals Court to proceed with IFP within 30 days after service of this Court's notice that your appellate IFP application was denied.

"How much time do I have to begin my appeal?

You must file your notice of appeal in the Federal District Court within 30 days after the judgment is · entered. For additional information regarding the time for filing a notice of appeal, see Federal Rule of Appellate Procedure 4 (a). There are many other steps to beginning and proceeding with your appeal, but they are governed by the Appeals Court Local Rules and the Federal Rules of Appellate Procedure, which are beyond the scope of this Guide.

May I request an appointment of counsel on appeal?

Yes, but your request should be filed with the Federal Court of Appeals. Be warned that there is no statutory or constitutional right to counsel on appeal in a habeas case.

PETITION FOR RELIEF FROM A CONVICTION OR SENTENCE
BY A PERSON IN STATE CUSTODY
(PETITION UNDER 28 U.S.C. § 2254 FOR A WRIT OF HABEAS CORPUS)

INSTRUCTIONS

1. To use this form, you must be a person who is currently serving a sentence under a judgment against you in a state court. You are asking for relief from the conviction or the sentence. This form is your petition for relief.

2. You may also use this form to challenge a state judgment that imposed a sentence to be served in the future, but you must fill in the name of the state where the judgment was entered. If you want to challenge a federal judgment that imposed a sentence to be served in the future, you should file a motion under 28 U.S.C. § 2255 in the federal court that entered the judgment.

3. Make sure the form is typed or neatly written.

4. You must tell the truth and sign the form. If you make a false statement of a material fact, you may be prosecuted for perjury.

5. Answer all the questions. You do not need to cite the law. You may submit additional pages if necessary. If you do not fill out the form properly, you will be asked to submit additional or correct information. If you want to submit any legal arguments, you must submit them in a separate memorandum. Be aware that any such memorandum may be subject to page limits set forth in the local rules of the court where you file this petition.

6. You must pay a fee of $5. If the fee is paid, your petition will be filed. If you cannot pay the fee, you may ask to proceed in forma pauperis (as a poor person). To do that, you must fill out the last page of this form. Also, you must submit a certificate signed by an officer at the institution where you are confined, showing the amount of money that the institution is holding for you. If your account exceeds $_____, you must pay the filing fee.

7. In this petition, you may challenge the judgment entered by only one court. If you want to challenge a judgment entered by a different court (either in the same state or in different states), you must file a separate petition.

8. When you have completed the form, send the original and _____ copies to the Clerk of the United States District Court at this address:

Clerk, United States District Court for _____
Address
City, State Zip Code

If you want a file-stamped copy of the petition, you must enclose an additional copy of the petition and ask the court to file-stamp it and return it to you.

9. CAUTION: You must include in this petition all the grounds for relief from the conviction or sentence that you challenge. And you must state the facts that support each ground. If you fail to set forth all the grounds in this petition, you may be barred from presenting additional grounds at a later date.

10. CAPITAL CASES: If you are under a sentence of death, you are entitled to the assistance of counsel and should request the appointment of counsel.

150

PETITION UNDER 28 U.S.C. § 2254 FOR WRIT OF HABEAS CORPUS BY A PERSON IN STATE CUSTODY

United States District Court		District: Middle District of Alabama
Name (under which you were convicted): Jerry Wiggins		Docket or Case No.: CC99-1133
Place of Confinement: Hamilton A and I		Prisoner No.: 214723
Petitioner (include the name under which you were convicted) Jerry Wiggins	v.	Respondent (authorized person having custody of petitioner) Scotty Shaffer, Cpt.
The Attorney General of the State of: Alabama		

PETITION

1. (a) Name and location of court that entered the judgment of conviction you are challenging:

Circuit Court for Jefferson County Tenth Judicial Circuit Bessemer

Bessemer, AL

(b) Criminal docket or case number (if you know): CC99-1133

2. (a) Date of the judgment of conviction (if you know): _____

(b) Date of sentencing: 07/29/2000

3. Length of sentence: Fifty years

4. In this case, were you convicted on more than one count or of more than one crime? ☐ Yes ☑ No

5. Identify all crimes of which you were convicted and sentenced in this case:

Rape in the first degree

6. (a) What was your plea? (Check one)

☑ (1) Not guilty   ☐ (3) Nolo contendere (no contest)

☐ (2) Guilty   ☐ (4) Insanity plea

(b) If you entered a guilty plea to one count or charge and a not guilty plea to another count or charge, what did you plead guilty to and what did you plead not guilty to? ___N/A___

_____

_____

_____

_____

(c) If you went to trial, what kind of trial did you have? (Check one)

☑ Jury   ☐ Judge only

7. Did you testify at a pretrial hearing trial, or a post-trial hearing?

☑ Yes   ☐ No

8. Did you appeal from the judgment of conviction?

☑ Yes   ☐ No

9. If you did appeal, answer the following:

(a) Name of court: __Alabama Criminal Court of Appeals__

(b) Docket or case number (if you know): ___CR-00-0652___

(c) Result: __Affirmed__

(d) Date of result (if you know): __07/20/2001__

(e) Citation to the case (if you know): __837 So. 2d 887__

(f) Grounds raised: __Ineffective Assistance of Counsel__

_____

_____

_____

_____

_____

(g) Did you seek further review by a higher state court?   ☑ Yes   ☐ No

If yes, answer the following:

(1) Name of court: __unknown__

(2) Docket or case number (if you know): __unknown__

(3) Result: __Affirmed__

POST-CONVICTION RELIEF: THE ADVOCATE

(4) Date of result (if you know): _____

(5) Citation to the case (if you know): __unknown_____

(6) Grounds raised: ____Ineffective Assistance of Counsel_____

_____

_____

_____

(h) Did you file a petition for certiorari in the United States Supreme Court? ☐ Yes   ☑ No

If yes, answer the following:

(1) Docket or case number (if you know): _____

(2) Result: _____

_____

(3) Date of result (if you know): _____

(4) Citation to the case (if you know): _____

10. Other than the direct appeals listed above, have you previously filed any other petitions, applications, or motions concerning this judgment of conviction in any state court?   ☐ Yes   ☐ No

11. If your answer to question 10 was "Yes," give the following information:

(a)   (1) Name of court: __Jefferson County Tenth Judicial Circuit – Bessemer Criminal Division__

(2) Docket or case number (if you know): ___unknown_____

(3) Date of filing (if you know): __10/01/2002_____

(4) Nature of the proceeding: ___Post-Conviction Relief – Rule 32_____

(5) Grounds raised: ____Ineffective Assistance of Counsel_____

_____

_____

_____

_____

_____

_____

_____

(6) Did you receive a hearing where evidence was given on your petition, application, or motion?

☑ Yes   ☐ No

(7) Result: __Denied_____

(8) Date of result (if you know): 05/05/2005

(b) If you filed any second petition, application, or motion, give the same information:

(1) Name of court: N/A

(2) Docket or case number (if you know): _____

(3) Date of filing (if you know): _____

(4) Nature of the proceeding: _____

(5) Grounds raised: _____

_____

_____

_____

_____

_____

_____

_____

(6) Did you receive a hearing where evidence was given on your petition, application, or motion?

☐ Yes   ☑ No

(7) Result: _____

(8) Date of result (if you know): _____

(c) If you filed any third petition, application, or motion, give the same information: _____

(1) Name of court: N/A

(2) Docket or case number (if you know): _____

(3) Date of filing (if you know): _____

(4) Nature of the proceeding: _____

(5) Grounds raised: _____

_____

_____

_____

_____

_____

_____

_____

(6) Did you receive a hearing where evidence was given on your petition, application, or motion?

☐ Yes   ☐ No

(7) Result: _____

(8) Date of result (if you know): _____

(d) Did you appeal to the highest state court having jurisdiction over the action taken on your petition, application, or motion?

(1) First petition: ☑ Yes   ☐ No

(2) Second petition: ☐ Yes   ☐ No

(3) Third petition: ☐ Yes   ☐ No

(e) If you did not appeal to the highest state court having jurisdiction, explain why you did not:

_____

_____

12. For this petition, state every ground on which you claim that you are being held in violation of the Constitution, laws, or treaties of the United States. Attach additional pages if you have more than four grounds. State the facts supporting each ground. Any legal arguments must be submitted in a separate memorandum.

CAUTION: To proceed in the federal court, you must ordinarily first exhaust (use up) your available state-court remedies on each ground on which you request action by the federal court. Also, if you fail to set forth all the grounds in this petition, you may be barred from presenting additional grounds at a later date.

GROUND ONE: Mr. Wiggins' trial counsel, Mr. Shelton Perhacs, provided ineffective assistance of counsel to such a degree that he facilitated the conviction of his innocent client.

(a) **Supporting facts** (Do not argue or cite the law. Just state the specific facts that support your claim.):

SEE ATTACHED _____

_____

_____

_____

(b) If you did not exhaust your state remedies on Ground One, explain why:

SEE ATTACHED _____

_____

_____

_____

_____

(c) Direct Appeal of Ground One:

(1) If you appealed from the judgment of conviction, did you raise this issue?   ☐ Yes   ☐ No

(2) If you did not raise this issue in your direct appeal, explain why: _____

SEE ATTACHED _____

_____

(d) Post-Conviction Proceedings:

(1) Did you raise this issue through a post-conviction motion or petition for habeas corpus in a state trial court?

☑ Yes   ☐ No

(2) If your answer to question (d)(1) is "Yes," state:

Type of motion or petition: ___ SEE ATTACHED _____

Name and location of the court where the motion or petition was filed: _____

SEE ATTACHED _____

Docket or case number (if you know): _____

Date of the court's decision: _____

Result (attach a copy of the court's opinion or order, if available): _____

_____

_____

(3) Did you receive a hearing on your motion or petition?   ☑ Yes   ☐ No

(4) Did you appeal from the denial of your motion or petition?   ☑ Yes   ☐ No

(5) If your answer to question (d)(4) is "Yes," did you raise this issue in the appeal?   ☑ Yes   ☐ No

(6) If your answer to question (d)(4) is "Yes," state:

Name and location of the court where the appeal was filed: _____

SEE ATTACHED _____

Docket and case number (if you know it): _____

Date of the court's decision: _____

Results (attach a copy of the court's opinion or order, if available): _____

_____

(7) If your answer to question (d)(4) or question (d)(5) is "No," explain why you did not raise this issue:

N/A _____

_____

_____

(e) **Other Remedies:** Describe any other procedures (such as habeas corpus, administrative remedies, etc.) that you have used to exhaust your state remedies on Ground One: _____

N/A

GROUND TWO: Mr. Wiggins' post-conviction counsel's failure to raise additional issues relating to Petitioner's initial trial constitutes a *Strickland* violation by which this Court should grant habeas relief.

(a) **Supporting facts** (Do not argue or cite the law. Just state the specific facts that support your claim.):

SEE ATTACHED

(b) If you did not exhaust your state remedies on Ground Two, explain why: _____

(c) **Direct Appeal of Ground Two:**

(1) If you appealed from the judgment of conviction, did you raise this issue? ☑ Yes ☐ No

(2) If you did not raise this issue in your direct appeal, explain why: _____

(d) **Post-Conviction Proceedings:**

(1) Did you raise this issue through a post-conviction motion or petition for habeas corpus in a state trial court?

☑ Yes ☐ No

(2) If your answer to question (d)(l) is "Yes," state:

Type of motion or petition: RULE 32

Name and location of the court where the motion or petition was filed: _____

Docket or case number (if you know): _____

KELLY PATRICK RIGGS

Date of the court's decision: _____

Results (attach a copy of the court's opinion or order, if available): _____

_____

(3) Did you receive a hearing on your motion or petition?	☑ Yes	☐ No
(4) Did you appeal from the denial of your motion or petition?	☑ Yes	☐ No
(5) If your answer to question (d)(4) is "Yes," did you raise this issue in the appeal?	☑ Yes	☐ No

(6) If your answer to question (d)(4) is "Yes," state:

Name and location of the court where the appeal was filed: _____

SEE ATTACHED _____

Docket and case number (if you know it): _____

Date of the court's decision: _____

Results (attach a copy of the court's opinion or order, if available): _____

_____

(7) If your answer to question (d)(4) or question (d)(5) is "No," explain why you did not raise this issue:

N/A _____

_____

_____

(e) **Other Remedies:** Describe any other procedures (such as habeas corpus, administrative remedies, etc.) that you have used to exhaust your state remedies on Ground Two: _____

N/A _____

_____

GROUND THREE: _____ N/A _____

(a) **Supporting facts** (Do not argue or cite the law. Just state the specific facts that support your claim.):

_____

_____

_____

_____

_____

_____

_____

(b) If you did not exhaust your state remedies on Ground Three, explain why:

_____

_____

_____

_____

_____

(c) **Direct Appeal of Ground Three:**

(1) If you appealed from the judgment of conviction, did you raise this issue? ☐ Yes   ☐ No

(2) If you did not raise this issue in your direct appeal, explain why: _____

_____

_____

(d) **Post-Conviction Proceedings:**

(1) Did you raise this issue through a post-conviction motion or petition for habeas corpus in a state trial court?

☐ Yes   ☐ No

(2) If your answer to question (d)(1) is "Yes," state:

Type of motion or petition: _____

Name and location of the court where the motion or petition was filed: _____

_____

Docket or case number (if you know): _____

Date of the court's decision: _____

Result (attach a copy of the court's opinion or order, if available): _____

_____

_____

(3) Did you receive a hearing on your motion or petition?   ☐ Yes   ☐ No

(4) Did you appeal from the denial of your motion or petition?   ☐ Yes   ☐ No

(5) If your answer to question (d)(4) is "Yes," did you raise this issue in the appeal? ☐ Yes   ☐ No

(6) If your answer to question (d)(4) is "Yes," state:

Name and location of the court where the appeal was filed: _____

_____

Docket and case number (if you know it): _____

Date of the court's decision: _____

Results (attach a copy of the court's opinion or order, if available): _____

_____

(7) If your answer to question (d)(4) or question (d)(5) is "No," explain why you did not raise this issue:

_____

_____

_____

(e) **Other Remedies:** Describe any other procedures (such as habeas corpus, administrative remedies, etc.) that you have used to exhaust your state remedies on Ground Three:_____

_____

_____

GROUND FOUR: _____N/A_____

(a) Supporting facts (Do not argue or cite law. Just state the specific facts that support your claim.):

_____

_____

_____

_____

_____

_____

_____

If you did not exhaust your state remedies on Ground Four, explain why:

_____

_____

_____

_____

(c) **Direct Appeal of Ground Four:**

(1) If you appealed from the judgment of conviction, did you raise this issue? ☐ Yes   ☐ No

(2) If you did not raise this issue in your direct appeal, explain why: _____

_____

_____

(d) Post-Conviction Proceedings:

(1) Did you raise this issue through a post-conviction motion or petition for habeas corpus in a state trial court?

☐ Yes   ☐ No

(2) If your answer to question (d)(1) is "Yes," state:

Type of motion or petition: _____

Name and location of the court where the motion or petition was filed: _____

_____

Docket or case number (if you know): _____

Date of the court's decision: _____

Result (attach a copy of the court's opinion or order, if available): _____

_____

(3) Did you receive a hearing on your motion or petition?	☐ Yes	☐ No
(4) Did you appeal from the denial of your motion or petition?	☐ Yes	☐ No
(5) If your answer to question (d)(4) is "Yes," did you raise this issue in the appeal?	☐ Yes	☐ No

(6) If your answer to question (d)(4) is "Yes," state:

Name and location of the court where the appeal was filed: _____

_____

Docket and case number (if you know it): _____

Date of the court's decision: _____

Results (attach a copy of the court's opinion or order, if available): _____

_____

(7) If your answer to question (d)(4) or question (d)(5) is "No," explain why you did not raise this issue:

_____

_____

_____

(e) Other Remedies: Describe any other procedures (such as habeas corpus, administrative remedies, etc.) that you have used to exhaust your state remedies on Ground Four: _____

_____

_____

_____

161

13. Please answer these additional questions about the petition you are filing:

(a) Have all grounds for relief that you have raised in this petition been presented to the highest state court having jurisdiction?

   ☐ Yes   ☐ No

If your answer is "No," state which grounds have not been so presented and give your reason(s) for not presenting them: _____

_____

_____

_____

(b) Is there any ground in this petition that has not been presented in some state or federal court? If so, which ground or grounds have not been presented, and state your reasons for not presenting them: _____

_____

_____

_____

14. Have you previously filed any type of petition, application, or motion in a federal court regarding the conviction that you challenge in this petition?   ☐ Yes   ☑ No

If "Yes," state the name and location of the court, the docket or case number, the type of proceeding, the issues raised, the date of the court's decision, and the result for each petition, application, or motion filed. Attach a copy of any court opinion or order, if available.

N/A _____

_____

_____

_____

_____

15. Do you have any petition or appeal now pending (filed and not decided yet) in any court, either state or federal, for the judgment you are challenging?   ☐ Yes   ☐ No

If "Yes," state the name and location of the court, the docket or case number, the type of proceeding, and the issues raised.

N/A _____

_____

_____

_____

_____

_____

16. Give the name and address, if you know, of each attorney who represented you in the following stages of the judgment you are challenging:

(a) At the preliminary hearing: Shelton Perhacs

(b) At arraignment and plea: Shelton Perhacs

(c) At trial: Shelton Perhacs

(d) At sentencing: Shelton Perhacs

(e) On appeal: Mari Ellen Morrison

(f) In any post-conviction proceeding: Mari Ellen Morrison

(g) On appeal from any ruling against you in a post-conviction proceeding:

17. Do you have any future sentence to serve after you complete the sentence for the judgment that you are challenging?

☐ Yes ☑ No

(a) If so, give name and location of court that imposed the other sentence you will serve in the future:

N/A

(b) Give the date the other sentence was imposed:

(c) Give the length of the other sentence:

(d) Have you filed, or do you plan to file, any petition that challenges the judgment or sentence to be served in the future?

☐ Yes ☑ No

18. TIMELINESS OF PETITION: If your judgment of conviction became final over one year ago, you must explain why the one-year statute of limitations as contained in 28 U.S.C. § 2244(d) does not bar your petition. *

Actual Innocence and Ineffectiveness of post-conviction counsel, see *Buck v Davis*, 580 U.S.

KELLY PATRICK RIGGS

_____
_____
_____
_____
_____
_____
_____
_____
_____
_____
_____
_____
_____
_____
_____
_____
_____
_____
_____
_____

*The Antiterrorism and Effective Death Penalty Act of 1996 ("AEDPA") as contained in 28 U.S.C. § 2244(d) provides in part that:

(1) A one-year period of limitation shall apply to an application for a writ of habeas corpus by a person in custody pursuant to the judgment of a State court. The limitation period shall run from the latest of –

(A) the date on which the judgment became final by the conclusion of direct review or the expiration of the time for seeking such review.

(B) the date on which the impediment to filing an application created by State action in violation of the Constitution or laws of the United States is removed, if the applicant was prevented from filing by such state action.

(C) the date on which the constitutional right asserted was initially recognized by the Supreme Court, if the right has been newly recognized by the Supreme Court and made retroactively applicable to cases on collateral review; or

(D) the date on which the factual predicate of the claim or claims presented could have been discovered through the exercise of due diligence.

(2) The time during which a properly filed application for State post-conviction or other collateral review with respect to the pertinent judgment or claim is pending shall not be counted toward any period of limitation under this subsection.

164

Therefore, the petitioner asks that the Court grant the following relief: Vacate, set aside or correct sentence; in order that petitioner receives a new trial.

or any other relief to which petitioner may be entitled.

_____
Signature of Attorney (if any)

I declare (or certify, verify, or state) under penalty of perjury that the foregoing is true and correct and that this Petition for Writ of Habeas Corpus was placed in the prison mailing system on _____ (month, date, year).

Executed (signed) on _____ (date).

_____
Signature of Petitioner

If the person signing is not petitioner, state relationship to petitioner and explain why petitioner is not signing this petition.

_____

_____

_____

_____

KELLY PATRICK RIGGS

IN THE UNITED STATES DISTRICT COURT
FOR THE NORTHERN DISTRICT OF ALABAMA
SOUTHERN DIVISION

JERRY WAYNE WIGGINS, Petitioner, v. SCOTTY SHAFFER, CPT., Defendant.	§ § § § § § §	Case no.:

PETITIONER'S BRIEF IN SUPPORT OF PETITION UNDER 28 U.S.C. § 2254 WRIT OF HABEAS CORPUS FOR A PERSON IN STATE CUSTODY

INTRODUCTION

This brief is respectfully submitted by the Petitioner, Jerry Wayne Wiggins (hereinafter Mr. Wiggins) *pro se*, in support of his accompanying Petition for Writ of Habeas Corpus for a person in state custody under the Antiterrorism and Effective-Death Penalty Act (AEDPA), as codified in 28 U.S.C. § 2254.

BACKGROUND

Following a trial in the State of Alabama, in the Circuit Court for Jefferson County Tenth Judicial Circuit – Bessemer Division, Mr. Wiggins was convicted on one count of first-degree rape on July 24, 2000. Mr. Wiggins received a fifty-year sentence. Mr. Wiggins appealed the conviction to the Alabama Criminal Court of Appeals, arguing ineffective assistance of counsel. On July 20, 2001, the court affirmed the conviction *per curium*. On October 1, 2002, Wiggins filed his first Rule 32 petition in which he alleged:

(1) that trial counsel had been ineffective;

(2) that appellate counsel had been ineffective for fourteen claims;

(3) that the trial court never formally accepted the jury's verdict;

(4) that the sentence imposed exceeds the maximum authorized by law;

(5) that the trial court erred by conducting a guilty plea hearing at the same time as his sentencing hearing and that doing so was "fundamentally unfair."

(6) that the trial court was without jurisdiction to render judgment or to impose sentence in his case because he said he was not present at every stage of the proceedings against him;

(7) that he was denied a fair trial by the loss of exculpatory evidence; and

166

(8) that the trial court erred in refusing his request that the judge recuses himself.

On December 16, 2002, the State filed a detailed response in which it argued that Wiggins' contentions both were precluded from appellate review and were without merit. An evidentiary hearing was held on May 5, 2005, and the following day the trial court summarily denied Wiggins's petition. On appeal, Wiggins reasserts the claims he asserted in his petition to the trial court and contends that the trial court is required to state specific reasons for denying his petition and that he is entitled to a new trial based upon the allegations and evidence presented in this petition.

Although the circuit court conducted an evidentiary hearing, it made no specific findings in the summary denial of Wiggins's Rule 32 petition it issued on May 6, 2005. On January 11, 2008, the Supreme Court denied certiorari review, without opinion (1070025).

GROUND ONE

Mr. Wiggins' trial counsel, Mr. Sheldon Perhacs, provided ineffective assistance of counsel to such a degree that he facilitated the conviction of his innocent client.

SUPPORTING FACTS: Jerry Wiggins grew up in Midfield Alabama where life with his parents involved a bait-and-tackle shop and a car lot. As life went on, Jerry moved to Birmingham and got married to his high school sweetheart, and they had two children. Jerry developed and grew in the community two businesses. One was named Environmental Carpet Cleaning and the other was Total Pest Elimination. Jerry lived comfortably with his family and was skilled in many areas that involved martial arts and mechanics. Holidays, birthdays, and events were always around the family and things with the family seemed normal.

Jerry met Norma Booth at a young age; she was the aunt of his wife Andrea. Life progressed, business was doing well, and Jerry purchased a house located at 1780 Cargile Dr. Oak Grove, Al 35006. As time progressed, Mr. and Mrs. Wiggins began having marital problems that involved an extramarital affair between Mrs. Wiggins and an unnamed man. In or around 1995 or 1996 Ms. Booth was over at the Cargile house visiting for a couple of weeks. Mr. Wiggins was watching an adult movie in his bedroom and Norma Booth come into the room and started making sexual advances towards him. After several sexual advances, Mr. Wiggins was effectively seduced, and he gave in to having sex with Ms. Booth.

Mr. Wiggins and Ms. Booth had an uninterrupted relationship for almost 3 years. On or about November 28, 1998, Norma Booth arrived at the residence of Jerry and Andrea Wiggins, at 7086 Lou George Loop Bessemer, Al 35022, under the ruse of assisting with the children. Neither Mrs. Wiggins nor the children were at home and when Mr. Wiggins returned home from work he was left alone with

Ms. Booth. Ms. Booth began a conversation with Mr. Wiggins about whether he remembered what happened at the Oak Grove house. She asked Mr. Wiggins if he wanted to have sex again and he agreed. Mr. Wiggins took a shower, when he returned to the living room Ms. Booth laid back on the couch and slid her jogging pants off. They started having sex. Ms. Booth started to experience some pain and asked Mr. Wiggins to stop. Mr. Wiggins stopped and removed the condom. He started to put it in the garbage can and Ms. Booth directed him to dispose of it elsewhere. Mr. Wiggins took it outside where he routinely burned trash.

Mr. Wiggins remained outside and decided to work in his garden, tilling compost for the next year's growth. When Mr. Wiggins returned to his home, he found Ms. Booth naked on his couch using her personal massager intimately on herself. When Ms. Booth discovered that Mr. Wiggins had returned, she asked him if he wanted to try having sex again. Mr. Wiggins declined, stating that his ex-wife, Mrs. Wiggins, would soon be there and together Mr. and Mrs. Wiggins were taking their children to Century Plaza.

When Mrs. Wiggins arrived, she drove Ms. Booth to her home, twenty-five minutes away. Mr. and Mrs. Wiggins proceeded to Century Plaza with their children and returned hours later. Later that evening two Jefferson County Sheriff's Deputies Showed up at Mr. Wiggins' home. They stated that someone reported that a sexual assault occurred at his residence.

Ms. Booth reported that she had been raped by Mr. Wiggins and that he broke the door down of his own home to commit the alleged assault. Mr. Wiggins was later arrested and charged with the crime.

Mr. Wiggins was formally charged and indicted by an Alabama Grand Jury.

Mr. Wiggins hired Attorney Sheldon Perhacs in preparation for trial. During the pre-trial investigation, the defense found that Ms. Booth recanted her story and admitted to having consensual sex with Mr. Wiggins, rather than having been raped. In her second statement, Ms. Booth admitted to using the massager on herself and that it caused sharp pain. Ms. Booth's second statement was recorded by Detective Mike Yarbrough and the defense was made aware of the existence of Ms. Booth's second recorded statement. During the discovery phase of the trial, however, The State of Alabama failed to turn over the recorded statement to the defense. Ms. Booth's conflicting statements not only served to call the veracity of her testimony into question, but they also raise a reasonable doubt as to the guilt of Mr. Wiggins. Thus, The State of Alabama withheld exculpatory evidence and effectively undermined the confidence in the outcome of the trial.

Ms. Booth's second statement had the propensity to not only raise a reasonable doubt, but to also give a plausible explanation for her injuries as self-inflicted wounds.

Mr. Wiggins' attorney, Sheldon Perhacs provided constitutionally ineffective assistance of counsel by refusing to explore the content of Ms. Booth's second statement. Additionally, Mr. Perhacs failed to object to the State's failure to provide all discovery material to the defense. Ms. Booth's second statement was exculpatory evidence that shed light on Mr. Wiggins' innocence. The State's refusal to turn Ms. Booth's second statement over to the defense is a Brady Rule violation.

DISCUSSION

Mr. Wiggins now files his petition and accompanying brief to this Court to challenge his state sentence Under 28 U.S.C. § 2254. Mr. Wiggins has exhausted all the applicable state remedies, including direct appeals as well as writs for post-conviction relief. He now seeks relief on two grounds. In addition to the grounds raised in the petition; Mr. Wiggins also raises issues of law regarding the ineffective assistance of trial and post-conviction counsel, both of which constitute *Strickland* violations.

A Petitioner has exhausted all available state remedies relating to the thirteen grounds for habeas corpus he raised, and now respectfully requests this Court grant relief from state conviction based on each.

In his petition in support of a writ of habeas corpus under 28 U.S.C. § 2254, Mr. Wiggins raises two grounds on which his trial counsel erred in his performance. Pursuant to 28 U.S.C. § 2254, Mr. Wiggins exhausted all state avenues for relief before bringing his petition to this Court. Specifically, the AEDPA precludes any federal court, absent exceptional circumstances, from granting relief under habeas corpus unless the petitioner has exhausted all available relief under state law. See 28 U.S.C. §2254(b)(1); see also, *O'Sullivan v. Boerckel*, 526 U.S. 838, 842-44 (1999). To exhaust all available state remedies, the petitioner must "fairly presen[t] federal claims to the state courts in order to give the State the opportunity to pass upon and correct alleged violations of its prisoners' federal rights," *Duncan v. Henry*, 513 U.S. 364,365 (1995). Here, Mr. Wiggins filed a direct appeal, a motion for post-conviction relief, and a state petition for a writ of Certiorari. All three remedies sought resulted in erroneous and unfavorable decisions. The two grounds Mr. Wiggins raises in his 28 U.S.C. § 2254 petition are all addressed by one or more of the exhausted state remedies he sought prior to the petition.

Having exhausted available state remedies for both grounds raised in his petition for writ of habeas corpus, Mr. Wiggins now respectfully requests this Court grant him relief from his state conviction. In addition to the grounds mentioned above, Mr. Wiggins also requests that this Court take notice of the *Strickland* violations resulting from ineffective assistance of trial and post-conviction counsel. Even under the AEDPA's strict requirements for habeas relief, the Petitioner's ineffective assistance of trial and post-conviction counsel claims are sufficient to warrant this Court's grant of his petition for writ of habeas corpus under *Strickland v. Washington*.

Under the AEDPA, a federal court may not grant habeas relief for a state court conviction unless the conviction "resulted in a decision that was contrary to, or involved an unreasonable application of, clearly established Federal law…or resulted in a decision that was based on an unreasonable determination of the facts considering the evidence presented in the State court proceeding," 28 U.S.C. § 2254(d).

Clearly established federal law has been interpreted to only include United States Supreme Court holdings "as of the time of the relevant state-court decision," *Williams v. Taylor*, 529 U.S. 362, 412 (2000). Ineffective assistance of counsel under the *Strickland* regime was a clearly established federal law by the time of Mr. Wiggins' conviction. See *Williams*, 529 U.S. at 391; see also *Strickland v. Washington*, 466 U.S. 668 (1984). Therefore, a petitioner must be granted habeas relief if the state supreme court's denial of his ineffective assistance claims was "contrary to or involved in an unreasonable application of" the *Strickland* doctrine. 28 U.S.C. § 2254(d). Violation of the right to the effective assistance of counsel under *Strickland* has two key components. See *Strickland*, 466 U.S. at 687. First, a petitioner must establish that their "counsel's performance was deficient," *id.* This specifically requires the petitioner to show that their counsel's errors were to such a degree that their performance to did not satisfy the fundamental guarantee to counsel under the Sixth Amendment. See *Id.*; see also U.S. Const. Amend. VI. Second, the petitioner must show that their counsel's performance "prejudiced the defense," *Strickland*, 466 U.S. at 687. This requires a showing that "there is a reasonable probability that, but for counsel's unprofessional errors, the result of the proceeding would have been different," *id.* at 694. A reasonable probability is characterized in *Strickland* as a probability "Sufficient to undermine the confidence in the outcome," *id.* The trial counsel's ineffective assistance is characterized in several distinct instances which in totality constitute a *Strickland* violation by which this Court should grant habeas relief. As iterated below, his trial counsel erred in several distinct instances. Specifically, the petitioner notes the following errors:

- Failure to properly investigate and introduce alternative defense evidence to rebut the untrustworthy testimonies of Norma Booth;

- Failure to question, seek out, speak to, or depose four potential witnesses to corroborate the defense's claims that the testimony of Norma Booth was untrustworthy

- Failure to adequately prepare for trial;

- Failure to pursue the discovery of a second recorded statement, by Norma Booth in which she recants her claim of rape, which was not provided to the defense by the State's Attorney.

In *Williams*, the United States Supreme Court addressed an AEDPA-based habeas petition that involved the *Strickland* doctrine. See *Williams*, 529 U.S. at 390-399. There, the petitioner, Williams, argued that his trial counsel failed to discover or offer mitigating evidence to the jury, *id.* In his opinion for the Court, Justice Stevens characterized these failures as a clear demonstration that Williams's "counsel did not fulfill their ethical obligation to conduct a thorough investigation," *id.* at 364.

Here, like in *Williams*, Mr. Wiggins' trial counsel failed to fulfill his ethical obligation to conduct a thorough investigation that would have constituted effective counsel under *Strickland*. In their totality, Mr. Wiggins' trial counsel provided ineffective assistance because he failed to address the four issues outlined above which constitutes deficient performance to a degree that violates Mr. Wiggins' guarantee of counsel under the Sixth Amendment. See *Strickland*, 466 U.S. at 687. Furthermore, there is more than a reasonable probability that, in their totality, the four failures outlined above prejudiced Mr. Wiggins' defense. See *id.* It is not a far stretch to conclude that the four failures constituted unprofessional errors, and that but for these errors, there may have been a different outcome.

Because Mr. Wiggins' trial counsel was both deficient in performance and prejudiced his defense, it rose to the level of ineffective counsel under *Strickland*. As such, Mr. Wiggins requests that this Court grant his petition for habeas relief under 28 U.S.C § 2254.

GROUND TWO

Mr. Wiggins' post-conviction counsel's failure to raise additional issues relating to Petitioner's initial trial constitutes a *Strickland* violation by which this Court should grant habeas relief.

SUPPORTING FACTS: Mr. Wiggins filed his first motion for state post-conviction relief, a Rule 32 motion, in *pro se* on October 1, 2002. On that motion, Mr. Wiggins was granted a hearing and appointed counsel, William R. Blanchard, to represent his claims. Mr. Blanchard, however, failed to investigate Mr. Wiggins's claims and he proceeded to court without taking the time to refine Mr. Wiggins *pro se* motion. Additionally, Mr. Blanchard failed to discover that at trial Mr. Wiggins' trial counsel failed to present an alternative theory to the State's case in chief. Had the trial counsel raised Mr. Wiggins's alternate theory of the case and presented the additional evidence and testimony, the outcome of Mr. Wiggins's trial would have been different.

Mr. Blanchard also failed to identify that trial counsel was deficient for failing to pursue the obvious Brady Rule violation concerning the second victim statement where Ms. Booth withdrew her previous statement accusing Mr. Wiggins of rape.

In addition to the errors made by Mr. Wiggins's defense counsel, his public post-conviction counsel failed to raise additional issues of relevance in his Rule 32 hearing. While courts must generally presume that post-conviction counsel's performance is sufficient, this presumption may be rebutted if it is outside the range of reasonable professional assistance. See *Strickland*, 466 U.S. at 689. Appellate counsel's presumption of effectiveness will be overcome where the "ignored issues are clearly stronger than those presented," *Smith v. Robbins*, 528 U.S. 259, 288 (2000) (quoting *Gray v. Greer*, 800 F.2d 644, 646 (7th Cir. 1986)).

In many states and at the federal level, claims of trial, sentencing, and appellate ineffectiveness must be raised through post-conviction proceedings. Wiggins's case, however, he filed for post-conviction relief in *pro se* and then suffered from the ineffectiveness of his appointed post-conviction counsel.

Thus, Mr. Wiggins' post-conviction lawyer failed to raise a claim of ineffective assistance that likely could have won. In *Martinez v. Ryan*, 566 U.S. 1 (2012) and *Trevino v. Thaler*, 133 S. Ct. 1911 (2013), the Supreme Court held that ineffective assistance in a STATE post-conviction proceeding can allow "substantial," procedurally defaulted claims of ineffective assistance of counsel to be raised for the first time in a 28 U.S.C. § 2254 petition. The Court also held that failure to raise a "substantial" claim of ineffective assistance because of a prisoner's "lack of counsel" in a post-conviction proceeding may also excuse a procedural default. Because Mr. Wiggins' trial counsel was both deficient in performance and prejudiced his defense, it rose to the level of ineffective counsel under *Strickland*. As such, Mr. Wiggins requests that this Court grant his petition for habeas relief under 28 U.S.C § 2254.

CONCLUSION

Given the aforementioned petition for writ of habeas corpus under 28 U.S.C. § 2254 and the additional *Strickland* violations outlined above, Mr. Wiggins respectfully requests that this Court review and approve his writ and require relief from his state conviction pursuant to, and appropriate under, the AEDPA. See 28 U.S.C. § 2254.

Respectfully submitted this _____ day of April 2022. By:

X_____
Jerry Wiggins, *pro se*
AIS# _____
Hamilton Aged and Infirmed
223 Dr. Sasser Dr.
Hamilton, AL 35570

CERTIFICATE OF SERVICE

I the undersigned do hereby certify that I have served a copy of the forgoing petition on all parties, via U.S. Mail, first-class postage prepaid, as required by rule and law.

Respectfully submitted this _____ day of April 2022. By:

X_____
Jerry Wiggins, *pro se*
AIS# _____
Hamilton Aged and Infirmed
223 Dr. Sasser Dr.
Hamilton, AL 35570

UNITED STATES DISTRICT COURT
FOR THE NORTHERN DISTRICT OF ALABAMA
SOUTHERN DIVISION

JERRY WAYNE WIGGINS, Petitioner,	§ § §	
v.	§ §	Case no.: 2:22-cv-00494-MHH-HNJ
SCOTTY SHAFFER, et al., Respondents.	§ § § §	

ORDER TO SHOW CAUSE

In reviewing Petitioner Jerry Wiggins's petition for writ of habeas corpus, filed pursuant to 28

U.S.C. § 2254, the court notes the petition appears to be a successive petition under 28 U.S.C. §

2244(b). The Antiterrorism and Effective Death Penalty Act of 1996 ("AEDPA") provides, in pertinent

part:

(b) (1) A claim presented in a second or successive habeas corpus application under section 2254 that was presented in a prior application shall be dismissed.

(2) A claim presented in a. second or successive habeas corpus application under section 2254 that was not presented in a prior application shall be dismissed unless –

(A) the applicant shows that the claim relies on a new rule of constitutional law, made retroactive to cases on collateral review by the Supreme Court, that was previously unavailable; or

(B) (i) the factual predicate for the claim could not have been discovered previously through the exercise of due diligence; and

(ii) the facts underlying the claim, if proven and viewed in light of the evidence as a whole, would be sufficient to establish by clear and convincing evidence that, but for constitutional error, no reasonable factfinder would have found the applicant guilty of the underlying offense.

(3) (A) Before a second or successive application permitted by this section is filed in the district court, the applicant shall move to the appropriate court of appeals for an order authorizing the district court to consider the application.

28 U.S.C. § 2244(b).

Even if Wiggins satisfies § 2244(b)(2)(B) through the presentation of new evidence not previously

discoverable, he must still comply with § 2244(b)(3)(A) prior to filing a successive petition. That

provision deprives the district court of jurisdiction and requires the dismissal of a "second or

successive" petition unless the applicant first obtains authorization from the appropriate court of

appeals. See, *e.g.*, *Magwood v. Patterson*, 561 U.S. 320, 330-31 (2010) ("If an application is 'second or successive,' the petitioner must obtain leave from the court of appeals before filing it with the district court."); *Burton v. Stewart*, 549 U.S. 147, 152 (2007) (*per curiam*) (holding the district court lacked jurisdiction to entertain second habeas petition because petitioner failed to obtain authorization from the appellate court).

Wiggins challenges his 2000 conviction for first-degree rape in the Circuit Court of Jefferson County, Alabama, Bessemer Division (Doc. 1 at 1). Wiggins filed at least one prior federal habeas petition regarding the conviction challenged in the instant petition. See *Jerry W. Wiggins v. C. Price, et. al.*, No. 2:08-cv-00155-KOB-HGD (N.D. Ala. 2008).[1] The court denied Wiggins's prior habeas petition on the merits on November 19, 2008[2] (08-155 Doc. 13).

The instant petition appears to be successive for purposes of 28 U.S.C. § 2244(b)(2). Pursuant to 28 U.S.C. § 2244(b)(3)(A), this court lacks jurisdiction to consider a successive habeas petition without authorization from the Eleventh Circuit Court of Appeals ("Eleventh Circuit"). *Farris v. United States*, 333 F.3d 1211, 1216 (11th Cir. 2003) (*per curiam*) ("Without authorization [from the Eleventh Circuit], the district court lacks jurisdiction to consider a second or successive petition."). Wiggins does not allege he sought or received authorization from the Eleventh Circuit to file the instant petition. (See Doc. 1).

Accordingly, the court **ORDERS** Wiggins to **SHOW CAUSE** within **14 days** of the entry date of this Order why his petition should not be dismissed as successive due to his failure to obtain the requisite authorization from the Eleventh Circuit.

The court **DIRECTS** the Clerk of Court to mail a copy of this Order to Wiggins.

DONE and ORDERED this 16th day of May 2022.

HERMAN N. JOHNSON, JR.
UNITED STATES MAGISTRATE JUDGE

---

[1] *See* United States v. Rey, *811 F.2d 1453, 1457 n.5 (11th Cir. 1987)* ("A court may take judicial notice of its own records and the records of inferior courts."); McBride v. Sharpe, *25 F.3d 962, 969 (11th Cir. 1994)* (stating the district court could take judicial notice of its own records in habeas proceedings).

[2] On March 20, 2009, the Eleventh Circuit Court of Appeals granted in part and denied in party Wiggins's motion for a certificate of appealability in his prior petition (08-155 Doc. 18). On August 21, 2009, the Eleventh Circuit Court of Appeals affirmed the district court's denial of Wiggins's § 2254 habeas petition (08-155 Doc. 19 at 7).

UNITED STATES DISTRICT COURT
FOR THE NORTHERN DISTRICT OF ALABAMA
SOUTHERN DIVISION

JERRY WAYNE WIGGINS, Petitioner,	§ § §	
v.	§ §	Case no.: 2:22-cv-00494-MHH-HNJ
SCOTTY SHAFFER, et al., Respondents.	§ § § §	

PETITIONER'S ANSWER TO SHOW CAUSE

Mr. Wiggins shows that good cause exists for his recent filing of a petition for a Writ of Habeas Corpus because the claims he raised therein have never been raised in a previous writ and that the claims were not available to him at the time of the previous filing. In 28 U.S.C.:2244(B)(l) it clearly states that:

"A claim presented in a second or successive habeas corpus application under section 2254 **that was presented in a prior application shall be dismissed**."

In Mr. Wiggins' application, the claims he raised could not have been raised in his original 2254 application because the ruling had not yet been made by the supreme court of the United States.

In the second round of Mr. Wiggins' petition, he claimed that his post-conviction counsel had provided deficient performance. Moreover, Mr. Wiggins' post-conviction counsel was so deficient that he failed to perform the most basic task of refining Mr. Wiggins's claims. Had his post-conviction counsel performed any investigation at all he would have discovered that the State of Alabama brazenly violated the Supreme Court's famed Brady Rule.

In most cases, a defendant has the right to obtain from the prosecution all exculpatory evidence and discovery material. Mr. Wiggins, however, was deprived of that right, and thus deprived of a fair trial. This failure was not objected to by his trial counsel and was not raised in a direct appeal. Shortly after, Mr. Wiggins filed a *pro se* petition for collateral review and was appointed counsel, Mr. Wiggins' post-conviction counsel failed to investigate Mr. Wiggin's case for potential claims or at the bare minimum refine the *pro se* petition filed by Mr. Wiggins himself. Mr. Wiggins then filed for habeas review in federal court in a *pro se* petition which was decided on November 19, 2008. See *Jerry W. Wiggins v. C. Price, et. al.,* No. 2:08-cv-00155-KOB-HGD. Because of constitutionally ineffective assistance of counsel, Mr. Wiggins has yet to date received a full and fair hearing on his unresolved claims.

The Supreme Court of The United States held that "Where, under state law, ineffective assistance of trial counsel claims must be raised in an initial review collateral proceeding, a procedural default will not bar a federal habeas court from hearing those claims if, in the initial review collateral proceeding, there was no counsel or counsel in that proceeding was ineffective." See *Martinez v. Ryan*, 566 U.S. 1 (2012).

As illustrated, Mr. Wiggins' claim for ineffective assistance of counsel could not have been ripe for review in a Federal Court until after the Supreme Court's holding of *Martinez* in 2012.

CONCLUSION

Wherefore, the above premises considered, Mr. Wiggins moves this court to allow his unresolved claims to proceed to a full and fair review.

Respectfully submitted this 30th day of May 2022. By:

X_____

Jerry Wiggins, *pro se*
AIS# _____
Hamilton Aged and Infirmed
223 Dr. Sasser Dr.
Hamilton, AL 35570

CERTIFICATE OF SERVICE

I the undersigned do hereby certify that I have served a copy of the foregoing petition on all parties, via U.S. Mail, first-class postage prepaid, as required by rule and law.

Respectfully submitted this 30th day of May 2022. By:

X_____

Jerry Wiggins, *pro se*
AIS# _____
Hamilton Aged and Infirmed
223 Dr. Sasser Dr.
Hamilton, AL 35570

CHAPTER SEVEN

PETITIONS FOR ALABAMA STATE PRISONERS UNDER RULE 32

Negotiating Alabama's criminal justice system after your conviction can be a pain in the butt. As you will figure out, the law is always evolving. Many changes in the law will lead to a right to file for post-conviction relief.

In Alabama, Rule 32 of the Alabama Rules of Criminal Procedure governs state post-conviction challenges to a conviction or sentence.

"[A]ny defendant who has been convicted of a criminal offense" may petition the Alabama state courts for post-conviction relief. Alabama law requires that the convicted person who seeks post-conviction relief – the "petitioner" – must be imprisoned or actually restrained of his or her liberty in order for an order to be issued.

While any restraint that precludes freedom from action is sufficient, and actual confinement in jail or prison is not necessary, a person who is on parole is not considered sufficiently restrained of his or her liberty to be entitled to post-conviction relief.

A post-conviction proceeding is different from a "direct appeal" in a criminal case. In Alabama, a defendant who is convicted of a criminal offense after a trial in a district or circuit court may appeal the judgment of conviction to the Court of Criminal Appeals and the Supreme Court of Alabama. This appeal – sometimes referred to as a "direct appeal" – is generally limited to a review of the trial record for errors committed during the pre-trial and trial proceedings. Thus, the direct appeal is generally limited to issues that are "in the record."

In contrast, a post-conviction proceeding focuses on claims that are based on facts that are "outside the record" and, therefore, could not have been raised on direct appeal.

It is important to know which claims can be raised in a post-conviction proceeding. Rule 32.1 of the Alabama Rules of Criminal Procedure defines the kind of issues that can be considered in a post-conviction proceeding in Alabama. Specifically, a petitioner can seek post-conviction relief on the ground that:

(1) the Alabama and/or Federal Constitution requires a new trial, a new sentence, or other relief;

(2) the trial court was without jurisdiction to render judgment or to impose a sentence.

(3) the sentence imposed exceeds the maximum sentence authorized by law or is otherwise not authorized by law;

(4) the petitioner is being held in custody after his or her sentence has expired; or

(5) newly discovered material facts exist which establish that the petitioner is innocent of the crime for which he or she was convicted or should not have received the sentence that he or she received.

Examples of issues that are commonly raised in state post-conviction proceedings include the following:

(1) trial or appellate counsel rendered ineffective assistance of counsel;

(2) the State failed to disclose exculpatory or impeachment evidence;

It should be noted that the Alabama Court of Criminal Appeals has held that when a Brady claim is first presented in a Rule 32 petition (instead of on direct appeal), the petitioner can prevail on the claim only if it involves "newly discovered evidence" as defined under Rule 32.1 (e).

(3) the State presented perjured testimony;

(4) juror misconduct;

(5) the defendant was incompetent to stand trial;

(6) the court lacked jurisdiction to render judgment or enter a sentence; and

(7) innocence.

However, even if an issue is of the kind that could be raised in an Alabama state post-conviction proceeding, the court's consideration of the issue may be precluded for various procedural reasons.

For those of you who are wondering, let me say, yes: Ineffective assistance of counsel claims are generally and appropriately raised for the first time in an initial Rule 32 petition. Claims of ineffective assistance of counsel require the petitioner to show both "deficient performance" (that it was objectively unreasonable when judged against prevailing professional norms) and "prejudice" (that there is a reasonable probability that the outcome would have been different). Because the evidence that supports these allegations is generally not contained in the trial record, it is necessary to present such evidence in a post-trial proceeding. However, if the claim could have been raised at trial or on direct appeal, the claim may be barred.

Such claims can, however, be raised in subsequent federal habeas corpus proceedings. Section Six of this book addresses raising state claims in Federal Court, in habeas corpus proceedings, that have been "exhausted" in state court.

Know also that there is a deadline for filing a state post-conviction petition in Alabama: Rule 32.2(c) of the Alabama Code of Criminal Procedure sets out the applicable statute of limitations for filing a state post-conviction petition in Alabama.

The deadline depends on whether the conviction was appealed or not. If it was appealed, then the deadline is based on whether a petition for *certiorari* was filed in the Alabama Supreme Court. As will become clear below, calculating this extremely important deadline is a complicated matter.

As a general rule, the statute of limitations for filing a Rule 32 petition is one year from the date when the conviction became "final" in state court. Pursuant to Rule 41 of the Alabama Rules of Appellate Procedure, the date that the conviction became "final" is (1) the date that the certificate of judgment was issued (if the conviction was appealed) or (2) the date on which the time to take an appeal lapse (if no appeal was taken).

If the conviction was not appealed to the Alabama Court of Criminal Appeals, the Rule 32 petition must be filed within one year after the time for filing an appeal expired. If the conviction was appealed to the Alabama Court of Criminal Appeals, the Rule 32 petition must be filed within one year of the issuance of the "certificate of judgment" by the Alabama Court of Criminal Appeals. When the certificate of judgment issues will, in turn, depend on whether or not a petition for *certiorari* to the Alabama Supreme Court was filed.

If a petition for *certiorari* to the Alabama Supreme Court was filed, the timely filing of the petition for *certiorari* stays the issuance of the certificate of judgment by the Alabama Court of Criminal Appeals. In that case, the certificate of judgment issues the following:

(1) if the Alabama Supreme Court denies certiorari (as is usually the case): on the date that the Alabama Supreme Court denies *certiorari*;

(2) if the Alabama Supreme Court grants *certiorari* and an application for rehearing is filed: on the date when rehearing is denied; or

(3) if the Alabama Supreme Court grants *certiorari* and an application for rehearing is not filed: on the date when the time for filing a rehearing application expires.

It is important to note that the filing of a petition for *certiorari* to the United States Supreme Court – as opposed to the filing of a petition for *certiorari* to the Alabama Supreme Court – has no effect on the calculation of the deadline for filing a Rule 32 petition.

Thus, the only date relevant to determining the state statute of limitations is the date on which the conviction became final in the Alabama state courts, which is calculated as explained above. Rule 41 specifies that the certificate of judgment is not due to be issued until several days after the conviction itself becomes final.

However, because of the potential for delay or other notice problems, the safe practice is to begin counting the one year on the date that the Alabama Supreme Court issues its final ruling – whether it is a denial of *certiorari* or denial of rehearing. Indeed, Rule 41 provides that if the Alabama Supreme Court denies rehearing without substantially modifying its decision, the certificate of judgment will be issued immediately.

Where the petitioner's claim is based on facts that the petitioner could not have discovered earlier – for example, where the prosecution suppressed evidence, making it impossible to raise the claim until the evidence came to light – the deadline for raising the claim in a Rule 32 petition is either six months after the discovery of this evidence or one year after issuance of the certificate of judgment (as described above), whichever is later.

A person who pled guilty is also eligible to challenge the validity of the guilty plea in post-conviction proceedings. While the entry of a guilty plea generally waives claims of constitutional violations that occurred prior to entry of the plea, a person who pled guilty may challenge the validity of the plea itself in a Rule 32 petition. A guilty plea is not valid if it was not knowingly, intelligently and voluntarily made.

If a prisoner is unable to afford an attorney, he or she has a right to the appointment of counsel in state post-conviction proceedings in Alabama.

If a court does not summarily dismiss a petition for post-conviction relief and determines that counsel is necessary to assert a petitioner's rights, it must appoint counsel. In other words, while a petitioner does not have a right to counsel for the purpose of filing a petition, a court may determine that counsel must be appointed for future proceedings following the submission of a petition if the court does not summarily dismiss that petition.

I know I have said a lot so far, but know that there is much more to know. In the rest of this chapter, I've listed a number of rules, laws, and sample motions for you to follow. Also, know that this is not a stand-alone chapter. This book is of a series that contains a lot of information that will help you in filing for post-conviction relief under Rule 32 of the Alabama Rules of Criminal Procedure.

In this chapter, I also include how your former attorney might defend himself against your claims under Rule 32.1. I know this sounds like I'm helping your lawyer defend himself, but I assure you that I include it so you don't fall down the same "Rabbit-Hole." I also included a very familiar Alabama State

32 Motion for you to review. I've changed the names to protect the reputation of the petitioner and his family. But know that I include it so you can see how detailed a winning petition must be. This is how detailed your petition must be as well.

ALABAMA RULES OF CRIMINAL PROCEDURE
Rule 32. Post-conviction remedies

Rule 32.1. Scope of remedy.

Subject to the limitations of Rule 32.2, any defendant who has been convicted of a criminal offense may institute a proceeding in the court of original conviction to secure appropriate relief on the ground that:

(a) The constitution of the United States or of the State of Alabama requires a new trial, a new sentence proceeding, or other relief.

(b) The court was without jurisdiction to render judgment or to impose a sentence.

(c) The sentence imposed exceeds the maximum authorized by law or is otherwise not authorized by law.

(d) The petitioner is being held in custody after the petitioner's sentence has expired.

(e) Newly discovered material facts exist which require that the conviction or sentence be vacated by the court, because:

    (1) The facts relied upon were not known by the petitioner or the petitioner's counsel at the time of trial or sentencing or in time to file a post-trial motion pursuant to Rule 24, or in time to be included in any previous collateral proceeding and could not have been discovered by any of those times through the exercise of reasonable diligence;

    (2) The facts are not merely cumulative to other facts that were known;

    (3) The facts do not merely amount to impeachment evidence;

    (4) If the facts had been known at the time of trial or of sentencing, the result probably would have been different; and

    (5) The facts establish that the petitioner is innocent of the crime for which the petitioner was convicted or should not have received the sentence that the petitioner received.

(f) The petitioner failed to appeal within the prescribed time from the conviction or sentence itself or from the dismissal or denial of a petition previously filed pursuant to this rule and that failure was without fault on the petitioner's part.

A petition that challenges multiple judgments entered in more than a single trial or guilty plea proceeding shall be dismissed without prejudice.

[Amended eff. 8-1-2002; Amended 1-13-2005, eff. 6-1-2005.]

Committee Comments

Post-conviction petitions may be filed in the court of original conviction by any defendant who has been convicted of a criminal offense. Rules 32. G(a), 32.7(a), and 32.10(a) recognize that these petitions may be filed in municipal courts; such post-conviction relief, however, will rarely be sought since a defendant is entitled to appeal a municipal-court conviction to the circuit court for a trial *de novo*.

Note from the reporter of decisions: The order adding the Committee Comments to Rule 32.1, effective January 9, 2001, is published in that volume of Alabama Reporter that contains Alabama cases from 778 So.2d.

Note from the reporter of decisions: The order amending Rule 32.1, effective August 1, 2002, is published in that volume of Alabama Reporter that contains Alabama cases from 810 So.2d.

Note from the reporter of decisions: The order amending Rule 32.1(f) and Rule 32.2 (c), and adopting the Court Comment to Amendment 32.2(c), effective June 1, 2005, is published in that volume of Alabama Reporter that contains Alabama cases from 890 So.2d.

WHAT IS A RULE 32 PETITION?

A Rule 32 Petition is a method by which your client, having exhausted or waived his appeals, can petition to have his conviction set aside.

It is a collateral attack.

It is a new attack – a petition. You have the burden of proof. It is *not* an appeal. Trust me, it will become an appeal later.

A Rule 32 petitions are filed with the trial court that adjudicated the client (Rule 32.5). A Rule 32 petitions require a filing fee or an *in forma pauperis* claim (Rule 32.6(a)).

A Rule 32 petitions are winnable!

A RULE 32 SEEKS TO VOID A CONVICTION ... PERIOD

Rule 32 petitions seek relief from a conviction. There are two results:

A conviction which is voidable is voided, *i.e.*, the court lacked jurisdiction to even try, much less convict the Defendant. A Rule 32, if won, sets him free.

A conviction which was obtained in violation of due process, *i.e.,* ineffective assistance of counsel, is set aside and the Defendant is given a new trial.

Make sure your client understands that a new trial means a new trial. This is important. Many Defendants think this is a ticket to freedom.

GROUNDS FOR A RULE 32 PETITION

A complete list of grounds include:

☐ The Constitution of the United States or of the State of Alabama requires a new trial, a new sentence proceeding, or other relief (Rule 32.1(a)).

☐ The court was without jurisdiction to render judgment or impose sentence (Rule 32.1(b)). This one actually has some teeth and is more common than you might think.

☐ The sentence imposed exceeds the maximum sentence authorized by law or is otherwise not authorized by law (Rule 32.1(c)).

☐ The petitioner is being held in custody after the petitioner's sentence has expired. (Rule 32.1(d)).

☐ Newly discovered material facts exist that require the conviction or sentence be vacated by the court because:

   a) the facts relied upon were not known by the petitioner or his counsel at the time of trial or sentencing or in time to file a post-trial motion;

   b) The facts are not merely cumulative;

   c) The facts do not merely amount to impeachment evidence;

   d) If these facts had been known at trial, the result would have been different (This is important!); and

   e) The new facts establish that the petitioner is innocent of the crime for which he was convicted. This is usually the weakest grounds to rely on.

☐ Ineffective assistance of counsel such that, but not for the deficient performance of the lawyer, the result of the case would have been different.

☐ Last, but not least, the petitioner failed to appeal within the prescribed time, but the failure was not his fault.

(See *Maples v. Thomas*, 565 U.S.___ (2012), in which an Alabama death row inmate's Rule 32 was filed out of time, dismissed, dismissal upheld, and the SCOTUS said he was not at fault because his attorneys had withdrawn from the case, and he didn't know it. The Court said the attorneys had "abandoned" Maples.)

TIME BAR

Rule 32 petitions must be filed within *one year* of the certificate of judgment if there was an appeal or within *one year* of the date of sentencing if the Defendant pleaded guilty and didn't appeal.

If the claim is jurisdictional, the time bar does not apply.

If you file an out-of-time Rule 32 petition and the State doesn't raise the issue of the statute of limitations before the trial court's ruling, it is waived.

Note: the State can raise the time bar at any time prior to the trial court's ruling.

ISSUE PRECLUSION

A Petitioner will not be given relief if his petition is based upon

1) Any issue which may be raised on direct appeal or by a post-trial motion under Rule 24;

2) Any issue which was raised or addressed at trial;

3) Any issue which could have been raised or addressed at trial but was not;

4) Any issue which was raised or addressed on appeal or in previous collateral attacks (Rule 32.2).

PLEADINGS
SPECIFICITY IS REQUIRED.

Rule 32 pleadings must be pled with *specificity*. Mere allegations and "notice pleading" language is insufficient. You must state the "who," "what," "when," "where," "how" and "why's" of your petition (Rule 32.69(b)).

Cite the record with specificity if you're citing the record. If it's a clerk's record, cite it as (C-Page #). If it's the transcript of the reporter, cite it as (R-Page #).

If you're quoting someone, quote the person verbatim and cite the place in the record where the quote occurs.

No mere conclusions of fact or law are sufficient.

The fastest way to lose your Rule 32 is to use notice pleading language and mere conclusions. The judge can deny the Rule 32 petition without a hearing if the petition doesn't contain specific recitations of facts. The judge needs only to cite that there was no specificity of facts and you're on your way to the appeals courts to try to prove the judge abused his discretion, or, better yet, file an amended petition and be specific.

VERIFIED PLEADING

Rule 32 petitions *must* be signed by the *client,* verified, and notarized (Rule 32.6 (a)). The Rule says it can be verified with the attorney's notarized signature, but I make my clients sign it. I'm not the party, they are.

The affidavit must be pled with *specificity.* I drag my mouse and copy the allegations of the pleadings into the affidavit in their entirety, with grammar changes to make it an affidavit, and have the client sign the petition, which I notarize.

PROPER FILING AND RESPONSE

The *petitioner* must pay a filing fee (Rule 32. 6(a)), or file for *in forma pauperis* status. The date of filing is the date of the filing of the petition *and* the payment of the fee or the declaration of *in forma pauperis* status, not the day it is granted.

No $200.00 or *in forma pauperis* request, you risk dismissal. Courts have said you can "amend" and pay the fee or file the *in pauperis* request.

The *petitioner* must serve a copy of the Petition upon the State/Respondent (Rule 32. 6 (a)).

The *petition* case number is the trial CC case number with a .60 suffix on it. This denotes that this is your Rule 32 petition and not some post-judgment motion.

The State/Respondent *shall* respond to the petition within 30 days of service of the Rule 32 petition (Rule 32.7).

Some judges will order the State doesn't need to respond. I've run into this. I made a mistake once and forced the State to respond. I should have held my cards. Why? If the State does not respond, then your facts are taken as undisputed.

If you want to force a response: File a petition for writ of mandamus for the Court of Criminal Appeals to order the trial judge to require the State to respond. This is a good tactic when the State has hidden evidence or failed to turn over discovery.

APPOINTMENT OF COUNSEL

Rule 32.7(c) provides:

"Appointment of Counsel. If the court does not summarily dismiss the petition, and if it appears that the petitioner is indigent or otherwise unable to obtain the assistance of counsel and desires the assistance of counsel, and it further appears that counsel is necessary to assert or protect the rights of the petitioner, the court shall appoint counsel."

You'll see appointed counsel on inmate petitions, mostly. Good luck with that one.

The "right to appointed counsel" is discretionary. Trial courts will fight you on this one. You might also see appointed counsel on capital cases. All others pay cash.

BURDEN OF PROOF

The *petitioner* has the burden of proving the allegations in the Rule 32 petition.

Remember, if the *State/Respondent* fails to answer, the facts contained in the *petition* are deemed undisputed.

The *State* has the burden of proving if an issue is precluded.

DISCOVERY

You have the right to conduct discovery in a Rule 32 petition.

EVIDENCE/EXPERTS

The *Petitioner* has the burden of proof.

If your issue is ineffective assistance of counsel, hire an expert. An expert is an experienced trial lawyer you know who can testify cogently about the grounds of your petition.

In ineffective assistance of counsel cases, you must have a lawyer opine that the lawyer at trial flat stunk and was so ineffective that if he had been effective, there would have been a different result.

It is not an argument about strategy. It's an argument about competency.

Do not handle Rule 32 petitions if you are one of those Rotary Club, Kiwanis Club, or join everything club kind of lawyers who want to be liked. Rule 32 petitions will make you unpopular. You've got to be rather brutal to win a Rule 32 petition. You've got to prove the trial lawyer failed to act when he should have acted or acted when he should have remained silent or failed to object when he should have or objected when he should have shut up, etc.

IF YOU'RE THE TARGET OF A RULE 32

You did your best for Client X at trial. You lost. Client X appealed. Conviction is affirmed. Now you're in the crosshairs. Client X has filed a Rule 32.

What do you do? First, breathe. Rule 32 doesn't affect your malpractice insurance. It doesn't affect your standing among your fellow lawyers. It doesn't mean you have to worry about a bar complaint or any censure.

Rule 32 is merely a tactic by Client X to get a new trial or the conviction voided.

You *will* be called to testify. Smile, be affable. And here's the secret: Answer with "you're right. I could've done that better." Here's why:

The State has to defend the Rule 32 petition. The State comes to the defense attorney and says, "We'll defend you. You did a great job." The State wants to prop you up to make sure it doesn't lose the Rule 32 hearing, so you are now their star witness.

Remember, a Rule 32 claim voids the attorney/client privilege. At this point, you can testify to anything your client said during the representation, but should you?

So, the State wants you to be their star witness, but you're an attorney. Your first responsibility is to your client, right? It's not about you. It's about the client's right to attack his conviction.

So, as you are questioned, if the petitioner has an issue and facts that show you made a mistake during your representation, simply say, "I could've done that better." Admit your mistakes. We all make them. Be honest.

I've had two Rule 32 petitions filed against me in 18 years of practice. Both times, other lawyers came in as experts and talked about me as if I was stupid. In both cases, I came in and testified truthfully.

One was a case where a man was convicted of sodomizing his two children. I'd gotten two hung juries, and my client was convicted after the third jury trial. The client claimed I was ineffective. His Rule 32 lawyer savaged me all day long during the hearing and focused on a point in the trial where he felt my cross-examination of a witness was lacking. I simply said, "You're right. I could have done that better." The judge denied the Rule 32 petition because the Court said my cross-examination was cogent and did not constitute ineffective assistance.

The other case was a drug distribution case. The client was convicted as a habitual offender and sentenced to life plus 5 plus 5. The plus 5s were for selling in a housing project next to a school. During the trial, we presented an entrapment defense. I explained to my client that he had to testify if we used an entrapment defense. When it came time for the Client to testify, he froze. I took him into the hallway and explained to him that he had to testify because an entrapment defense has the element that you don't deny that you sold the drugs, but you were entrapped into it. He refused to testify.

I went in and asked for a mistrial on the grounds that my client had misunderstood that he had to testify, and the judge denied it. The jury later convicted my client.

During the Rule 32 hearing, the lawyer tried to make me seem incompetent, of course. I testified truthfully that my client had insisted on the entrapment defense and froze when it came time to testify. I admitted that I "could have done that better," agreeing with the lawyer that I should never have allowed my client to use the entrapment defense if there was a chance he'd freeze up.

In *both* cases, the Rule 32 petitions were denied and, in both cases, the appellate courts upheld the denials.

My practice did not suffer one whit as a result of either petition.

So, aside from Rule 32 petitions being a giant inconvenience for the lawyer accused of being ineffective, there is no threat to your practice.

My opinion is you always side with the client. If he wins a new trial, you've upheld the oath you took to defend your clients.

APPEAL

Any party may appeal the decision of a circuit court according to the procedures of the Alabama Rules of Appellate Procedure to the Court of Criminal Appeals upon taking a timely appeal as provided in Rule 4, Alabama Rules of Appellate Procedure. Any party may appeal a decision of a district or municipal court according to the existing procedure. (Rule 32.10(a)).

PETITIONER RELEASE

The petitioner shall not be released on bond pending appeal by either party. Release of the petitioner on bond pending a retrial after an order requiring retrial has become final, or after the time for filing an appeal from such an order has lapsed, shall be governed by the laws and rules governing release on bond pending an initial trial (Rule 32.10 (b)).

APPELLATE COURT STANDARD OF REVIEW

The standard for reviewing a circuit court's judgment denying a Rule 32 petition is as follows:

"[When the facts are undisputed and an appellate court is presented with pure questions of law, that court's review of ruling in a post-conviction proceeding is *de nova*; however, where there are disputed facts in a post-conviction proceeding and the circuit court resolves those disputed facts, the standard of review on appeal is whether the trial judge abused his discretion when he denied the petition." See *Ex parte Woods*, 957 So.2d 533 (Ala. 2006); *Jackson v. State*, 963 So.2d 150 (Ala.Crim.App. 2006); In *Hyde v. State*, 950 So.2d 344 (Ala.Crim.App. 2006).

"[When reviewing a circuit court's denial of a Rule 32 petition we apply an abuse-of-discretion standard." See *Davis v. State*, ___ So.2d ___, 2008 WL 902884 (Ala.Crim.App. 2008), citing *Elliott v. State*, 601 So.2d 1118, 1119 (Ala.Crim.App. 1992).

The "plain-error standard of review does not apply in Rule 32 petitions." See *Hill v. State*, 695 So.2d 1223 (Ala.Crim.App.1997); *Neeley v. State*, 642 So.2d 494 (Ala.Crim.App.1993). *Boyd v. State*, 913 So.2d 1113, 1122 (Ala.Crim.App. 2003); *Ex parte White*, 792 So.2d 1097, 1098 (Ala. 2001); *Elliott v. State*, 601 So.2d 1118, 1119 (Ala.Crim.App. 1992).

GROUNDS FOR REMAND

The bulk of appeals court remands are for these reasons:

1) Petition not barred by time limitations or preclusion grounds. Judges will often mistakenly rule a petition is time-barred when the claim is jurisdictional, where there is no time bar.

2) Petition is not procedurally barred. Judges often will cite this in a summary dismissal of the petition without a hearing, only to have the appeals courts remand the petition for a hearing.

3) The trial judge failed to enter an order setting out the reasons for summary dismissal and the facts on which the summary dismissal is based. The judge must be specific, too.

4) The trial judge summarily dismissed the petition without an evidentiary hearing where grounds as specifically plead clearly showed a meritorious claim.

5) The trial judge held an evidentiary hearing but failed to make written findings of fact stating the Court's ground for denial of relief for each claim. Judge will often summarize, rather than point-by-point deny each claim. This will get the case remanded.

6) The trial judge failed to make written findings of fact in a claim of ineffective assistance of counsel. The trial judge is required to make a ruling as to the specific issues relating to the claim of ineffective assistance.

7) The trial judge abused his discretion by not allowing a Rule 32 petition to be amended.

CASE LAW

SUBJECT MATTER JURISDICTION

Absent payment of the filing fee or approval of the *in forma pauperis* declaration, the circuit court does not acquire subject matter jurisdiction. The refusal of the circuit court to accept a petition is not a final judgment and cannot, therefore, support an appeal. Mandamus, and not appeal, is the proper method by which to compel the circuit court to determine whether to authorize the petitioner to proceed *in forma pauperis*. See *Goldsmith v. State*, 709 So.2d 1352 (Ala. Crim; App.1997), cited in *Goodwin v. State* 720 So.2d 1050 (Ala.Crim.App. 1998).

The circuit court lacked subject-matter jurisdiction to consider a petition for post-conviction relief, where the circuit court did not grant the petitioner's request to proceed *in forma pauperis* and the petitioner did not pay the filing fee. See *Smith v. State*, 918 So.2d 141 (Ala.Crim.App. 2005), citing *Ex parte McWilliams*, 812 So.2d 318 (Ala. 2001); *Ray v. State*, 895 So.2d 1063 (Ala.Crim.App. 2004); *Ex parte St. John*, 805 So.2d 684 (Ala. 2001); *Goldsmith v. State*, 709 So.2d 1352 (Ala.Crim.App. 1997).

CERTIFICATE OF WARDEN OR PRISON OFFICER

A prison inmate was not entitled to proceed *in forma pauperis* with respect to his petition for post-conviction relief, or to waiver of filing fee on a petition, because he failed to provide the court with a certificate of the warden or prison official of the correctional facility in which he was incarcerated showing the balance of his inmate account for 12 months preceding the filing of his post-conviction petition, as required by Rule 32.6(a), Ala.R.Crim.P.32(6). See *Ex parte Washington*, 855 So.2d 1138 (Ala.Crim.App. 2003).

ACCEPTANCE OF IN FORMA PAUPERIS APPLICATION OR RECEIPT OF FILING FEE

A remand to the circuit court was required for the determination of whether a post-conviction relief petitioner paid the circuit court filing fee or whether the circuit court granted the petitioner's request to proceed in forma pauperis, Rule 32.6 Ala.R.Crim.P. See *Broadway v. State*, 881 So.2d 1068 (Ala.Crim.App. 2003).

A review of the record shows it is unclear whether the circuit court had jurisdiction to rule on the petition, the case was remanded for the circuit court to make specific written findings as to whether *in forma pauperis* granted or filing fee paid, *Maxwell v. State*, 897 So.2d 426 (Ala. Crim. App.2004).

Remanded to the Circuit court to make specific, written findings as to whether it actually granted the petitioner's request to proceed *in forma pauperis* or whether the petitioner paid the filing fee. See *Broadway v. State*, 881 So.2d 1068 (Ala.Crim.App. 2003) and *Jackson v. State*, 854 So.2d 157 (Ala.Crim.App. 2002).

Trial court's order requiring an inmate to pay the filing fee for his first petition for post-conviction relief, which was issued in apparent response to the inmate's filing of a second petition for post-conviction relief, was untimely. The order was issued nine months after the trial court had summarily dismissed the first petition, rather than upon dismissal of the first petition, *Ex parte Ward*, 957 So.2d 449 (Ala. 2006).

"Access to the courts is a fundamental tenet of our judicial system; legitimate claims should receive a full and fair hearing no matter how litigious the plaintiff may be," *in re Oliver*, 682 F.2d 443, 446 (3rd Cir.1982)." See also *Ex parte Coleman*, 728 So.2d 703 (Ala.Crim.App. 1998), and *White v. State*, 695 So.2d 241 (Ala.Crim.App. 1996).

DENIAL OF REQUEST FOR PROCEED IN FORMA PAUPERIS

The Court of Criminal Appeals will issue a writ of mandamus directing a trial court to state its reasons for denying a prisoner's request to proceed *in forma pauperis* on his post-conviction relief petition. See *Ex parte Amerson*, 849 So.2d 1001 (Ala.Crim.App. 2002).

VENUE/JURISDICTION

Rule 32.6 (b) requires a hearing by the court of original conviction because the circuit judge has personal knowledge of the facts underlying the allegations in the petition, he may deny the petition without further proceedings so long as he states the reasons for the denial in a written order," *Sheats v. State*, 556 So.2d 1094, 1095 (Ala.Crim.App. 1989), cited in *Gilmore v. State*, 937 So.2d 547 (Ala.Crim.App. 2005).

The judge who presided over the trial or other proceedings and observed the conduct of the attorneys at the trial or other proceedings need not hold a hearing on the effectiveness of those attorneys based on the conduct that he observed. See *Ex parte Hill*, 591 So.2d, 462, 463 (Ala. 1991).

The circuit court was not the court where the defendant was convicted, thus court lacked authority or jurisdiction to dispose of a petition for post-conviction relief and should have transferred the case to the county where the conviction occurred, *Sloan v. State*, 780 So.2d 805 (Ala.Crim.App. 2000).

If a post-conviction petition is filed in the wrong court, the circuit court in which the petition is filed must transfer the petition to the circuit court of the original conviction, rather than dismiss the petition. See *Barker v. State*, 766 So.2d 988 (Ala.Crim.App. 2000).

Upon determining that a petition for writ of habeas corpus should have been pursued as a petition for post-conviction relief in the court where the petitioner was convicted, the trial court should have transferred the petition to the court of the original conviction, rather than dismissing it. See Rule 32.5 Ala.R.Crim.P., *Long v. State*, 673 So.2d 856 (Ala.Crim.App. 1995).

AMENDED PETITIONS

When a post-conviction petition styled as a petition for writ of habeas corpus is filed and the allegations raised in the petition are cognizable in a proceeding under Rule 32, Ala.R.Crim.P., the cause should be entertained in the court of original conviction and the petitioner should be given the opportunity to file a petition in the proper form as required by Rule 32.G (a). See *Glover v. State*, 615 So.2d 1331(Ala.Crim.App.1993); *Drayton v. State*, 600 So.2d 1088 (Ala.Crim.App. 1992).

In *Smith v. State*, 918 So.2d 141 (Ala.Crim.App. 2005), [T]he "second sentence in Rule 32.6(a) specifically contemplates that defects in the form of the petition are not grounds for dismissal of the petition but are readily curable by amendment, and both the Supreme Court and this Court have held that defects in the form of a Rule 32 petition in no way implicate the jurisdiction of the circuit court," *Smith v. State*, 918 So.2d 141 (Ala.Crim.App. 2005). See, *e.g.*, *Davis v. State*, 784 So.2d 1082 (Ala.Crim.App.2000); *Norwood v. State*, 770 So.2d 1113 (Ala.Crim.App. 2000); *Young v. State*, 667 So.2d 141 (Ala.1995).

SUFFICIENCY OF PLEADING

Once a petitioner has met his burden of pleading so as to avoid summary disposition pursuant to Rule 32.7(d), Ala.R.Crim.P., he is then entitled to an opportunity to present evidence in order to satisfy his burden of proof, *Murray v. State*, 922 So.2d 961 (Ala.Crim.App. 2005), quoting *Ford v. State*, 831 So.2d 641 (Ala.Crim.App. 2001). See also *Tolbert v. State*, 953 So.2d 1269 (Ala.Crim.App. 2005) [quoting *Boyd v. State*, 746 So.2d 364, 406 (Ala.Crim.App. 1999).

"It is not the pleading of a conclusion which, if true, entitle[s] the petitioner to relief. It is the allegation of facts in the pleading which, if true, entitles the petitioner to relief. After facts are pleaded, which, if true, entitle the petitioner to relief; the petitioner is then entitled to an opportunity, as provided in Rule 32.9, to present evidence proving those alleged facts," *Lancaster v. State*, 638 So.2d 1370, 1373 (Ala.Crim.App. 1993).

Petitioner failed to satisfy the specificity and pleading requirements under the criminal rules governing post-conviction procedure, and, thus, the trial court was "under no obligation to conduct an evidentiary hearing on his petition," because the defendant "failed to cite any law that would have prevented the circuit court from merely receiving the indictment, as opposed to proceeding with the case, pending appeal from juvenile court," *Baker v. State*, 907 So.2d 465 (Ala.Crim.App. 2004),

DISMISSAL OF MERIT-LESS PETITIONS

Trial court can proceed to address the issues and dispose of the petition where the petition clearly does not have merit. See *Ex parte Maddox*, 662 So.2d 915 (Ala. 1995).

Rule 32.7(d), Ala.R.Crim.P. also takes precedence, in some cases, over Rule 32.6(a), Ala.R.Crim.P. requirement that the petition is filed on the "proper form." "Our blind adherence to the holding of *Drayton v. State*, 600 So.2d 1088 (Ala.Crim.App. 1992), is a literal exaltation of form over substance. It is ridiculous to remand this cause so that the appellant will have the opportunity to file a petition in the proper form that will be promptly dismissed," 662 So.2d at 915.

It would be an exaltation of form over substance to remand [this] case to the circuit court so that the court could return the petitions to the appellant, and so the appellant could refile three separate petitions that, for the reasons set forth above, will be promptly dismissed. See *Heulett v. State*, 842 So.2d 741 (Ala.Crim.App. 2002).

DATE OF FILING OF PETITION BY INMATE

A Rule 32 petition was deemed filed on the date it was placed in the prison mail system to be mailed to the circuit court clerk, despite the fact that the date stamp supplied by the clerk indicated the petition was not "filed" until six months after the date on which it was mailed. See *Rash v. State*, 968 So.2d 552 (Ala.Crim.App. 2006).

RULE 32 FILING WHILE DIRECT APPEAL PENDING

When a defendant files a Rule 32 petition while a direct appeal is pending in the Court of Criminal Appeals, The Court will notify the circuit court to hold the Rule 32 petition in abeyance pending the outcome of the appeal. "Or the appellate court may remand, thus staying the appeal of the petitioner's conviction and transferring jurisdiction to the circuit court to adjudicate the Rule 32 petition. After adjudication, a return to remand would be submitted to this court, and the parties would be allowed to submit issues for review of the circuit court's action on the Rule 32 petition," *Barnes v. State*, 621 So.2d 329 (Ala. Crim. App.1992).

The Court of Criminal Appeals granted Wilson's motion, stayed the appeal, and transferred jurisdiction of the cause to the circuit court for adjudication of the Rule 32 petition. The Court ordered the circuit court to dispose of the petition and ordered the court reporter to supplement the record on appeal with a transcript of the Rule 32 proceedings. See *Wilson v. State*, 830 So.2d 765 (Ala.Crim.App.2001), (citing *Barnes*.)

OUT OF TIME APPEAL

"It is clear from the wording of Rule 32.1(f), that the out-of-time-appeal provision applies only to situations where the notice of appeal is untimely," *State v. Carruth*, ___So.2d___, 2008 WL 2223060 (Ala.Crim.App. 2008).

VERIFICATION

"The failure to comply with the verification requirement provided in Rule 32.6(a) Ala. R. Crim. P is not a jurisdictional defect that deprives the trial court of subject matter jurisdiction," *Smith v. State*, 918 So.2d 141 (Ala.Crim.App. 2005).

Failure to comply with the verification requirements of Rule 32.6(a) Ala.R.Crim.P. was not a defect that operates to deprive the circuit court of subject-matter jurisdiction to consider the merits of a Rule 32 petition. The Court noted that "permitting a verification defect to be cured by amendment without requiring the dismissal of the petition for lack of jurisdiction serves to promote the primary policy objectives underlying the verification requirement, ensuring that the averments in the petition are based on merit and truth and protecting against the filing of frivolous petitions without sacrificing judicial economy," *Smith v. State*, 918 So.2d 141 (Ala.Crim.App. 2005), overruling to that extent *Kelley v.*

State, 911 So.2d 1125 (Ala.Crim.App. 2004)4, *Coleman v. State*, 911 So.2d 1099 (Ala.Crim.App. 2004) 5; and *Thornton v. State*, 859 So.2d 458 (Ala.Crim.App. 2003).

The petitions were not properly verified as required by Rule 32.6(a) in *Brooks v. State*, 929 So.2d 491 (Ala.Crim.App. 2005.

Failure to comply with the verification requirements of Rule 32.6(a) was not a defect that would deprive the circuit court of subject-matter jurisdiction to consider the merits of the petition, and the defect is waived if not raised. See *Smith v. State*, 918 So.2d 141 (Ala.Crim.App. 2005).

The issue of whether the petition by the capital murder petitioner was properly verified was waived because the State did not object to the lack of proper verification. See *Loggins v. State*, 910 So.2d 146 (Ala.Crim.App. 2005).

JURISDICTIONAL ISSUES RIGHT TO COUNSEL

Post-conviction petitioner's claim that he was arraigned without his counsel present was a jurisdictional claim not subject to the procedural bars set forth in the Rules of Criminal Procedure. See *Castillo v. State*, 925 So.2d 284 (Ala.Crim.App. 2005).

JURY NOT SWORN

A claim that the jury venire and the petit jury were not sworn is a jurisdictional issue because a verdict rendered by jurors who have never been sworn is a nullity. See *Barclay v. State*, ___So.2d___, 2008 WL 902887 (Ala.Crim.App. 2008); *Ex parte Benford*, 935 So.2d 421 (Ala.Crim.App. App. 2006); *Brooks v. State*, 845 So.2d 849, 850-851 (Ala.Crim.App. 2002).

"It cannot be presumed from a silent record that the jury was sworn; there must be in the record some affirmative showing that the oath was administered to the jury," *Barclay v. State*, ___So.2d ___, 2008 WL 902887 (Ala.Crim.App. 2008) citing *Ex parte Deramus*, 721 So.2d 242 (Ala. 1998).

ILLEGALLY SENTENCED

The contention that the sentence exceeds the maximum authorized by law raised a jurisdictional issue. See *Steele v. State*, 911 So.2d 21, 31 (Ala.Crim.App. 2004). "When a sentence is clearly illegal or is clearly not authorized by statute, the defendant does not need to object at the trial level in order to preserve that issue for appellate review," *English v. State* 954 So.2d 1136 (Ala.Crim.App. 2006); *Hunt v. State* 659 So.2d 998 (Ala.Crim.App. 1994); *Ex parte Brannon*, 547 So.2d 68 (Ala.1989).

A challenge to an illegal sentence is not precluded by the limitations period or by the rule against successive petitions. See *Jones v. State*, 724 So.2d 75, 76 (Ala.Crim.App.1998).

An illegal sentence can be challenged at any time because when a trial court imposes an illegal sentence, it has exceeded its jurisdiction and the sentence is void. See *Henderson v. State*, 895 So.2d 364, 365 (Ala.Crim.App. 2004).

Defendant's claim that the trial court was without jurisdiction to sentence him as a habitual felony offender after he was convicted of child abuse (a misdemeanor offense) was a jurisdictional claim not subject to the time bar of the post-conviction relief rule. See *Mosley v. State*, ___ So.2d ___ 2007 WL 2459379 (Ala.Crim.App. App. 2007).

HABITUAL FELONY ACT ENHANCEMENT

Post-conviction petitioner's claim that the record did not affirmatively reflect that he was sentenced under the Habitual Felony Offender Act was procedurally barred, because the claim did not have jurisdictional implications, and it was not raised on appeal. See *Murray v. State*, 922 So.2d 961 (Ala.Crim.App. 2005). See also, *Pilgrim v. State*, 963 So.2d 697 (Ala.Crim.App. 2006).

Petitioner was entitled to a hearing on his second petition for post-conviction relief alleging that the 15-year sentence imposed for second-degree theft of property exceeded the maximum sentence authorized by statute, despite the State's contention that the sentence was properly imposed pursuant to the Habitual Felony Offender Act and that the petition was successive. The statute authorized a maximum sentence of ten years for the defendant's offenses, and the record contained no indication that the defendant was sentenced as a habitual felony offender. See *Barnes v. State*, 708 So.2d 217 (Ala.Crim.App. 1997).

"Rule 32. 1(b) provides for post-conviction relief where the court was without jurisdiction to render judgment or to impose a sentence. A claim of a lack of jurisdiction to render judgment or to impose sentence is not precluded as a basis for relief by Rule 32.2, even though the question of jurisdiction could have been but was not raised at trial or on appeal," *Barnes v. State*, 708 So.2d 217 (Ala.Crim.App. 1997).

DOUBLE JEOPARDY CLAIM

A claim, raised in the defendant's fourth petition for post-conviction relief, that the defendant's convictions for both felony murder and the underlying felony offense of robbery violated the constitutional guarantee against double jeopardy, which was raised in defendant's fourth petition for post-conviction relief, was not subject to preclusion because it implicated the subject matter jurisdiction of the trial court. See *Edwards v. State*, 907 So.2d 1077 (Ala.Crim.App. 2004).

NO CRIMINAL OFFENSE

Petitioner's claim that the offense of "attempted robbery" did not exist under Alabama law, raised a jurisdictional issue, and therefore, the petitioner's post-conviction claim that the trial court lacked jurisdiction to accept his guilty plea to a nonexistent offense was not subject to a procedural bar for having failed to raise the claim at trial or on direct appeal. See *Conner v. State*, 955 So.2d 473 (Ala.Crim.App. 2006).

Evidence is not newly discovered for purposes of a post-conviction relief claim, where the accused knew of the evidence but did not mention it to his counsel. See *Woods v. State*, 957 So.2d 492 (Ala.Crim.App. 2004).

A capital murder defendant who alleged in a petition for post-conviction relief that he was entitled to a new trial based on newly discovered evidence, specifically that newly discovered material facts proved that the gun recovered from his mother's home was not the gun used in the murders, was not entitled to relief. The Court of Criminal Appeals held that the evidence presented at the evidentiary hearing was cumulative to the evidence that was presented at trial and thus, would not have changed the outcome of the trial. See Rules 32.1(e) and 32.3 Ala.R.Crim.P., *Hinton v. State*, ___So.2d.___2006 WL 1125605 (Ala.Crim.App. 2006).

A party who files a petition for post-conviction relief based on newly discovered evidence cannot go back after the trial to secure what he considers to be a more qualified expert. Allowing a party to do so would be contrary to the post-conviction relief requirement that evidence was not merely cumulative to facts that were known. See Rule 32.1(e)(2) Ala.R.Crim.P., *Hinton v. State*, ___So.2d.___, 2006 WL 1125605 (Ala.Crim.App. 2006).

A post-conviction claim that the State withheld exculpatory evidence was procedurally barred where the defendant proffered no facts showing that the claim was based on newly discovered evidence and the claim could have been raised at trial and on direct appeal. See *Madison v. State*, ___ So.2d.___, 2006 WL 2788983 (Ala.Crim.App. 2006).

SUCCESSIVE PETITIONS

"We now interpret Rule 32.2(b) as federal courts interpret habeas corpus petitions to mean that new claims in subsequent petitions are barred as being successive unless 'the petitioner shows both that good cause exists why the new ground or grounds were not known or could not have been ascertained through reasonable diligence when the first petition was heard, and that failure to entertain the petition will result in a miscarriage of justice." See Rule 32.2(b) Ala.R.Crim.P. *Whitt v. State*, 827 So.2d 869 (Ala.Crim.App. 2001), overruled *Blount v. State*, 572 So.2d 498 (Ala.Crim.App.1990). Not successive unless a prior petition is decided.

EXCEPTIONS TO ISSUE PRECLUSION

JURISDICTIONAL CLAIMS

Jurisdictional claims are not "precluded by the limitations period or by the rule against successive petitions," *Coleman v. State* 927 So.2d 883 (Ala.Crim.App. 2005); *Grady v. State*, 831 So.2d 646, 648 (Ala.Crim.App. 2001), quoting *Jones v. State*, 724 So.2d 75, 76 (Ala.Crim.App. 1998).

The petitioner raised nine claims in his Rule 32 petition but because the petitioner's claim was filed outside the statutory limitations period provided in Rule 32.2 (c), the Court of Criminal Appeals could only consider the jurisdictional claim that the trial court was without jurisdiction to render the judgment or to impose the sentence and that the sentence imposed exceeded the maximum authorized by law. See *Edmond v. State*, 954 So.2d 608 (Ala.Crim.App. 2006).

NON-JURISDICTIONAL CLAIMS

Insufficiency of evidence to support the defendant's guilt beyond a reasonable doubt pursuant to § 13A-S-42, applicable to capital cases, "is a non-jurisdictional defect that, when adequately preserved in the trial court, may, despite [the] guilty plea … be raised on direct appeal," *in Ex parte Booker*___ So.2d.___, 2008 WL 1838299 (Ala. 2008), overruling *Elder v. State*, 494 So.2d 922 (Ala.Crim.App. 1986). Scc also *Davis v. State*, 682 So.2d 476 (Ala.Crim.App.1995), *Benton v. State*, 887 So.2d 304 (Ala.Crim.App. 2003), and *Cox v. State*, 462 So.2d 1047 (Ala.Crim.App. 2003).

STATUTE OF LIMITATIONS

One-year limitations period governing petitions for post-conviction relief was not a jurisdictional bar; rather, the limitations period was an affirmative defense that could be waived if not raised. See *Ex parte Ward*, ___ So.2d. ___, 2007 WL 1576054 (Ala. 2007).

FILING OF PETITION OF IN FORMA PAUPERIS

Date of filing is the date when *in forma pauperis* petition was submitted, not when it was granted. See *Hyde v. State*, 950 So.2d 344 (Ala.Crim.App. 2006), overruling *Clemons v. State*, ___ So.2d.___, 2003 WL 22047260 (Ala.Crim.App. 2004).

INEFFECTIVE ASSISTANCE OF COUNSEL.

"To sufficiently plead an allegation of ineffective assistance of counsel, a Rule 32 petitioner not only must 'identify the [specific] acts or omissions of counsel that are alleged not to have been the result of reasonable professional judgment,' *Strickland v. Washington*, 466 U.S. 668, 690 [104 S.Ct. 2052, 8 L.Ed.2d 674] (1984), but must also plead specific facts indicating that he or she was prejudiced by the acts or omissions, *i.e.*, facts indicating that there is a reasonable probability that, but for the counsel's unprofessional errors, the result of the proceeding would have been different. A bare allegation that prejudice occurred without specific facts indicating how the petitioner was prejudiced is not sufficient." See Rule 32.6(b) Ala.R.Crim.P., *Madison v. State*, ___ So.2d ___,2006 WL2788983 (Ala.Crim.App. 2006).

Trial counsel is presumed effective. In reviewing claims of ineffective assistance, the standard of review is the *Strickland v. Washington*, 466 U.S. 668 (1984), a standard requiring the petitioner to show "1) that counsel's performance was deficient; and 2) that the petitioner was prejudiced by the deficient performance," *Davis v. State*, ___ So.2d ___, 2008 WL 902884 (Ala.Crim.App. 2008).

"To sufficiently plead an allegation of ineffective assistance of counsel, a Rule 32 petitioner not only must 'identify the [specific] acts or omissions of counsel that are alleged not to have been the result of reasonable professional judgment,' *Strickland v. Washington*, 466 U.S. 668, 690, 104 S.Ct. 2052, 80 L.Ed.2d 674 (1984), but also must plead specific facts indicating that he or she was prejudiced by the acts or omissions, *i.e.*, facts indicating 'that there is a reasonable probability that, but for counsel's unprofessional errors, the result of the proceeding would have been different,' 466 U.S. at 694, 104 S.Ct. 2052. A bare allegation that prejudice occurred without specific facts indicating how the petitioner was prejudiced is not sufficient," *McNabb v. State* ___ So.2d ___, 2007 WL 2459405 (Ala.Crim.App. 2007).

INEFFECTIVE COUNSEL AND INVOLUNTARY GUILTY PLEA

It is well settled that claims of ineffective assistance of counsel and involuntary guilty plea may be presented for the first time in a timely filed Rule 32 petition. See *Murray v. State*, 922 So.2d 961, 965 (Ala.Crim.App. 2005), cited with approval in *Johnson v. State*, ___ So.2d ___, 2007 WL 2459965 (Ala.Crim.App. 2007).

Claims of ineffective assistance of counsel raised for the first time in his post-conviction petition were not procedurally barred. The defendant did not file a direct appeal; therefore, his post-conviction petition was the first opportunity to challenge the counsel's performance. See *Kelley v. State*, ___ So.2d. ___ 2007 WL 1866749 (Ala.Crim.App. 2007).

BURDEN OF PROOF

At the pleading stage, a petitioner must provide "a clear and specific statement of the grounds upon which relief is sought, Rule 32.6(b), Ala.R.Crim.P. Once a petitioner has met the burden of pleading so as to avoid summary disposition pursuant to Rule 32.7(d), Ala.R.Crim.P., he is then entitled to an opportunity to present evidence in order to satisfy his burden of proof," *Ford v. State*, 831 So.2d 644 (Ala.Crim.App. 2001), cited with approval in *Kelley v. State*, ___ So.2d ___, 2007 WL 1866749 (Ala.Crim.App. 2007).

"The petition must contain a clear and specific statement of the grounds upon which relief is sought including full disclosure of the factual basis of those grounds. A bare allegation that a constitutional right has been violated and mere conclusions of law shall not be sufficient to warrant any further proceedings," *Boyd v. State*, 913 So.2d 1113 (Ala.Crim.App. 2003). "The burden of pleading under Rule 32.3 and Rule 32.6(b) is a heavy one. Conclusions unsupported by specific facts will not satisfy the requirements of Rule 32.3 and Rule 32.6(b). The full factual basis for the claim must be included in the petition itself. If assuming every factual allegation in a Rule 32 petition to be true, a court cannot determine whether the petitioner is entitled to relief, the petitioner has not satisfied the burden of pleading under Rule 32.3 and Rule 32.6(b)," 913 So.2d 1113 at 1125 (Ala.Crim.App. 2003).

Claim challenging lethal injection as a method of execution did not meet the specificity requirements of the Rule of Criminal Procedure and the pleading requirements of the rule governing the burden of proof. The court concluded that the "defendant's argument was largely speculative in nature and was replete with vague and hypothetical allegations that the method could cause pain, and the defendant did not actually allege that the execution procedure, if properly performed, caused an unacceptable or unconscionable level of pain," *McNabb v. State*, ___ So.2d ___, 2007 WL 2459405 (Ala.Crim.App. 2007).

It is not the pleading of a conclusion in a petition for post-conviction relief which, if true, entitles the petitioner to relief, it is the allegation of facts in the pleading which, if true, entitles a petitioner to relief, *Tolbert v. State*, 953 So.2d 1269 (Ala.Crim.App. 2005).

PROSECUTOR/STATE'S RESPONSE TO CLAIMS

The Court explained that due process required the State to plead the procedural bars that it maintains apply to the claims in a Rule 32 petition to give "the petitioner the notice he needs to attempt to formulate arguments and present evidence to 'disprove [the] existence [of those grounds] by a preponderance of the evidence.'" Because the State's compliance with Rule 32.3 is mandatory, if the State fails to comply with the rule, it waives the application of the procedural bars, and an appellate court cannot sua sponte apply the procedural bars to claims in the petition unless "exceptional circumstances" are present. See *Ex parte Rice*, 565 So.2d 606 at 608 (Ala. 1990). See also, *Nicks v. State*, 783 So.2d 895 (Ala.Crim.App. 1999).

Procedural bars to post-conviction relief contained in criminal procedure rules are not jurisdictional, and, thus, they can be waived. Only in extraordinary circumstances can such a waiver be overcome by an appellate court acting *sua sponte*, Rule 32.2(a) Ala.R.Crim.P. The State can avoid most of the issues created by an appellate court's *sua sponte* application of Rule 32 procedural bar by exercising due diligence and care when answering a post-conviction petition," *Ex parte Clemons*, ___ So.2d. ___, 2007 WL 1300722 (Ala. 2007), abrogating *Davis v. State*, ___ So.2d ___, 2006 WL 510508 (Ala. 2006).

Note: In *McNabb v. State*, ___ So.2d ___, 2007 WL 2459405 (Ala.Crim.App. 2007), the Court of Criminal Appeals concluded that the appellate court's *sua sponte* application of the pleading requirement in Rule 32.6(b) did not conflict with the Alabama Supreme Court's holding in *Ex parte Clemons*, ___ So.2d ___ 2007 WL 1300722 (Ala. 2007). This conclusion was based on the following distinction: "Because Rule 32.3 limits the State's burden of pleading to 'grounds of preclusion,' and [we note that] only those provisions in Rule 32.2 entitled 'Preclusion of Remedy' fall within such a description, the pleading requirement in Rule 32.6(b), and Rule 32.7(d) governing summary disposition do not fall within the 'Preclusion of Remedy' as discussed in *Ex parte Clemons*."

HARMLESS ERROR

Prosecutor's failure to file a response to the defendant's petition for post-conviction relief was held to be a "harmless error," on the basis that the facts supporting the grounds for precluding the defendant from obtaining relief by his petition were beyond dispute, and thus the prosecutor's response could not have assisted the defendant in formulating any plausible argument or presenting any evidence to disprove the grounds for denial of his petition. See *Young v. State*, 600 So.2d 1073 (Ala.Crim.App. 1992),

The issue of "harmless error" was also considered in *Ex parte Clemons*, ___ So.2d ___, 2007 WL 300722 (Ala. 2007). The State failed to plead the applicability of the procedural bars of Rule 32.2(a) to the petitioner's claims of ineffective assistance of trial counsel, and the trial court did not apply the procedural bars when it addressed those claims. The Court of Criminal Appeals, however, applied the mandatory procedural bars and thus did not address the merits of the petitioner's claims. The question for the Supreme Court was whether the *sua sponte* application of the procedural bars by the appellate court had "probably injuriously affected substantial rights" of the State or the petitioner. The Alabama Supreme Court held, that because it was obvious from the record that the procedural bars were applicable and nothing in the record established that the petitioner's or the State's substantial rights would be injuriously affected, the *sua sponte* application of Rule 32.2(a) procedural bars by the Court of Criminal Appeals was harmless.

AMENDED PETITIONS

"[A] petitioner does not have the unfettered right to file endless amendments to a Rule 32 petition. The right to amend is limited by the trial court's discretion to refuse to allow an amendment if the trial court finds that the petitioner has unduly delayed filing the amendment or that an amendment unduly prejudices the State," *Ex parte Jenkins*, 972 So.2d 159 (Ala. 2005). See also *Ex parte Rhone*, 900 So.2d 455 (Ala. 2004).

Undue delay and undue prejudice cannot be applied to restrict the petitioner's right to file an amendment clearly provided for in Rule 32.7 simply because it states a new claim that was not included in the original petition. See *Ex parte Jenkins*, 972 So.2d 159 (Ala. 2005).

NO RELATION BACK

Relation-back doctrine should not preclude an inmate from filing an amendment to a Rule 32 petition that asserts claims not raised in the original petition, *Ex parte Jenkins*, 972 So.2d (159 (Ala. 2005).

Restricting a Rule 32 petitioner's right to file an amendment by applying principles found in the Alabama Rules of Civil Procedure, such as the relation-back doctrine, should be the subject of careful consideration by the Standing Committee on the Alabama Rules of Criminal Procedure. We decline to rewrite the Rules of Criminal Procedure by sanctioning the incorporation of the relation-back doctrine into those rules when nothing of that nature presently appears in them. See *Ex parte Woods*, 957 So.2d 533 (Ala. 2006).

A petitioner seeking to amend a petition for post-conviction relief does not have an initial burden of showing diligence in filing the amendment or that the facts underlying the amendment were unknown to him before the filing of the original petition, *Ex parte Rhone*, 900 So.2d 455 (Ala. 2004) overruling *Cochran v. State*, 548 So.2d 1062 (Ala.Crim.App. 1989.)

MULTIPLE CONVICTIONS

Where the allegations in a Rule 32 petition make reference to multiple judgments entered in one proceeding (and which is likewise reflected in the court record), the circuit court should consider the claims as they relate to all of the convictions and make specific findings of fact as required by Rule 32.9(d) Ala.R.Crim.P. and *Davis v. State*, ___ So.2d ___, 2007.WL 4463923 (Ala.Crim.App. 2007).

The trial court should have dismissed the defendant's petition for post-conviction relief without prejudice rather than ruling on its merits, where the defendant challenged, in a single petition, convictions for assault and sodomy that were entered in separate proceedings. See *Carr v. State*, 884 So.2d 932 (Ala.Crim.App. 2004).

EVIDENTIARY HEARINGS

Rule 32 petitioner is not automatically entitled to an evidentiary hearing on any and all claims raised in his petition. A trial court may summarily dismiss a petition for post-conviction relief when a simple reading of the petition shows that, assuming every allegation of the petition is correct, the petition is without merit or is precluded. See *Sullivan v. State*, 944 So.2d 164 (Ala.Crim.App. 2006), citing *Boyd v. State*, 913 So.2d 1113 (Ala.Crim.App. 2003).

After the facts are pleaded, if true, entitles a post-conviction petitioner to relief, the petitioner is then entitled to an opportunity to present evidence proving those alleged facts. See *Hodges v. State*, ___ So.2d. ___, 2007 WL 866658 (Ala. Crim. App. 2007).

Where a petition appears meritorious on its face, a circuit court judge must conduct an evidentiary hearing on a petition for post-conviction relief. See *Rash v. State*, ___ So.2d. ___, 2006 WL 3123521 (Ala.Crim.App. 2006).

Inmate filing a post-conviction petition seeking an out-of-time appeal from the denial of his two previous petitions was entitled to an evidentiary hearing on his claim that his failure to appeal the denial of previous petitions was through no fault of his own because he timely mailed notices of appeal, which were apparently lost in the mail and never received by the circuit clerk. The Court noted that the claim was sufficiently pleaded, and his factual allegations were unrefuted by the State. See *Poole v. State*, ___ So.2d ___, 2007 WL 1519008 (Ala.Crim.App. 2007). See also *Fox v. State*, ___ So.2d. ___, 2007 WL 2460048 (Ala.Crim.App. 2007).

RIGHT TO COUNSEL

Federal ruling:
No provision of the Constitution requires the appointment of counsel for inmates who seek post-conviction relief in state courts. See *Murray v. Giarratano*, 482 U.S. 1, 1-09 S.Ct. 2765, 106 L.Ed.2d 1 (1989)

Alabama ruling:
"There is no requirement that indigent petitioners be furnished counsel regarding post-conviction proceedings." See *Ex parte Cox*, 451 So.2d 235, 237 (Ala.1983), cited in *Mayes v. State*, 563 So.2d 38 (Ala.Crim.App. 1990) and *Ingram v State*, ___ S0.2d ___, 2006 WL 2788984 (Ala.Crim.App. 2006).

The Alabama Rules of Criminal Procedure permit a trial court to appoint counsel to represent an indigent petitioner in a post-conviction proceeding if it 'appears that counsel is necessary to assert or protect the rights of the petitioner. In instances where counsel is provided, such an appointment occurs only after a petition has been filed,'' *Ex parte Jenkins*, 972 So.2d 159 (Ala. 2005).

SUMMARY DISPOSITION OF PETITION

If the court determines that the petition is not sufficiently specific, is precluded, or fails to state a claim, or that no material issue of fact or law exists which would entitle the petitioner to relief under this rule and that no purpose would be served by any further proceedings, the court may either dismiss the petition or grant leave to file an amended petition. Leave to amend shall be freely granted. Otherwise, the court shall direct that the proceedings continue and set a date for a hearing (Rule 32.7(d)).

SUMMARY DISPOSITION OF TIME-BARRED, NON-JURISDICTIONAL CLAIMS

Trial court could summarily deny the defendant's petition for post-conviction relief without a hearing where the petition that was filed after the limitations period had expired raised only non-jurisdictional claims, and the defendant did not assert equitable tolling in his petition. See *Davenport v. State*, ___ So.2d ___, 2007 WL 4463946 (Ala.Crim.App. 2007),

SUMMARY DISPOSITION – PERSONAL KNOWLEDGE

"[T]he fact that a circuit court judge ruling on a petition for post-conviction relief is not required to conduct an evidentiary hearing on a petitioner's claims of ineffective assistance of trial counsel if that judge personally observed the conduct of counsel, does not relieve that judge of the responsibility of entering a sufficiently specific order addressing each of the petitioner's claims of ineffective assistance of trial counsel," In *Lucious v. State*, ___ So.2d ___, 2007 WL 2459973 (Ala.Crim.App. 2007).

"[I]f the circuit judge has personal knowledge of the actual facts underlying the allegations in the petition, he may deny the petition without further proceedings so long as he states the reasons for the denial in a written order," *Sheats v. State*, 556 So.2d 1094, 1095 (Ala.Crim.App. 1989). See also *Dobyne v. State*, 805 So.2d 733, 740-41 (Ala.Crim.App. 2000) and *Payne v. State*, 791 So.2d 383, 394 (Ala.Crim.App. 2000).

REQUIREMENT OF WRITTEN ORDER

Despite the heavy caseload under which the trial courts of this State toil and that Rule 32 petitions add to that already heavy burden, Rule 32.9(d) requires the trial court to make specific findings of fact relating to each material issue of fact presented. See *Long v. State* ___ So.2d ___, 2008 WL 902883 (Ala.Crim.App. 2008). See also *Ex parte Walker*, 652 So.2d 198 (Ala. 1994) and *Smith v. State*, 665 So.2d 954 (Ala.Crim.App. 1994).

"It is to do likewise if it finds that a particular allegation fails to state a claim or to present any material issue of fact or law that would entitle [the petitioner] to relief. In other words, the court's written findings are to address individually each claim not precluded by Rule 32.2," *Dedeaux v. State*, 976 So.2d 1045 (Ala.Crim.App. 2005).

However, a written order is required even when no evidentiary hearing is conducted and the judge has relied upon personal observations to dismiss the petition. See *Lucious v. State*, ___ So.2d. ___, 2007 WL 2459973 (Ala.Crim.App. 2007).

In dismissing a Rule 32 petition, a court need not specify the reasons, but if the record on appeal is insufficient to show the basis of the denial, the cause will be remanded for such a determination. See *Henderson v. State*, 570 So.2d 879 (Ala.Crim.App. 1990).

The trial court's failure to make specific, written findings of fact regarding the defendant's claims in denying his petition required a remand for the trial court to make such findings. See Rule 32.9(d) Ala.R.Crim.P. and *Hawthorne v. State* ___ So.2d ___, 2007 WL4463941 (Ala.Crim.App. 2007).

The court must make specific findings of fact relating to each material issue of fact presented in an evidentiary hearing on the defendant's petition for post-conviction relief. See *Wiggins v. State*, ___ So.2d. ___ 2006 WL 1121210 (Ala.Crim.App. 2006).

Trial court's failure to make specific findings of fact supporting its dismissal of the defendant's post-conviction petition warranted remand. The Rules of Criminal Procedure required the court, if it conducted an evidentiary hearing on a post-conviction petition, to make specific findings of fact relating to each material issue of fact presented. See *Getz v. State*, ___ So.2d. ___, 2006 WL 2788976 (Ala.Crim.App. 2006).

If a court's findings on a petition for post-conviction relief are based on the court's personal knowledge of the underlying guilty plea proceedings, then the order should so state. See *Harris v. State*, 814 So.2d 1003 (Ala.Crim.App. 2001).

IN THE CIRCUIT COURT OF CULLMAN COUNTY
STATE OF ALABAMA

JOHN L DOE, Petitioner	§ § §	Case No._____
vs.	§ § §	
STATE OF ALABAMA, Respondent	§ § §	

PETITION FOR RELIEF FROM SENTENCE OF DEATH
UNDER RULE 32 OF THE ALABAMA RULES OF CRIMINAL PROCEDURE

John L. Doe, *pro se*, respectfully petitions this Honorable Court for relief from his sentence of death. The Constitutions of the United States and of the State of Alabama require a new sentencing proceeding pursuant to Rule 32 of the Alabama Rules of Criminal Procedure.

PROCEDURAL HISTORY

A. Trial and Sentencing

1. On September 26, 1987, John Doe was convicted of the capital offense of murder during a robbery under § 13A-5-40 (a)(2), Code of Alabama (1975), in the Circuit Court of Cullman County.

2. On September 28, 1987, a sentencing hearing was conducted, and the jury returned an advisory verdict in favor of death by a vote of 11 to 1.

3. The judge held a pre-sentence hearing on November 9, 1987, and sentenced John Doe to death in the electric chair on December 1, 1987.

B. Direct Appeal

4. The Court of Criminal Appeals affirmed the conviction and sentence on June 16, 1989, *Doe v. State*, 564 So. 2d 453 (Ala. Cr. App. 1989).

5. That decision was affirmed by the Supreme Court of Alabama on March 23, 1990, *Ex parte Doe*, 564 So. 2d 469 (Ala. 1990).

6. The United States Supreme Court denied John Doe's petition for writ of certiorari to the Alabama Supreme Court on December 3, 1990, *Doe v. Alabama*, 112 L. Ed. 2d 579 (1990).

C. Post-Conviction Relief Petition

7. In December 1990, John Doe obtained new counsel, Bernard E. Harcourt, to represent him in a state post-conviction challenge to his conviction and sentence of death.

8. A Rule 32 state post-conviction petition on behalf of John Doe was filed on December 3, 1991.

9. Pre-trial hearings on the Rule 32 petition were held on March 6, 1995, and January 8, 1996.

10. During this period, John Doe, also challenged two prior convictions from the state of Tennessee that were used as aggravating circumstances at his Alabama death penalty sentencing hearing. That petition was denied by the Tennessee circuit court. In February 1997, the Tennessee Court of Criminal Appeals affirmed the denial of relief. John Doe's request to the Tennessee Supreme Court for discretionary review was denied in March 1997. On June 16, 1988, John Doe filed a petition for writ of habeas in a federal district court in Tennessee. The petition was dismissed, and the Sixth Circuit affirmed and denied John Doe a certificate of appealability on March 17, 1999. The United States Supreme Court denied his petition for *writ of certiorari*.

11. On December 6, 1999, the court denied John Doe's Rule 32 petition in an 89-page proposed order that had been filed with the court three days before by the Alabama Attorney General with the caption "PROPOSED MEMORANDUM OPINION." When the judge signed and issued the order, he made no changes to it, including leaving the caption "PROPOSED MEMORANDUM OPINION."

12. On February 1, 2002, the Alabama Court of Criminal Appeals affirmed the denial of Mr. Doe's Rule 32 petition, *John Doe v. State*, 913 So. 2d 460 (Ala. Cr. App. 2002).

13. On April 19, 2002, the Alabama Court of Criminal Appeals denied John Doe's application for rehearing, *John Doe v. State*, 2002 Ala. Crim. App. LEXIS 3242 (2002).

14. The Alabama Supreme Court denied John Doe's timely filed certiorari petition on May 20, 2005.

D. Federal District Court

In May 2006, John Doe filed for federal habeas corpus. The district court denied the petition in full, *Doe v. Allen*, 2013 WL 1282129 (N.D. Ala. 2013). The district court refused to grant a certificate of appealability on any issues.

E. Eleventh Circuit Affirms and Supreme Court Denies Certiorari

The Eleventh Circuit granted a certificate of appealability. Eight months after the argument, the Eleventh Circuit affirmed, *Doe v. Comm'r*, 620 F. App'x 752 (11th Cir. 2015).

17. The U.S. Supreme Court denied John Doe's petition for writ of certiorari. See *Doe v. Allen* 137 S. Ct. 39 (2016).

F. State's Motion to Set a Date of Execution for John Doe

18. On June 23, 2017, the State moved the Supreme Court of Alabama to set a date of execution for John Doe.

19. On August 25, 2017, the Alabama Supreme Court ordered the State to allow John Doe to undergo a medical examination by his medical expert, Dr. Mark Heath, to find out his venous condition. The Court also ordered that John Doe provide weekly status updates to the Court.

20. John Doe filed weekly status updates with the Alabama Supreme Court on September 1, 2017; September 8, 2017; September 15, 2017; September 22, 2017; September 29, 2017; and October 2, 2017. On October 2, 2017, John Doe also filed an answer with the Alabama Supreme Court addressing the question of the impossibility of John Doe's venous access.

21. The Alabama Supreme Court ordered the State to respond, which it did on October 10, 2017, and John Doe filed a supplemental response on October 11, 2017.

22. On December 13, 2017, the Supreme Court of Alabama entered an order, without having a hearing, authorizing John Doe's execution on February 22, 2018.

G. John Doe's § 1983 Suit

23. The same day that an execution date was set, John Doe filed a § 1983 complaint in the United States District Court for the Northern District of Alabama, *Doe v. Dunn*, 2018 WL 723104 (N.D. Ala. Dec. 13, 2017).

24. On January 31, 2018, after an evidentiary hearing, the District Court denied the state's motion for summary judgment and granted John Doe's motion for a stay of execution, *Doe v. Dunn*, 2018 WL 723104 (N.D. Ala. Feb. 6, 2018), Doc. 30.

25. On February 13, 2018, the Eleventh Circuit reversed the stay. It ordered the District Court to move forward with the case, immediately appoint an independent medical expert to evaluate John Doe fully, and then make factual findings by Tuesday, February 20th, *Doe v. Dunn*, No. 18-10473 (11th Cir. Feb. 13, 2018).

26. On February 19, 2018, the independent medical expert's report was distributed to the parties.

27. On February 20, 2018, the District Court denied John Doe's motion for a stay and permitted the execution to move forward. However, the judge conditioned this on the defendant's agreement to not attempt peripheral venous access through John Doe's upper extremities. Defendants agreed to only attempt to obtain peripheral venous access through John Doe's lower extremities, *Doe v. Dunn*, 2:17-cv-02083-KOB (N.D. Ala. Feb. 20, 2018).

28. On February 22, 2018, the Eleventh Circuit affirmed, *Doe v. Comm'r*, 2018 WL 1020051 (11th Cir. Feb. 22, 2018).

29. On the evening of February 22, 2018, at around 8:45 PM, the U.S. Supreme Court denied John Doe's motion for a stay of execution and a petition for writ of certiorari. See *Doe v. Dunn*, 583 U. S. ___ (Feb. 22, 2018).

H.   State's Failed Attempt to Execute John Doe on February 22, 2018

30. On February 22, 2018, around 8:45 pm CST, following the United States Supreme Court's denial of his application for a stay, the state of Alabama began the execution of John Doe via intravenous lethal injection at Holman Correctional Facility.

31. Prior to being brought to the execution chamber, John Doe had not been given his regular pain medication, Tylenol-Codeine No.3, at his regularly scheduled time. Normally, John Doe would receive three doses of his medication daily. On February 22, 2018, John Doe was not given his evening dose of medication, typically administered around 6:00 pm. Not surprisingly, John Doe's usual pain resulting from his cancer became substantially worse before he entered the execution chamber that night.

32. After the U.S. Supreme Court lifted its temporary stay of execution, John Doe was taken into the execution chamber and strapped onto the lethal injection gurney. Two members of the execution team entered the execution chamber and immediately began to work on John Doe, below his knees, on both the left and right sides. The two members of the execution team worked at the same time, each taking one side of John Doe's body, in an attempt to find a vein anywhere in his lower extremities for peripheral venous access.

33. The execution team inserted needles and/or catheters multiple times into his left and right legs and ankles, each time forcing the needles into his lower extremities. In at least two of these attempts, an execution team member inserted a needle into John Doe's leg and kept the needle in his leg for several minutes, moving it around in a painful and futile attempt to enter John Doe's veins. Throughout this process, John Doe felt painful stretching, pressure, and burning sensations. At one point, the execution team turned John Doe over onto his stomach on the gurney, slapping the back of his legs to try to generate a vein.

34. After multiple, repeated attempts at peripheral venous access, the execution personnel stated aloud that they could not establish access. With peripheral access unavailable, other execution team members next attempted central venous access. An unidentified man, wearing a business suit and no protective covering besides gloves, attempted venous access, while an unidentified woman, also in a business suit and no protective covering besides gloves, operated the ultrasound machine.

35. The execution team used an ultrasound to locate veins before attempting access with needles and/or catheters. The staff only attempted central venous access in John Doe's right groin.

Multiple times, the execution team tried to insert a needle or catheter into John Doe's right groin, causing severe bleeding and pain. The staff put a pad on his groin to absorb the blood and had to change the pad during the procedure when the pad became completely soaked with blood. The woman operating the ultrasound machine had to change her gloves several times because they were bloody.

36. Throughout these excruciating hours, John Doe experienced extreme fear and psychological distress. In addition to the already distressing situation of anticipating his own death, John Doe was subjected to not only physical agony but also psychological torture from the uncertainty and cruelty resulting from hours of attempted execution. While the execution team was working on the central line in his groin, John Doe was praying that the team would successfully establish access so that he would simply die, and the pain would stop.

38. The execution was ultimately terminated at approximately 11:27 pm CST, or at least that was when counsel was notified. However, even after it was announced in the execution chamber that the execution was terminated, the man attempting central line access insisted that he be allowed to continue. He suggested continuing with central venous access in John Doe's right groin, or trying elsewhere on his lower extremities, despite being told that the execution had been terminated and that he should cease any further attempts. Only after being repeatedly told that the execution could not continue did the man give up. A bandage was then taped to John Doe's right groin.

39. After the execution was terminated, John Doe was unstrapped, and correctional officers lifted him up off the gurney. When his feet hit the floor, John Doe collapsed in agony. Unable to stand or walk on his own, John Doe had to be held up by the correctional officers and carried back to his cell.

40. John Doe was brought to the infirmary shortly after the execution was terminated, where the bandage on his groin was replaced. John Doe told the doctor on staff that he was in excruciating pain, but he was not given any pain medication until around 3:00 am or 4:00 am CST.

41. After the botched execution, John Doe urinated blood. He reported painful and bloody urination during the hours and days after the execution, evidence that the IV team likely punctured his bladder while attempting central line access.

42. Since February 22, 2018, John Doe has suffered not only physically but also emotionally. He has had nightmares and flashbacks in which he pictures himself lying on the gurney again, being subjected again to the torturous pain that occurred on February 22, 2018. John Doe has been traumatized and lives in fear that ADOC will subject him to another painful and botched execution.

43. Just days after John Doe's botched execution, the medical personnel at Holman Correctional Facility determined that he has lymph infections in his right groin and armpit, and they prescribed antibiotics.

I. John Doe's Other Litigation to Prevent Any Further Execution Attempts on Him by Any Means or Methods as Violative of the United States and Alabama Constitutions

44. On March 5, 2018, John Doe also filed a petition for writ of habeas corpus in the U.S. District Court of the Northern District of Alabama: John Doe has requested that the federal district court hold

his proceedings in abeyance until he is able to fully pursue what remedies are available to him in the state courts.

45. On March 5, 2018, John Doe also filed an amended complaint in his ongoing § 1983 lawsuit in the U.S. District Court of the Northern District of Alabama seeking relief on these grounds as well.

JURISDICTION

This Is a Valid Successive Petition Under Rule 32

46. Rule 32 prohibits successive petitions, unless the exception in Rule 32.2(b)(2) applies, which provides that a successive petition is permitted if:

[T]he petitioner shows good cause exists why the new ground or grounds we're not known or could not have been ascertained through reasonable diligence when the first petition was heard, and that failure to entertain that petition will result in a miscarriage of justice. See Ala. Rules Crim. Pro. 32.2(b).

47. John Doe's current circumstances fall squarely within the scope of this exception. The factual predicate: including the events and activities giving rise to the underlying claims in this petition, did not arise until February 22, 2018. Prior to that evening, including when he filed his first Rule 32 petition, John Doe had no way of knowing, no matter how much due diligence was used, that these grounds necessary to challenge his death sentence would arise.

48. Moreover, the serious and profound circumstances surrounding this petition demand consideration. John Doe survived an excruciating experience where the State attempted to execute him via means and methods that John Doe had repeatedly warned them would risk a dangerous, painful, and bloody procedure. Still, despite this notice, the state went forward and subjected John Doe to the torturous attempt to execute him. Out of this arise the grounds for this petition, warranting significant consideration of his challenge for relief from his sentence of death.

FACTS IN SUPPORT OF GROUNDS FOR RELIEF

49. No one in the history of capital punishment in the United States has gone through what John Doe was subjected to on February 22, 2018. No one in the history of the death penalty in this country has been led into the execution chamber, strapped onto the execution gurney in the execution chamber, had the execution team insert needles and catheters into his peripheral veins, had the execution team then insert needles and catheters into his central veins, and ultimately had the execution terminated and walked out of the execution chamber. No one has ever gone through this. John Doe is the only person in American history that has ever been subjected to execution by lethal intravenous injection of his peripheral and central veins and lived.

50. But John Doe survived this ordeal only after being subjected to hours of prolonged unnecessary pain and a dangerous, bloody procedure to find a vein in his feet, ankles, shin, or groin, in what amounted to nothing less than the torture of John Doe.

51. The brutal consequences of what took place in the execution chamber in the Holman Correctional Facility on February 22nd were entirely foreseeable to the state of Alabama. That the execution team would be unable to find a vein and that any attempt to find veins would lead to a painful and bloody process was all presented, documented, and proved to the state of Alabama for months leading up to the execution.

52. For at least seven months, John Doe had repeatedly explained to the state of Alabama that, as a result of his serious medical conditions, he lacks any usable veins for intravenous access for purposes of lethal injection. He warned the State that any attempt at execution requiring intravenous access would result in a risky, painful, and bloody procedure that would amount to cruel and unusual punishment.

53. Beginning in June 2017, when the State moved the Supreme Court of Alabama to set an execution date for John Doe, Mr. Doe actively litigated the issues surrounding his medical conditions, specifically his venous access and cancer. The Alabama Supreme Court ordered the State to allow John Doe to undergo a medical evaluation in August 2017, and John Doe filed weekly status updates with the Alabama Supreme Court until October 2017.

54. On December 13, 2017, the same day that the Alabama Supreme Court set John Doe's execution date, John Doe filed a 42 U.S.C. § 1983 complaint in the District Court for the Northern District of Alabama, challenging the state of Alabama's method of execution, as applied to him, on Eighth Amendment grounds.

55. On February 6, 2018, the District Court for the Northern District of Alabama denied the defendant's motion for summary judgment and granted a stay of John Doe's execution. The Eleventh Circuit subsequently vacated the District Court's stay of execution and ordered the District Court to immediately arrange for a medical examination of John Doe.

56. The District Court promptly appointed an independent medical expert and arranged for a physical examination of John Doe's veins and potential lymphadenopathy, which occurred on February 16, 2018. Based on the results of the medical examination, the District Court determined that the defendants could proceed with the execution of John Doe but required that the defendants stipulate to not attempt to access any peripheral veins in John Doe's upper extremities. John Doe appealed the District Court's decision to the Eleventh Circuit.

57. On February 21, 2018, before returning a decision, the Eleventh Circuit requested that the defendants provide affidavits, within six hours, stating that: (1) they agreed to follow the stipulation made to the District Court; (2) ultrasound technology and an "advanced-level practitioner" would be present during the execution; and (3) they were, in fact, capable of administering an intravenous line through John Doe's veins in his legs. The defendants submitted one affidavit from Warden Cynthia Stewart confirming, in one-line answers, each item that the Eleventh Circuit requested.

58. On February 22, 2018, the day of John Doe's scheduled execution, the Eleventh Circuit affirmed the District Court's denial of John Doe's request for a preliminary injunction, permitting the execution to go forward.

59. After the Eleventh Circuit's decision, John Doe filed a petition for writ of certiorari and an application for a stay of execution in the United States Supreme Court. The Court imposed a temporary stay of execution, which was lifted at approximately 8:45 pm CST on February 22, 2018. The Court denied John Doe's petition for writ of certiorari and motion for stay of execution, with Justice Ginsburg and Justice Sotomayor dissenting. The execution was permitted to proceed.

60. On February 22, 2018, at approximately 11:30 pm CST, the defendants terminated John Doe's execution after hours of attempting to establish venous access. The execution warrant subsequently expired at midnight.

61. These months of litigation put the defendants on notice that Mr. Doe's medical conditions would make lethal injection particularly challenging and dangerous.

GROUNDS SUPPORTING THE PETITION FOR RELIEF

I.   A SECOND ATTEMPT TO EXECUTE JOHN DOE, BY ANY MEANS OR METHODS, IS A VIOLATION OF THE STATE AND FEDERAL CONSTITUTIONAL PROHIBITIONS AGAINST CRUEL AND UNUSUAL PUNISHMENT: EIGHTH AND FOURTEENTH AMENDMENTS TO THE U.S. CONSTITUTION; ART. I, SECTION 15 OF THE ALABAMA CONSTITUTION.

62. John Doe incorporates by reference all facts and allegations detailed throughout this Petition.

63. On February 22, 2018, John Doe was escorted out of the execution chamber around 11:30 PM. This was after he underwent hours of torturous pain while the state of Alabama's execution team used all permissible means to execute him.

64. John Doe bears no responsibility whatsoever for the executioners' failure. Throughout the attempt to execute him, John Doe remained cooperative and did nothing to obstruct the execution team.

65. Nor was the state of Alabama's failure to execute John Doe the result of an accident or an "isolated mishap." Instead, it was the consequence of a deliberate and intentional act to try to execute John Doe no matter what it took and how much unnecessary pain it caused – including going into the

right groin even though the executioners knew from the District Court's independent medical examination that he has abnormal lymph nodes there and that the executioners should not attack his right groin. For seven months prior to the execution, the state of Alabama was aware that John Doe's medical conditions made his veins inaccessible or unusable for intravenous access for purposes of lethal injection.

66. John Doe repeatedly warned the state of Alabama – through state and federal litigation and through filed clemency applications with the Governor – that lethal injection would be impossible in light of his negligible venous access. For seven months, he repeatedly explained that his veins, as a result of his cancer, cancer treatment, age, and prior intravenous drug use, did not permit the venous access necessary for lethal injection; and that his abnormal lymph nodes from his lymphoma would interfere with central venous access. He pleaded with the state of Alabama to not subject him to the dangerous, painful, and bloody execution that would take place if attempted.

67. Even after the court-appointed independent medical expert confirmed John Doe's claims that he had no peripheral venous access in his upper extremities and identified abnormal lymph nodes in his right groin, the state still proceeded with lethal injection targeting his right groin. It ignored the concerns of experts, who had reviewed the medical report and called for "further workup/comment" on the abnormal lymph nodes that were identified.

68. The state of Alabama guaranteed that it could succeed in executing John Doe using only peripheral intravenous access through John Doe's lower extremities, despite evidence – and even an admission in court – that the Alabama Department of Corrections had never attempted an execution via this method in the history of Alabama's lethal injection system, meaning, in particular, that the execution team had no practice or prior experience with this method.

69. Despite clear notice since the summer of 2017 that significant problems would result if lethal IV injection was attempted, the state of Alabama completely disregarded this information, and the significant risk posed, choosing instead to proceed with the attempted execution of John Doe via lethal IV injection on February 22, 2018.

70. The evening of the execution, John Doe remained strapped to the execution gurney in the execution chamber while the execution team – for hours – unnecessarily and painfully prodded and jabbed John Doe with needles in a fruitless attempt to find a vein.

71. When it was deemed impossible to obtain peripheral venous access, the execution team then turned to the second method of execution that the state of Alabama had never used before. It attempted to obtain central venous access through John Doe's right groin. This decision to try for central venous

access only in John Doe's right groin was made despite the independent medical expert's report that this was the very location where John Doe had abnormal lymph nodes. Yet rather than avoid this area, the execution team deliberately attempted to obtain central venous access only through his right groin. Like peripheral access, the multiple attempts to obtain central venous access also failed, but only after it resulted in a bloody and unnecessarily painful procedure.

72. Though John Doe was strapped to the gurney for hours, in significant pain from the attempts to find a peripheral vein in his lower extremities and then an attempt to find a central vein in his right groin, the execution team had no intention of stopping. Rather, it sought to continue inflicting this unnecessarily painful and bloody procedure on John Doe. Even when the execution officially was terminated, a member of the execution team held on to John Doe's right groin, and then his ankles, insisting that more attempts at forcing a needle into his flesh would finally be successful. This insistence to continue in attempting to execute John Doe can only be considered a purpose to inflict unnecessary pain and suffering on him.

73. John Doe, strapped to the execution gurney, lay in pain, a bloody mess from the waist down, as he faced the prospect of a slow, lingering death. The trauma inflicted upon John Doe cannot be measured.

74. The U.S. Supreme Court has previously described punishments to be unconstitutionally cruel "when they involve torture or a lingering death," *In re Kemmler*, 136 U.S. 436, 447 (1890), or when they "involve the unnecessary and wanton infliction of pain," *Rhodes v. Chapman*, 452 U.S. 337, 346 (1981). It has also demanded that punishment accord with "the dignity of man," *Hope v. Pelzer*, 536 U.S. 730, 738 (2002) (quoting *Trop v. Dulles*, 356 U.S. 86, 100 (1958)). What was imposed on John Doe does not fall within this society's standards for a constitutional execution. See *Woodson v. North Carolina*, 428 U.S. 280, 288 (1976) ("The Eighth Amendment stands to assure that the State's power to punish is 'exercised within the limits of civilized standards.'").

75. The U.S. Supreme Court has also previously stated that "a series of abortive attempts" at execution raise an Eighth Amendment claim, *Baze v. Rees*, 553 U.S. 35, 50 (2008); see also *Glass v. Louisiana*, 471 U.S. 1080, 1085-86 (1985) (noting the potential unconstitutionality that "would be presented ... if the Court were confronted with a series of abortive attempts").

76. To attempt the second execution in light of the torturous circumstances inflicted on John Doe during the first attempt would be unconstitutional under both the federal and state constitutions. Precedent is clear when "unnecessary and wanton infliction of pain" is inflicted, *Rhodes*, 452 U.S. at 346, or when the method of execution "involve[s] torture or a lingering death," *In re Kemmler*, 136 U.S.

at 447, the Eighth Amendment's prohibition against cruel and unusual punishment is violated. It would, therefore, be unconstitutional to subject John Doe to a second attempted execution.

77. Previously, the U.S. Supreme Court has recognized only one exception to this well-established principle of constitutional law – namely, when the first execution is impossible to complete because of an "isolated mishap" or an accident. See *Louisiana ex rel. Francis v. Resweber*, 329 U.S. 459,464 (1947) (noting specifically that the "fact that an unforeseeable accident prevented the prompt consummation of the sentence" does not bar a second execution) (emphasis added). However, John Doe's case does not fall into that exception by any stretch of the imagination. The failed execution here was caused by the state's deliberate decision to disregard the significant risk, raised for months prior to the execution, of a botched and bloody execution. The courts that have most recently considered this issue agree: "To hold that Plaintiff's claim is not plausible based on *Resweber* would thus be an erroneous application of case that has shown its age in at least one relevant, core aspect. Over sixty years after *Resweber*, another Supreme Court plurality recognized that under an Eighth Amendment analysis, a series of abortive execution attempts could potentially indeed, present an unconstitutional violation." See *Broom v. Strickland*, 2010 WL 3447741, at *2 (S.D. Ohio Aug. 27, 2010) (citing *Baze*, 553 U.S. at 50) (noting, as well, that *Resweber'* s precedential value is in question because it was only a plurality decision).

78. John Doe's case falls under the rule, not the exception, of *Resweber* since his execution did not fail because of an accident or "isolated mishap." Nothing unforeseeable impeded the state's attempt to execute John Doe. Rather, the execution failed because the state decided to proceed by methods that it knew or should have known, based on the information provided by counsel months prior, would be unsuccessful. The state, therefore, chose to inflict significant physical and psychological unnecessary pain on John Doe.

79. Moreover, it is not even clear that the *Resweber* exception, decided by a plurality opinion in 1947, remains good law today. The U.S. Supreme Court has repeatedly stated that the meaning of the Eighth Amendment continues to evolve along with society's current prevailing norms. What forms of cruel and unusual punishment it protects against, the Court has explained, "must change as the basic mores of society change" and is based on "the evolving standards of decency that mark the progress of a maturing society," *Kennedy v. Louisiana*, 554 U.S. 407, 419 (2008); see also *Trop v. Dulles*, 356 U.S. 86, 101 (1958). This determination, therefore, "necessarily embodies a moral judgment," *Kennedy*, 554 U.S. at 420 (citing *Furman v. Georgia*, 408 U.S. 238, 382 (1972) (Burger, C.J., dissenting)). Applying this analysis, it is likely that under society's current prevailing norms, attempting a second execution,

particularly in light of a torturous first attempt, would violate the Eighth Amendment under all circumstances and, therefore, puts into question whether the *Resweber* exception decided more than seventy years ago, remains a valid exception to what would otherwise be seen as a cruel series of abortive attempts inflicting a lingering death.

80. What was inflicted on John Doe was a form of torture. The circumstances of this case – the state's prior notice that his veins were inaccessible for lethal injection, the state's insistence to proceed with the execution, the state's attack on his right groin where there were abnormal lymph nodes, the state's use of two never-before-used methods of execution, and the execution team's unwillingness to stop inflicting pain even after repeated failed attempts and the execution was called off – reflect a deliberate and intentional purpose to inflict pain upon.

81. To subject John Doe to a second execution would subject him to a torturous experience of physical and psychological unnecessary pain. Therefore, further attempts to execute John Doe by any means or methods would violate the Eighth and Fourteenth Amendments of the U.S. Constitution and Article I, section 15 of the Alabama Constitution.

82. John Doe is entitled to an order from this court setting aside his death sentence and releasing him from death row and into Alabama's general prison population. He is also entitled to temporary, preliminary, and permanent injunctive relief against any further attempts by the state to execute him again by any means or methods. He is also entitled to declaratory relief that it would be unlawful for the state to make any further attempts to carry out a death sentence on John Doe. His death sentence may no longer be carried out by any means or methods without violating the constitutional rights identified herein.

11. TO ATTEMPT THE SECOND EXECUTION OF JOHN DOE WOULD VIOLATE THE STATE AND FEDERAL CONSTITUTIONAL PROHIBITION AGAINST DOUBLE JEOPARDY: FIFTH AND FOURTEENTH AMENDMENTS TO THE U.S. CONSTITUTION; ARTICLE I, SECTION 9 OF THE ALABAMA CONSTITUTION.

83. John Doe hereby incorporates all facts and allegations made in this petition.

84. The Fifth Amendment, applied to the states through the Fourteenth Amendment, states that no person shall "be subject for the same offense to be twice put in jeopardy of life or limb." Article I, section 9 of the Alabama Constitution states that "no person shall, for the same offense, be twice put in jeopardy of life or limb." These clauses guarantee John Doe both federal and state protections against Double Jeopardy, which includes the right not to face a second attempted execution.

85. The U.S. Supreme Court has cautioned that "multiple punishments for the same offense" violates the Double Jeopardy Clause. See *U.S. v. Halper*, 490 U.S. 435, 441 (1989); see also *North*

Carolina v. Pearce, 395 U.S. 711, 717 (1969), overruled on other grounds. This protection, it explained, "has deep roots in our history and jurisprudence," *Halper*, 490 U.S. at 440; see *Ex parte Lange*, 28 Wall. 163, 21 L. Ed. 872 (1874) ("If there is anything settled in the jurisprudence of England and America, it is that no man can be twice lawfully punished for the same offense.").

86. There is no question that the state already placed John Doe "in jeopardy of his life or limb" on the evening of February 22, 2018. Under John Doe's conviction and sentence to death, the state had the authority to proceed with the execution of John Doe (though the measures it took, in its attempt to execute him, went well beyond what is constitutional).

87. On the evening of February 22, 2018, the state brought John Doe into the execution chamber, where the entire process of execution was to take place. In the execution chamber, John Doe was strapped onto the lethal injection gurney, where he lay for hours, had the execution team insert needles and catheters into his peripheral veins, had the execution team then insert needles and catheters into his central veins, and ultimately had the execution terminated and walked out the execution chamber. But for hours, the execution team executed John Doe. The execution process was well and fully underway.

88. A second attempt to execute John Doe, for the same conviction, would again, place him "in jeopardy of life or limb." This contravenes the very words and purpose of the Double Jeopardy Clause in the Fifth Amendment of the U.S. Constitution and Article I, section 9 of the Alabama Constitution. See *Resweber*, 329 U.S. at 461-4.

89. The U.S. Supreme Court has permitted a second attempt at execution only when the first execution fails due to "an accident, with no suggestion of malevolence, prevent[ing] the consummation of a sentence," *Resweber*, 329 U.S. at 463. It found in that specific case, where the result was unforeseeable, that a second execution does not implicate double jeopardy concerns.

90. The attempted execution of John Doe, however, did not fail because of an accident. The State was repeatedly warned through litigation in state and federal court, as well as applications for clemency to the Governor, that intravenous access for purposes of lethal injection would be impossible and, more so, cruel.

91. Moreover, throughout the hours of the execution, none of the medical equipment necessary to complete the execution malfunctioned, nor in any way impeded the state's execution. *Cf. Resweber*, 329 U.S. at 461 (noting that because of a "mechanical difficulty," the electrocution chair failed and "death did not result"). The state of Alabama had additional equipment above and beyond the protocol – an ultrasound – in the execution chamber specifically for John Doe's execution, and still the execution team could not successfully execute him. This was not due to an accident of any sort. This was an

attempt to execute someone, knowing it would inflict significant unnecessary pain and suffering, despite clear notice of the likely consequences.

92. John Doe is entitled to an order from this court setting aside his death sentence and releasing him from death row and into Alabama's general prison population. He is also entitled to temporary, preliminary, and permanent injunctive relief against any further attempts by the state to execute him again by any means or methods. He is also entitled to declaratory relief that it would be unlawful for the state to make any further attempts to carry out a death sentence on John Doe. His death sentence may no longer be conducted by any means or methods without violating the constitutional rights identified herein.

III. IMPOSITION OF THE DEATH PENALTY UNDER THE CIRCUMSTANCES OF THIS CASE WOULD VIOLATE ARTICLE I, SECTIONS 1, 9, 13, 15, AND 17 OF THE ALABAMA CONSTITUTION.

93. John Doe hereby incorporates all facts and allegations made in this petition.

94. This case appears to be a case of first impression in the state of Alabama. This Court should examine each allegation as it relates to the specific provisions of the Alabama Constitution. Under the Alabama Constitution, any attempt to execute John Doe again is cruel and unusual under Article 1, section 15; violates due process under Article I, section 13; constitutes double jeopardy under Art. I, section 9; violates his right to habeas corpus under Article I, section 17; violates his right to life under Article I, section 1; and violates his right to equal protection under Article I, section 1.

95. The Alabama Constitution may provide more protection for John Doe than the federal constitution.

96. John Doe is entitled to an order from this court setting aside his death sentence and releasing him from death row and into Alabama's general prison population. He is also entitled to temporary, preliminary, and permanent injunctive relief against any further attempts by the state to execute him again by any means or methods. He is also entitled to declaratory relief that it would be unlawful for the state to make any further attempts to carry out a death sentence on John Doe. His death sentence may no longer be carried out by any means or methods without violating the constitutional rights identified herein.

CONCLUSION

97. John Doe seeks relief under Rule 32, as a matter of state and federal law, to set aside his death sentence and prohibit the state from attempting any further execution of him by any means or methods.

98. John Doe should be granted temporary, preliminary, and permanent injunctive relief against any further attempts by the state to execute him again by any means or methods.

99. Discovery and an evidentiary hearing to develop the facts and law more fully is hereby requested.

100. This Court should find that a remedy for the state and federal constitutional violations alleged herein is required.

101. Petitioner John Doe further requests that this Court grant all relief, legal and equitable, that it deems appropriate.

Respectfully submitted, on this 5th day of March 2018. By:

X_____

John L. Doe, *pro se*
AIS#_____

CERTIFICATE OF SERVICE

I hereby certify that on March 5, 2018, I served a copy of the attached pleading to all parties, via U.S. Mail as required by rule and law.

X_____

John L. Doe, *pro se*

ABOUT THE AUTHOR

Kelly Patrick Riggs is best known as the author of *The Post-Conviction Relief Series*. He is a former prisoner who discovered his life's passion while serving a prison sentence for a crime he did not commit. Since his release, he has pledged himself to serve the people who need him most, people who need something better out of life: the American prisoner.

FREEBIRD PUBLISHERS

Thanks for your interest in Freebird Publishers!

We value our customers and would love to hear from you! Reviews are an important part in bringing you quality publications. We love hearing from our readers-rather it's good or bad (though we strive for the best)!

If you could take the time to review/rate any publication you've purchased with Freebird Publishers we would appreciate it!

If your loved one uses Amazon, have them post your review on the books you've read. This will help us tremendously, in providing future publications that are even more useful to our readers and growing our business.

Amazon works off of a 5 star rating system. When having your loved one rate us be sure to give them your chosen star number as well as a written review. Though written reviews aren't required, we truly appreciate hearing from you.

Sample Review Received on Inmate Shopper

poeticsunshine

★★★★★ **Truly a guide**
Reviewed in the United States on June 29, 2023
Verified Purchase

This book is a powerhouse of information. My son had to calm/ground himself to prioritize where to start.

www.ingramcontent.com/pod-product-compliance
Lightning Source LLC
Chambersburg PA
CBHW080329270326
41927CB00014B/3147